CW00797931

A
Shillingsworth
of Promises

FRED HITCHCOCK

Woodfield

Published in 1997 by
WOODFIELD PUBLISHING, Woodfield House, Babsham Lane, Bognor Regis,
West Sussex PO21 5EL, UK.

© Fred Hitchcock, 1997

ISBN 0 873203 32 2

All rights reserved. No part of this publication may be reproduced or transmitted
in any form or by any means, electronic or mechanical, nor may it be stored in
any information storage and retrieval system, without prior permission from the
publisher.

Contents

Chapter 1   Youth Matters 4

Chapter 2   Newton Benoulli & Bullshit 46

Chapter 3   An Erk in Baghdad & Beyond 73

Chapter 4   The War (some lighter moments) 120

Chapter 5   Peace, sadness & a Cairo wedding 137

Chapter 6   Goodbye RAF, hello LAF 157

Chapter 7   Changing jobs, homes & gear 175

Chapter 8   Retirement, bereavement & reunion 199

1 ■ *Youth Matters*

As a Zeppelin was dropping its bombs over South East Kent, so Mrs Rose Hitchcock was dropping her second son Frederick. It was the early afternoon of October 13th 1915, and her target area was the front bedroom of a small terraced house, number 28 Cobden Road, in the old Cinque Port of Hythe. The impact made little impression at the time and, as the years passed by, the event became increasingly insignificant, for the world continued on its way, happily and totally unaware and unappreciative of what it had been blessed with. Mrs. Hitchcock herself was born on the fourth of January 1888 at Lambeth in London. The third eldest daughter of a family of eight, fathered by a very active London cabby, a Mr Gilbert who, after the death of his first wife, married again and had four more children. Hence, I suppose, the propensity of the young Fred to waggle his bum a bit in later life. The first Gilbert family lived in a state of seemingly permanent poverty, in a variety of lodgings in and around Lambeth. Constantly being thrown out onto the streets, together with their few miserable bits and pieces, for allowing a long sequence of rent days to come and go without consoling the landlord. The family, during these hard times, was fed mainly through and by various charities. Mother recalls her heartbreak when once, having to cross Lambeth bridge to reach the soup kitchen, she was reproached on her return because the anticipated meal was cold, greasy and inedible.

Clothing everyone was comparatively less difficult, there being in the area many second hand and cheapjack stalls. Here the choosing of the choicest items of footwear meant pairings which did not exactly match, known as halfpenny rights and penny lefts, or vice versa if fashion dictated.

Mr. Hitchcock was the fifth son of a family of eight brothers and one sister, living with mother-in-law and her son at 1 & 2 Wilton Road, Pimlico. Dad's father died at a comparatively young age from an excess of cheap booze and dear tobacco. His wife too suffered an early demise at the age of 32, and the lack of any real information on the history of his family leaves it only reasonable to assume that such sad and early deaths came about because of the constant struggles they had in trying to keep going under the 'normalities' of the time.

This potted history of the lifestyle of the family in the late nineteenth century gives some idea of the extreme poverty suffered by my immediate forebears. An era when poverty was actual and not just relative or assumed.

A SHILLINGSWORTH OF PROMISES

London in the early 1900s was certainly no place to be poor in, so at an early age Herbert, the middle son, made a trip to the Kent coast, to Hythe, in search of change, a job, and escape. It was early summertime in 1908 and he immediately fell in love with the town, situated as it was in that beautiful corner of the Kent coast where the sloping hills of the Roughs drop down and disappear into the flat green and golden fields of the mystic Romney Marshes. The sheer white chalk cliffs to the east from Folkestone to Dover and beyond dipping into sometimes blue and sometimes stormy grey seas, presented a sight which his tired and beauty starved London eyes absorbed greedily.

The screeching of the gulls as they soared, stalled and dived behind the home coming trawlers, the happy chatter of holiday makers, and the gentle rustle of shingle under the breaking waves as they washed the shore, were all new and wondrous sounds. This was reachable paradise and how easy it was to be overwhelmed by the beauty and tranquillity of the town itself, with its Elm lined Ladies' Walk; and the Royal Military Canal, also splendidly wooded with its own share of full grown Elms on its rising northern banks. All of which, together with the green fields of the cricket and football grounds, forming an attractive and fitting foreground to the old church on the hill, nestling comfortably and picturesquely amongst the narrow little streets of old, old Hythe.

Herbert had, of course, decided by this time that the location for his continuing earthly struggles had been pleasantly and satisfactorily settled. It only remained now to find a job, a home, and a wife.

The job, as a painter and decorator, was provided by a small firm of jobbing builders. The home, temporary of course, was found in Dental Street, as a lodger. The third element of his ambitions, a wife, was at least halfway satisfied in the form of a girl friend, Rose Gilbert, still living in London. A strugglingly composed letter, a halfpenny stamp, and a few minor exaggerations were enough to bring her, albeit somewhat doubting, on a new adventure and to separate lodgings, also in Dental Street.

No quadratic formula was required for the solving of Herbert's basic equation for salvation, for Rose immediately found work at the laundry in Dymchurch Road, ironing shirts and stiff starched collars. A skill she and a multitude of her sisters had learnt and practised in a laundry in Haydon's Road, Wimbledon.

Their courtship was brief and, due to the puritanical attitudes of their respective landladies, carried on out-of-doors, and those cold winter months were hardly conducive to comfortable courting. This was a great pity as both were of a romantic and loving disposition. However, the meeting places for the practical demonstration of their affections were romantic enough. The lych-gate of Saltwood church and the tree sheltered benches along the canal banks being the favourites, with probably others selected rather more randomly and urgently.

An early wedding was arranged. This took place at Newington church on 30th January 1909, a cold and snowy day. The poor horses slipping and sliding as they struggled to pull the carriage up the hill from Hythe, this route being more than a mite steep in places. It was not a world shattering event as the vicar, Rose, Herbert, the cabby, and the two horses were the only participants. But the newly espoused were quite happy and confident, for the return journey took them to 28 Cobden Road, a brand new mid-terraced house, a stone's throw from the sea, and taken at a rental of eight shillings per week, exclusive of rates.

The cold evenings on the canal benches fast became a memory. Herbert being aware that his loved one, on many a shivering night, curtailed the courting, and the timetable of the rattling horse-drawn trams along South Road, by saying it was time to go home, as the second from last tram was identified as the last. Herbert, having no watch, agreed. He too was cold and stiff, probably no doubt also in parts that were not yet licensed to receive the ameliorating treatment that marital status would soon confer.

The first born of the family, my elder brother Bert, arrived on the 17th of October 1912 and I, as already related, dropped in on October 13th 1915. A war baby and, as the mathematically minded may work out, a parting gift from Dad to Mum as in the first onrush of national fervour he left to join up and to do his bit. Unfortunately, being somewhat deaf, his acceptance into the army was delayed for quite some time. The parting gift none the less was just as lovingly cared for. Dad was called up eventually and became a proud member of the Pioneer Corps. His service was extended into the early post war years, when clearing the battle fields of unburied dead was part of his grisly duties. This appalling aspect of war's aftermath seems to mock the assertion made by both the Germans and us that 'God is on our side'. Maybe he was, for both sides have well-kept Military Cemeteries to prove it.

I can remember, however, his somewhat shamefaced and hesitant attempts to convey the horror of his stories with adroit or maladroit touches of black humour. How they chortled, he recalled, at the accidental disappearance into an old unmarked, but well filled, latrine pit of two live privates carrying one dead sergeant, which occasioned the observation that it wasn't every day that you could drop a sergeant right in it!

Father's return home late in 1919 was quite unexpected. No knock on the front door, just heavy steps on the linoleumed floor of the passage and then a sudden appearance at the door of the living room. Mother was sitting in front of the old black kitchen stove, and from the cuddled warmth of her lap I saw this unkempt man in strange clothes with his eyes alight with happiness. It was the sudden emotional outbreak of tears and laughter that surely imprinted this scene on my mind, for it became my earliest memory and the beginning of conscious existence.

The simple reason for existence is something that always puzzles me, and even given a lifetime's pondering no answer has yet seemed adequate. A trifle nihilistic maybe to say, 'Why be born if eventually you have to die?' What one does or will not do with one's life really doesn't matter only in so far as it might affect the life and living of those around one.

More simply, you are born and you die and you worry yourself to bloody death in between. Not forgetting of course to enjoy and savour the satisfying of all the senses and emotions that you possess. That, I suppose, is living. Dying is losing the capacity to do so.

And the hereafter? Is it a question of faith, fiction or hope? Everlasting life in the infinity of space is a concept which defeats the capacity of my mind to comprehend. It's a comforting theory though. Maybe sufficient to tranquillise the stresses and emphasise the joys of the usual three score years and ten that most of us suffer or enjoy, and to rationalise the reason for our human existence.

My existence continued, however, and at the age of four my academic career began. I was taken by my elder brother via the Stade Street entrance to the local infants' school, but nearing the gate I tore loose from his guiding hand, turned tail and ran for home. A moustachio'd barber, a Mr Griffiths, taking a breath of fresh air on the doorstep of his one roomed emporium, immediately sized up the situation, shot out a massive paw, grabbed me by my golden locks and restored me to the care and anger of big brother.

In a state of fear and torment, I remember passing through the doors of the school and being given into the care of a very large lady who put me onto a very low canvas bed in line with lots of other recumbent kids. She patted my head and told me it would soon be time to go home. I slept, then woke, then was allowed to wander home alone.

So passed my first day in the realms of academe, and from there on in I became a willing, sometimes attentive and sometimes inattentive victim, sometimes bored, but occasionally stimulated to high endeavour.

My days at the Infants are but happy memories, the taking of the school photograph being one of them. It eventually became a topic of family speculation when it was found with pinholes in all the heads except two, mine and the little girl who sat in front of me. All I could supply by way of explanation was that she never wore any knickers. A fact which, at that age, affected me not at all, as I thought little girls were just other small people, who for some unknown reason were different. So why no pinhole in her head? Was it the blossoming of some romantic notion or just some hidden concern? What I do recall, however, is when I put my hand up (in the traditional classroom fashion, I hasten to add) to tell Miss Dann that Daisy never wore anything under her dress, she took me to a corner of the classroom to whisper to me, "Some families can afford some things but not others." The bottom line in basic home economics, and a lesson to me to mind my own business.

Learning to read was part of the daily syllabus, using small books with little stories, written in large letters, each child reading a line or so until the teacher said, "Next".

Unfortunately the word 'next' occurred in the text of my two lines, and I was unable to read it.

"Next," she informed me. I sat down, thankfully.

"Stand up!" I stood up.

"Next," she again informed me. I sat down, wondering.

"Stand up!" It could have gone on forever, but realisation on her part, a smile, an explanation, and I was allowed to sit.

February 12th 1921, mid morning. Mother had excessive labour pains and her anguished cries alerted the neighbours. The doctor and then the midwife arrived, and almost immediately my second brother, a lightweight of some three pounds, was born. Mother and child were successfully brought through the ordeal by the dedication and skill of a caring doctor aided by one of those imperturbable, ever cheerful, cycling district midwives.

Tom in his very early days, being so small and weak, was cradled in an old shoe box. However, he survived well enough and, apart from a degree of inherited deafness, suffered no long term setbacks. As Tom's arrival was somewhat earlier than expected, Father was, of course, working as usual, decorating a flat on Marine Parade. I ran to tell him I had a brother.

He said, "Yes, I know son, what's with Bert?"

"Not Bert, Dad, a new one."

He beat me home by some two hundred yards. A while later, after being chided by the neighbours, "What, another boy?" he boastingly replied,

"Ah, it takes a real expert to put spouts on kettles. Any amateur can knock dents in them."

September 1921, at the age of six, rising seven, saw my transfer to the big boys' elementary school. I was in standard one which was under the control of the headmaster's wife, Mrs Molyneux, a tiny lady, kind and caring. She must have been a very good teacher, imprinting the multiplication tables on our minds until we could repeat them without fault up to the twelfth!

It was about this time too that it dawned on me that female figures also had some sort of peculiarly disturbing attraction. For I enjoyed playing on the beach with my pal Leslie who always seemed to have one or two little girls in tow. Of course, it wasn't long before we were playing 'looks', and having no sisters, it was an educational excitement to me, that for some reason died a quick death when she said, "I like Leslie's best. Yours is bigger, but it's not so pretty." She deemed this to be some sort of consolation I suppose.

In all innocence and feeling no shame, I told my parents as part of the family chat during supper, exactly what had happened and what had been said. I got no word of sympathy as expected, just a funny look from Mum and a raised eyebrow from Dad as he said, with a twinkle in his eye, "Don't worry, Lad." This I understood, but when he added, "It's the mechanics of the thing that matter," the relevance of that remark was wasted on me. Mother's funny look became threatening and Father bit deep into his chunk of mustard laden bacon fat, and said no more.

Back at school, standard one arithmetical problems revolved around simple applications of the recently assimilated tables, and were solved without difficulty, until one concerning herrings and florins was posed. I misread 'florins' as 'floorings' and just couldn't understand what carpets had to do with buying fish. I guessed the answer as twenty herrings per square yard, then got two out of ten for trying and an unscheduled lesson on bartering.

At this stage painting and drawing were attempted. Not being an exacting exercise, it seemed each child had very liberal scope to reproduce on paper what it thought it saw. Early expressionists? Not exactly; just trying to paint yellow bananas with brown spots then brown leaves with yellow spots, and how to join legs and arms to bodies. Meanwhile Mrs Molyneux tried to teach me in particular that real people did not have triangular heads or square feet, and they certainly did not have such long noses. Here she was fighting a losing battle as long noses were a family trait going back for decades, and they had already become a feature in all the mental images I had of my myriad aunts and uncles.

Before leaving this bottom class, learning the alphabet forwards and backwards had been accomplished, with difficulty and a few repetitive errors. This accomplishment had to be repeated at chatty family gatherings. What that did for my parents I don't know, but it left me feeling self conscious and tongue tied. To save myself prolonged embarrassment I soon learned to make mistakes, being then excused and allowed to leave. Usually to go to Leslie's to see if he could come out to play, hopefully with one of his many other little friends.

Leslie was also, at an early age, very conscious of the attractions of lovely ladies, and on many a Saturday afternoon he would easily inveigle me into going with him to the Picture Palace in the High Street. There to take a neck breaking twopenny seat as close to the thumping mood reflecting pianist as possible, to look in wonder at Greta Garbo, in astonishment at Hoot Gibson and Tom Mix, and hilarious contentment at Charlie Chaplin or Buster Keaton. And Leslie would drool incessantly on the way home over the attractions of the great Garbo, or any other screen beauty for that matter.

September 1922 brought a transfer to standard two and to Miss Stanford. The 'sweet lady' as she was nicknamed, because, if you were very good, you were rewarded with a butter ball, varying in size according to how good or clever she imagined you had been.

Writing, spelling and dictation were the predominant requirements at this stage, spelling being the most difficult, trying to get the correct juxtaposition of those awkwardly placed vowels and consonants.

My greatest success came when sitting in the back row, and being the last but one to be asked to spell the word 'Autumn'. I remembered the final 'n' which had so far been ignored. I was awarded a giant size butter ball and allowed to go home early. Father happened to be at home when I arrived, and he became curious as to why so early. I said Miss Stanford had sent me home because... And before I could explain he asked, "And what are you sucking?"

"One of her butter balls."

I promptly received a smart cuff around the ear. As mentioned before, Dad was a little deaf, and he had missed the first four words. It all finished well, however, for on realising the truth he gave me a halfpenny. A little while later I spent a consoling hour sitting on the little sea wall, enjoying the salt air and a bag of tiger nuts.

Nineteen twenty two and twenty three saw me through standards two and three, where I was introduced to the advancing complications of joined-up writing and involved arithmetic, and then on to composition, with its

A SHILLINGSWORTH OF PROMISES

nouns, verbs and picture forming adjectives. I wondered how we had all managed to talk and converse up until then, and be understood, without any knowledge of grammar or syntax whatsoever.

About this time and during the summer months I took to enjoying an early morning six o'clock dip in the sea. On occasions I would see the standard four class master doing the same thing. His early morning flounderings and the sight of his somewhat spindly legs seemed somehow to convince me that teachers were not exactly God's next door neighbours after all. From there on, although basically a shy boy, I became a little less tentative in my relationships with the heavenly bodies of the scholastic hierarchy. Family finances during these days, what with two boys at school and a sickly new arrival, were very strained. Father, as always, would do all the house maintenance, even making some items of furniture. The hall stand being built from the pine wood side frames of an old bed and bits of wood from a Tate and Lyle sugar box. The whole thing though, when completed with glove box, umbrella stand and small mirror, and with all the woodwork stained and polished, looked remarkably professional. It remained in full use until 1960, and every week without fail on Friday, the family's insurance books and nine pennies were put on the glove box in readiness for the collector. Mother ordained we would have to tighten our belts if necessary, to pay the insurance. Otherwise, what indignity we would all suffer if there was not enough money to provide a decent funeral for whichever one of us felt the need to have one.

The State in those days took only a seemingly incidental interest in the plight of the under privileged, creating an inherent desire to survive in some, and a sense of total helplessness in others. Thus the modern 'cradle to grave' Welfare State can be considered to be either degrading or an absolute social necessity, depending on the character, circumstance and effort of those involved.

Anyway the effort within our family was proportional according to age and size. So Father's share was hefty, and included all the boot and shoe repairing. His reward being an appreciative word from Mum together with a cuddle, and no doubt further rewards when feelings reached a higher degree of thankfulness and love.

The shoe repairing was done in the little concreted yard at the back of the house, using a small cast iron foot, chunks of hide, and a good flow of unique and not so unique language when things went wrong.

"Gnats' cocks are stronger than these bloody sprigs they sell nowadays," he moaned, adding, "And this bleeding leather never saw a cow's arse, it's like sodding cardboard."

That was part of a conversation I overheard between Dad and the milkman, for the milk was delivered to the back door in those days. Mother would sometimes go shy and red when dealing with Mr Jenkinson. This embarrassment was, however, only because she had to ask for time to pay, and not due to the fact that he was tall and good looking, which made playing the supplicant all that harder to do. However, Mother tried to avoid this by making a few pence from taking in washing from some four or five regular customers living in the big houses on the sea front.

I loathed the Monday washing days, the steamed up kitchen, the big zinc baths and the scrubbing board. But most of all the feeding of the ancient copper in the corner with all the old paper and cardboard boxes gathered during the week, together with any driftwood from the beach. That firehole was insatiable, stinking and sweat making. Not only that, it made me very dirty, which meant a full naked tubbing at the end of the day, in the kitchen, hopefully before it had cooled off too much.

It was my job to deliver the finished laundry, and a job I enjoyed wholeheartedly, for the landladies, bless them, would tip me a halfpenny or a penny on delivery. When or if this amounted to threepence, I would secretly, in the evening, regale myself with a 'twopenny piece and a penn'orth of chips', sitting at a stone topped table in Dray's fish and chip shop in Albert Lane. That is, until one sad evening Mother passed by and saw me and I had to explain. She scolded, "The neighbours will think I don't feed you, eating out of doors like that, and don't you think the money should help keep the family and not just one greedy little boy?"

I didn't think I was being greedy, just enjoying the fruits of honest labour. Needless to say, the fruits from then on dropped into Mum's ever ready purse, including the pips. I felt I was being squeezed.

My elder brother, during these years, became involved with the church choir, the Boy Scouts and some of the Girl Guides. Activities which did not affect me, being unable to sing for one thing, and too young for the other two. One thing we did have in common, however, was a desire to help out where we could with the family struggle to get by, avoiding at all costs any dependence on charity of any sort. But one sad sacrifice brother Bert had to make was to be refused permission to sit the scholarship examinations for the Grammar school. He was surely bright enough to have passed. He reached the top class, that is standard seven of the elementary school, at the age of twelve and then stagnated for two years before he could even begin to search for a job, which in the event proved more than somewhat difficult.

One of his help out jobs was for a retired army Major living in a largish house on Barrack Hill. In those days Hythe was of course a military town, being the home of the Small Arms School, which was situated between Dymchurch Road and the canal, its brick built married quarters, officers' and sergeants' messes being further along towards West Hythe. The rifle ranges, located between the sea and the coast road, skylined with their raised and numbered butts, made a very prominent and familiar landmark. The pop-pop-popping of small arms fire would be a sound all old Hythites would recognise instantly.

The nature of the job that Bert had found was to clean the Major's boots, including his riding boots and his wife's shoes, reporting for duty every morning at seven thirty sharp. He got a reprimand if late, or if the shine wasn't up to the required army bullshit standard. For this work he got three shillings for a five day week. He very quickly developed an intense dislike for 'them what live up on the hill' and soon after started talking about 'the exploitation of the toiling masses' and 'nothing to lose but his chains'. Then, come the revolution, and he would stick the riding boots right up his flaming arse, reflecting that all that shine would make the job that much easier.

However, none of this came to pass. He joined the Royal Navy, went through the war and the ranks, finishing up as a commissioned Lieutenant, convinced that people from all classes were virtually the same and that if you changed *en masse* the commissioned for the non-commissioned, or the director generals and managers for the workers, or vice versa, it would make absolutely no difference.

I would agree, adding that all political polemic was virtually useless, as it mostly reflected the background and environment into which each individual was born, with argument being tailored to fit inborn prejudices.

But back to the joys of childhood and 1924 when, at the age of eight, I was always hungry, and anxious about what Mum would conjure up for the next meal. Always a problem, particularly from Wednesday to Friday, the three days before pay day. Pay day, however, would see Dad come home about a quarter to six; and always with half a dozen doughnuts, a small slab of walnut toffee, and a large choux pastry eclair for Mum.

I looked forward to this weekly treat, and to the joy of handling my own Saturday penny, which more often than not turned out to be a halfpenny. But in those days a full penny would purchase a couple of hours of sweet sucking delight in the form of a gob-stopper (in a variety of colours) followed by a locust, which was a large, sweet, dried bean, shiny black in colour and very chewy in texture. And finally a sherbet dab to fizz away the stickiness. I often wonder to myself, as no doubt hundreds of my generation do, whatever happened to tiger nuts and locusts?

Anticipating probable mid-week catering problems, Mother would send me, large basket in hand, to call early Monday mornings at the back entrance in Chapel Street of Burch's High Street baker's shop, to buy four penn'orth of stale loaves, and 'any buns please' if they had any.

My basket was always amply filled (hence the big one, I suppose) by a gentle and, to me, somewhat elderly man, ghostly white in his large smock, his flour covered face smiling sympathetically. And he always ostentatiously added a doughnut, which was obviously more fresh than stale. On these occasions this bun disappeared *en route* home but, not being an experienced rogue I left a ring of sugar around my lips. Mother, no doubt elated by the success of the enterprise, and the ploy of using a big basket, made no comment, except to say, "Next time, wipe your mouth, your brother likes doughnuts too, you know."

Bert was now thirteen and too old to carry on with his weekly shopping chore, which was to go, on Wednesdays, to Wood's the pork butcher in the High Street, for three penn'orth of skin and bones. This, however, was a front door purchase, made during the day, and always very good value for money, enough to make a healthy thick stew for at least two meals. Sometimes a bit of a pig's head would be included, and from this Mum would make a mouth watering brawn.

I duly inherited this item of mid-week shopping, together with Bert's Saturday fruit and vegetable job, for which he used to be paid one shilling and sixpence. Mr Crump, who lived next door at number 30 Cobden road, which was the end house, ran a small weekend fruit and vegetable round, pushing his well loaded barrow around the streets, calling at all the houses for orders. So the job consisted of helping with the pushing, knocking on people's doors, enquiring if they needed anything, making up any orders, taking them back and collecting the money. The money taken was not all that heavy, but I never realised how weighty ten pounds of spuds, a large cauliflower and sundry pounds of fruit could be. It was an all-day job and by six o'clock I was absolutely knackered, dirty and hungry. And for that he gave me one shilling, saying I was smaller than my brother!

The next weekend at twelve o'clock I told him I would have to finish. He wanted to know why of course. I told him,

"I'm only small you know, and I'm tired, financially tired."

A SHILLINGSWORTH OF PROMISES

After a puzzled silence he said, "OK Son, one and sixpence then. Is that what you're getting at?"

"No, Mr Crump, two shillings."

The wrinkles on his face deepened as he almost smiled and actually said, "OK boy, OK boy."

But I had to do a little more of the pushing from then on, it's hard to get something for nothing in this world. It was another lesson learnt .

There was also more learning to be done at school for by 1925, I had arrived in standard five, and Mr Hawkins was the class teacher. He was keen and interesting and blessed with the patience and skill to activate the minds of his class. I liked him, and he certainly took pride in trying to get the utmost from his pupils.

Very elementary science and geometry were the new subjects. They immediately appealed to me, as there were no problems with interpretation and degree. Simply the learning of facts, functions and processes which seemed to have a logical and natural interdependence. The Arts, on the other hand, appeared to me to be the boggy breeding ground for the pseudo-intellectual. So I was doomed to be a non-intellectual at a very early age. My first science lesson, I remember, concerned the description and construction of a simple water pump, operated by a hand lever to draw water up from an underground supply. The sort that can be seen on a multitude of allotment gardens the length and breadth of the country, and familiar to every working class lad of those days.

One day I tried to impress my dear old Dad by trying to explain to him how the pump in the corner of his allotment worked. Impressed he was not, concerned yes, for it had not rained for some time, and his newly planted seedlings badly needed water.

"Now Lad, put all your scientific knowledge to the test, and get pumping on that handle." Obediently I pumped, and pumped, and pumped, but all I got from that old mechanical monstrosity were clanks and squeaks.

"What do we do now then, Lad?" he asked.

"Don't know, Dad. Maybe there's no water underneath. I could ask Mr Hawkins next week," I suggested.

"No need for that, Son, just get that old tin can there, fill it up with water from the canal, then empty it into that little hole on top of the pump." This I did, being careful not to spill a drop as it was all of seventy yards to the canal. I was invited to, "Try it now." Once more the pump clanked and squeaked and then spluttered, and then gurgled and then gave forth in spasmodic but full strength squirts of clear water. Astonished, I asked, "What made it work then, Dad?"

"I don't know, Son, exactly, but I think you'd better have another chat with your Mr. Hawkins. It's something about you can't suck up nothing, you got to fill it up first. Prime it with a taster – goes for lots of things in life, Son."

Doing the allotment was usually a shared Sunday morning pleasure, pushing the hand-cart full of tools to the Twiss Road site, and planning on the way exactly where and what we would be planting, or sometimes re-planting. For all we found one particular Sunday were two rows of evenly spaced holes, each hole being in the exact spot where two weeks before we had planted the peas. Father was nonplussed and I had no ideas to offer. The mystery was quickly solved, however, when three birds from the mass of Elm tree rookeries on the canal bank suddenly landed on an adjoining plot and systematically and without error uplifted each single pea our neighbour had planted, leaving a neat row of empty holes. Our own holes were duly re-seeded, but this time were amply protected with a cover of broken brush wood. This tip having been given to us by a watching, and more experienced 'allotmenter', together with some advice to get on to the council 'about them sodding rooks'.

With the morning's work done, the return trip home would almost invariably be interrupted for a 'quick one' at the Hope in Stade Street. If Father happened to be short on pennies then the return trip was made via the sea front, where there was no pub and no temptation. Despite the reason for the deviation, I preferred the sea front route, for going this way we were home sooner. And being hungry my mouth watered long before the actual smell of Mum's always excellent Sunday dinner filled my nostrils. Even now, writing this at the age of 75 my glands are salivating, triggered by a nostalgic activation of the olfactories. Nostalgia as a cure, or for re-activating other lost joys? It's an idea.

On one memorable short stop at The Hope on the way home, on a very hot day, Father decided to lace my usual lemonade with beer. Thinking, "Well, the boy's ten years old, he's tired so it'll liven him up a bit. It's only a couple of shandies anyway." I downed the drinks, enjoying the slight bitterness mixed with the tingle of the lemonade. On reaching home I immediately had to have a wee, ten minutes later another one, and then another. Mother gave me a peculiarly suspicious look and bent down to smell my breath.

"Haven't you got more sense than to give that ten year old beer?" came Mother's angry voice as she disappeared through the kitchen door, slamming it behind her.

A SHILLINGSWORTH OF PROMISES

I heard nothing but a few rumbling voices, as I dropped off to sleep, missing my dinner and waking about four hours later with the first of my many pub-induced headaches.

By 1925 the post war economic boom was on the wane, a growing crisis of overproduction with diminishing sales. Unemployment began to raise its ugly head and Father was sometimes a victim. It seemed that the bi-annual trip to Aunt May and Uncle Fred's for the Christmas knees-up was in jeopardy. But the family told us, "You find the fares and we will do the rest."

This trip to 10 Cowdrey Road, South Wimbledon, by train to Charing Cross, with a short walk down Villiers Street, underneath the arches to the Thames embankment, to wait for and ride on that wonder of wonders, a double decker electric tram all the way to Merton High Street, was then my joy of joys. A new world of lights, noise and traffic, a hectic mixture of trams, buses, and horse-drawn vehicles. I was spellbound and swivel-necked trying to read and appreciate a variety of huge and gaudy advertising hoardings, remembering the classics of course, The Bisto Kids, Cherry Blossom boot polish, Pear's soap, Swan Vestas and many others.

Aunt May's flat was the ground floor of a two storey terraced house comprising a front room, a middle bedroom, a tiny five foot square scullery with a back living room complete with the inevitable black kitchener. And of course an outdoor loo. There was a common front entrance with the top flat, the stairs running up from the passage, and used during the three day Christmas party for storing the beer crates, imprisoning poor old Mrs Hoddinot for the duration. This dear old soul I remember only too well. She was short, somewhat tubby, had a big wart on her chin and only two teeth, one up and one down. She also had a great liking for all children and for me in particular and would almost frighten me to death with her great halitosical hug of greeting, the first of which had me worried – it was the wart I think. However, she was always seemingly content and happy and enjoyed the party, tackling the stored crates from the top end, for the milk stout, her favourite tipple, was always on the highest stair within planned and easy reach.

The parties were nearly always successful and nearly always the same. Guaranteed plenty to drink, plenty to eat and plenty of noise. Cousin Rose playing the piano, Aunt May having a bash on it, massacring such old favourites as Mother Brown, My Old Man, Irish Eyes, The Stein Song, and any old alcoholic tune that came to mind. Then inevitably the 'sing, say or show' saga. Bare bums were ten a penny. Shy old Mum would edge away to find some glasses to wash, or to check on the sleeping babes, while Father would save himself with his inevitable 'butcher's dog' song.

"There was two-legs sitting on three legs, one leg in his hand, when up came four-legs, he bit two-legs and grabbed that one leg, understand?" The song goes on but my memory doesn't. I'm a leg adrift already I think.

Other mental movies come to me of my cousin Jim taking flashlight photographs, and setting fire to the paper decorations when holding his small tray of flash powder a little too close to a low slung paper bell. There was panic for a couple of seconds, invoking screams and shouts which quickly subsided when it was realised that there were enough half-filled glasses around to put out even a major conflagration.

Boxing day morning would bring the aftermath, with the front room stinking of stale beer, cigarette and cheap cigar smoke. The now cooled off, once sweaty recumbent figures would be fast asleep and open mouthed, in all kinds of pain inducing postures, all totally unaware of having been the victims of cousin Jim's burnt cork treatment, their faces streaked and blackened to hilarious unrecognisability. Really not a pretty sight.

We kids of course were bright as buttons, having been put to bed early the previous evening. All seven of us being loaded sideways onto the large bed at intervals, as fatigue overcame us. A mixture of boys and girls, happy in the arms of Morpheus. Cousin Alice though had other ideas. She was some two years older than I, and happened to be bedded next to me. Immediately I was being propositioned to have a cuddle like Rose and Willy do (they were in their twenties and engaged). I don't know where, when or what she had seen, but it involved a lot of wriggling about and left me feeling somewhat funny. I had not as yet read D.H. Lawrence, so my loins and their reactions were still a mystery to me.

The return trip to Hythe was never an anti-climax, and I became increasingly disillusioned with the visits to London as I became increasingly fond of life by the sea and in the beautiful countryside around my home. Sadly enough, it is now impossible to follow the path of many of my old well trodden and well remembered near to nature rambles.

Progress progresses, and people need homes. I don't begrudge any of them, and I feel happy that they have chosen to live in such lovely surroundings in which, no doubt, they too have discovered walks of their own that, because of the changed geography, would be unknown to me. That doesn't destroy the satisfaction and joy, however, that I get from remembering my lost routes. Following one in my mind's eye along the course of the Redbrooks Stream, with its tiny horseshoe lakes, formed in exactly the same way as those of large and famous rivers. Then to gather chestnuts at Forty Steps, before passing the isolated country cottage in the field beyond, surrounded by its ivy and chickens, and then on to Sandling Road where, from what is now the site of a girls' school one would have a clear view right across Hythe Bay to Dungeness point.

From Saltwood the choice of ways back to Hythe were many. Via Saltwood castle, passing the horse chestnut trees, thinking maybe of Thomas a Becket and those murdering sycophantic knights, through to Station Hill and down to Hythe. Or from Sandling Road down Darky cum Lovers' Lane (it was known as both). Or via Hillcrest Road going down by the church with its skull laden crypt, and then down underneath the Town Hall, across the High Street to the canal, by the old war time tank and band stand, across the bridge to Ladies' Walk, then to the sea front and home. The canal banks, the Elham valley, the Roughs, Lympne, the marshes and less well known localities would also be ideal places where a happy, armchair based nostalgic ramble could be enjoyed .

Nineteen twenty six came and with it the General Strike, and at the age of ten this was to me something which held the attention and deep concern of the grown-ups only. But I seem to remember my sympathies were with those who tried hard to keep things going. I didn't like the newspaper pictures of hate filled faces and raised fists threatening mayhem. Surely there were better ways of understanding and overcoming whatever were the root causes of the troubles. Looming up for me though were a few troubles of my own.

I had been among the limited number of children to be recommended to sit for the year's scholarship examination for entry to the Harvey Grammar School in Folkestone. Things, as usual, were hard at home, and Mother argued that, as Bert had had to forego his opportunity, because by leaving school at the age of fourteen he would contribute to his own upkeep, then I would have to do the same. Father, as usual, was neutral.

But living next door at number 26 was a retired gentleman's butler and his wife, a Mr and Mrs Simmonds. Mrs Simmonds had been in service as a lady's companion, so they were a comparatively worldly couple with, I imagine, enough income from the interest on their lifetime savings to allow them to enjoy a very quiet and inexpensive retirement. However, though living amongst the lower classes they weren't quite of the lower classes, a fact I think which triggered Mr. Simmonds's very pointed remark to my father. "You prevented your first son from having a good chance in life by refusing permission for him to sit the exams. Surely you are not going to be so hard, and if I may say so, so stupid, as to deny your second son the chance."

Father, I remember, repeated this one-way conversation to Mother, who was more than a little dumbfounded at being classified stupid, as all she had in mind was the welfare of the family. This needed money, and I should provide my share as soon as possible. She disappeared in high dudgeon to give that old interfering so and so a talking to. An hour later she returned, looking strangely pensive, and said to me,

"Do you really think you would like to go over there to Folkestone, to that posh school?" I simply said, "If I pass the exam – yes."

"OK then, you'd better pass the exam, go to the Grammar school, and make us all proud of you, especially him next door. If you don't you'll be in trouble, not from me, from him."

The next day Mr Simmonds called me into what he called his back parlour. The same room in our house was called the kitchen. He invited me to sit down, then spoke of grasping opportunities, and how it needed a good educational background to be a success in life; its rewards were great, and so on. I suppose as a demonstration of the veracity of his remarks he gave me a shilling, wishing me well, and hoping I wouldn't disappoint my Mum and Dad. I shyly thanked him and gave him a shilling's worth of promises, thinking 'He's not such a bad old soul after all.'

I returned next door wondering not how or if I was going to pass the exam, but whether I should tell Mum about my shilling. In the event I did and she said with the suspicion of a tear, "Keep it, Boy, but remember it's got to be earnt."

Further along the coast at Broadstairs, about this time I imagine, was another young boy with a father in the building trade. He too would be preparing for the scholarship exams. He was successful and finished up many years later re-arranging the furniture at 10 Downing Street. He also had something to do with the arrangements whereby the United Kingdom joined the European Economic Community, though the degree and nature of that union is still unsettled. What a great pity it was that he had to lose the battle with the miners, and subsequently the confidence of the electorate. An expert yachtsman, an accomplished conductor and a gourmet nosher of no mean repute. A very full life!

I too gained my scholarship. Where oh where did I go wrong? Thank God!

Of the actual examination I recall very little, except in one of the tests the letter 'N' had to be written upside down. It cost me anxious minutes of agony and irritation. Eventually I wrote it the right way up, that is, upside down! And I'm still not sure. The English paper gave me a choice of an essay on 'Power'. Very boldly I started by stating 'The power of nature will always be greater than the power of man.' I didn't know a lot about either, but it

A SHILLINGSWORTH OF PROMISES

gave ample scope for the mental meanderings of a ten year old. Exampling the ease with which the seas in their rage destroyed the man built Martello towers and also sank the mighty man made, unsinkable, *Titanic*.

I was interviewed and tested in the oral part of the examination by a Mr Forbes. A large man with a mass of beautiful grey hair and an encouraging smile, creating a very calming ambience, which helped my confidence no end. Here, I had to put into chronological order a number of historical events, and then followed some mental arithmetic involving very simple fractions; simple maybe, but at the time a half of an eighth, and fifteen per cent of three hundred seemed anything but simple.

A final interview with the headmaster accompanied by a parent, Mum of course, Father was in work and working, was in the nature of an introduction, also I think to ascertain the degree of financial assistance that each scholarship boy would be given. In my case help with fares to and from school was granted, pride preventing Mother making other requests. The fares were considered a bonus, obtaining free access to Grammar school education was the real prize.

My first day of attendance, early in September 1926, saw me waiting in the Red Lion Square, if not immaculately turned out, at least with no patches in sight, to catch the transport between Hythe and the Harvey Grammar School in Folkestone. This was provided by a privately owned charabanc, a solid-tyred, open topped relic, fighting senility and the daily wear and tear of twenty or so carefree and active youngsters. Conquering Sandgate Hill was always a chancy thing, the old vehicle struggling and spluttering almost to a halt at each double-declutched graunching gear change, before finally clanking its way to Cheriton Road to deliver its ribald passengers on time. A daily miracle.

The return journey was less hazardous, being partly downhill and with no estimated time of arrival. The driver puffed less frequently on his ever present and droopy Craven A, and the conductor was less likely to use his sealed leather money bag as a weapon of control or revenge. He was Christened, I remember, by some alliterating young wag as 'Bully, Biffer, Bruiser, Basher, Bert'.

My first reactions to my new school were very mixed. I missed the cosiness of the old single storeyed stone buildings, the homeliness of the teachers and the sense of belonging. The old church of England school was in our part of Hythe, and Hythe was my town. The 'Grammar' was more remote in both senses, the buildings large and modern, the teachers strange, and the atmosphere, though not exactly impersonal, had no real warmth. There was also a strict discipline, with its consequent punishments for the breaking of rules. This was alien to me as I always felt that being able to accept any request to do something, I did not need to be ordered to do it. Or to be required to subject myself to enforced disciplines backed up by punishment for non-compliance, because to my mind I didn't need the discipline in the first place.

The sense of strangeness with the teachers was of course soon replaced by a feeling of respectful familiarity for some and, not unnaturally, an intense dislike for others.

A really likeable one was Mr Emerson, the French teacher, or more precisely, the teacher of French, and, as would be expected, a dapper smallish man of infinite patience. The thought of learning to speak a foreign language intrigued and pleased me. Especially as, on a clear day, one could look across the Channel and actually see the land where people really spoke the language. I clearly remember the very first lesson. Forty minutes entirely taken up by an introduction to the five vowels as they would be pronounced by a Frenchman. Mr Emerson's intention was, with a class of thirty or so, to have each one in turn come out to his desk to stare intently at his mouth and tongue as he articulated each and every vowel, and then for the boy to repeat and repeat each one, until he had achieved some semblance of tonal similarity. The first lad, even after thirty odd minutes had not been able to get his tongue around the letter 'A' let alone the rest. I was the second boy called and, having been sitting in the front row, I had been listening intently and mouthing on my own. So with seeming ease I was able to repeat, with an acceptable accent, all five vowels. Mr Emerson turned to the class and said, "There you are, that's the way to speak French."

That evening at home, apropos nothing, I casually remarked to Mum and Dad, "I can speak French you know."

Father challenged, "Come on Son, let's have some then."

"Ah, er, ee, oh, yew" I parroted.

"That's not French my Son, that's bowel trouble."

Mother, suffering an attack of intuition, asked, "What's the difference?" How did she know that French lessons would, in the future, seem to me to be particularly '*emmerdantes*'?

The first year in Lower Three A grade passed quickly enough, but seemingly with not quite the same effortless assimilation of knowledge that had prevailed heretofore, for it was only Upper Three B into which I progressed. Here a sad attempt was made to enlighten, and introduce me to, the grammar and powers of the ancient language of Latin. Taught, strangely

A SHILLINGSWORTH OF PROMISES

enough, by a Mr Latimer who used not only his tongue but the edge of a wooden foot ruler to emphasise and convey his meanings. All to no avail, for Latin declensions would bore me to death. Bonus, Bona, Bonum – ad infinitum. The only residual bit of knowledge from a full year's tuition being my appreciation of how a charabanc became an omnibus and thence a bus. It wasn't even a matter of '*volo non valeo*', I just could not appreciate wasting brain power on something as dead as a dead language. The '*volo*' certainly did not apply and the '*non valeo*' remains a question. I never put it to the test, for after a year I chose geography instead.

Homework of course was always a test of strength, whether to enjoy to the full my free time, or to be seduced into sitting at home being good. The compromise usually, was to try to do any prep on the school bus, or in the few moments before the lesson began. This system created a lot of scope to enjoy and take part in the activities of local life, such as when, on some summer and autumn evenings the family would sit waiting and anticipating a mouth watering meal of a frying pan full of either sprats or mackerel. To be served hot and crisp with chunks of thickly cut bread. These fish would have spent the early afternoon swimming in shoals too close to the shore not to be spotted and netted by the ever vigilant local fishermen. Mainly the Griggs', Wires' and Blackmans', all large families of strong and weather beaten men, manning not only the fishing boats but also, when required, the lifeboat.

The sprats and mackerel in those days would be caught by encircling the shoals with nets which were cast over rollers attached to the sterns of small, sturdy rowing boats. The ropes from one end of the net would be held by men on the beach and the boat, having encircled the shoal, paying out the net meanwhile, would beach further along. Then both ends of the net would slowly be pulled ashore by the fishermen and a multitude of willing kids. Whose reward, after the main catch had been hauled in, would be a bucketful of fresh, wriggling fish, and eventually a tasty evening meal with the family.

Homework, though always considered to be an intrusion on one's private time, was of course at times reluctantly given some degree of priority. Such as when required for the end of term exams. These exams being designed to reveal any lack of attainment. At these times a period of intensive study would be undertaken in an attempt to forestall any such revelations being made. To this end we potential lunk heads would couple up to help each other out with question and answer sessions. My helpmate was a certain George Hilton, he was my age and my size, five foot and not much else, an only son, so we used his home on cramming nights.

He lived quite close to the Hythe Church of England school, in a very old cottage which stands to this day, as does the little stone wall nearby, surrounding a triangle of land between St Leonard's Road and Albert Road. I appreciated the quiet and homely atmosphere of that little cottage, the tiny rooms, the ever burning coke fire and Mrs Hilton's hot scones. She was a tiny Irish lady, kindliness personified, somewhat like an escaped nun. She had that air about her. Her thick Irish brogue entranced me, and sometimes puzzled me, as I didn't always get the exact gist of what this angel from Cork was saying. On the other hand Mr Hilton was not at all difficult to understand, a tall hard man with an acid tongue who had great trouble when angered, and that was often, in stringing five words together without three of them being swear words. A retired postman, a dedicated gardener, and an enemy of all those noisy brats from the school next door. An inveterate follower of the horses and, he claimed, a master interpreter of the form book. He was as gaunt as his wife was cuddly, and was not a man a little boy should argue with. So I didn't. Although I did once get the better of him, somewhat fortuitously it must be said.

Along the northern boundary of the large garden at the rear of his cottage was a tall stone, south facing wall, which was ideal for the cultivation of outdoor tomatoes, and the crop each year would be disposed of wholesale to the International Stores in the High Street. The growth and size of the crop was invariably encouraged by copious feedings of the plants with well rotted horse dung. This was gathered from the stables at the rear of the Duke's Head public house, some two hundred yards away across the school playing field which was itself part of the 'Green'. The collection of this manure called for maybe a dozen trips with an average size garden wheelbarrow. A job which was a little too much for the ageing pop Hilton, so he cut into his profits and paid George and I a shilling each to do it for him. George's bob went into his savings book, and mine mysteriously stayed in Pop's pocket as he took me aside and said, "How would you like to turn your shilling into, say, five shillings?"

"By doing what?" I wanted to know.

"It's like this if this afternoon I put your shilling on a horse at odds of four to one, then when it wins you will get four shillings winnings plus your own shilling back. That makes five shillings."

It all sounded a bit too easy to me. So I queried the 'when it wins' bit.

"The form book can't be wrong, can it?" he assured me and added, "Let me know what you want to do after dinner."

A SHILLINGSWORTH OF PROMISES

I couldn't make up my mind whether he was being crafty or helpful. I gave him the benefit of the doubt, but decided to look at the racing pages of Dad's paper and spike his guns by picking my own horse. That way I couldn't blame him if I lost, and my faith in human nature wouldn't be at risk. I searched the back pages and found an item headed 'Stable News', and listed beneath was the information I was looking for. It read: 'Manton – 3 o'clock – Lady Marjorie will win.' I thought in my innocence, if the trainer says it's going to win, that's as good as old Pop saying so. Whether Pop actually laid the bet or not I don't know, but the evening paper brought the confidently anticipated news that Lady Marjorie had won and, at odds of ten to one. I was pleased, Mum and Dad were very pleased, and Pop, he was more or less dumbfounded, only a few colourful words escaping his fluttering bottom jaw.

The following Saturday, a similar story, a different horse, Shipbourne, and at the same odds of ten to one. I was beginning to think, who requires an education? All you need is the back page of the *Daily Herald*. Fortunately for me it did not work out like that. Two more back breaking Saturday mornings humping horse shit, two sure tips from the 'Stable News', two 'will wins' which didn't, and I reluctantly realised it was the academic course for me, not the race course, and that there really wasn't an easily reachable rainbow's end. Pop though still went on chasing losers, growing monster tomatoes and keeping himself happy swearing his way out of disappointments. He also thereafter paid me in cash!

However, on the academic course my year in 4B saw the beginnings of my discontent with life at the Grammar school. Sadly, it stemmed from a sense of loyalty to my working class background, as I tried to make excuses for the resentment of my mates. The resentment showed itself in the normal childish way of name-calling, and the mocking of Grammar school uniforms and insignia. But it was enough to put doubt in my mind, indicating that perhaps I was getting ideas above my station.

Not only that, but those that had left school were already earning money, and were able to buy twopenny packets of fags, and even chocolate coconut squares from Mrs Crump's little wooden shop on the sea front, where now stands the Stade Court Hotel.

It was 1928 and I was thirteen years of age and experiencing the 'risings' of sexual awareness. I was becoming intrigued by the throbbings and the spattering of sperm, not realising that I was on the verge of developing the equipment, or power tool, which every man needs to fulfil his role in life. I also of course quickly became aware of the changing shapes of Dorothy, Kathleen, Phyllis and others, and of their liking for coconut squares, chat and flattery. I lost out to my working contemporaries and felt frustrated and resentful at having to suffer the unrelieved pangs of teenage sexual hunger, brought on by a surfeit of education and unfair competition.

I also suffered at school. For it was about this time on a windy and miserable November day, during the afternoon break, that I took shelter from the elements by standing under a window on the lee side of the main school building. Other kids, more boisterous and uncaring than I, were playing soccer with some unfortunate's school cap, which happened to land at my feet. I picked it up, intending to return it to its owner, another scholarship lad, whose parents could probably ill afford the expense of a new cap. At this moment the window above me flew open and the voice of the headmaster angrily ordered me to go immediately to his study.

He had been watching the game and meant to use me as an example, accusing me of being an active participant, and maybe the ringleader. In spite of my protests and explanation, I was ordered there and then to bend over. I received six sonking whacks across my arse from an expert. For later, when checking the damage to the receiving area, it was like looking at a fleshy hot cross bun, as all six strokes had landed on the same spot precisely. An accurately performed miscarriage of justice, and it hurt both morally, physically and psychologically.

I began to think that life was becoming just a little confusing, not knowing whether to concentrate on higher or lower things, a head versus penis situation. Looking back in retrospect the result would seem to be a draw, though not exactly nil – nil, becoming more like an away win as I grew older.

It was 1929 and my personal period of disappointment and depression coincided with the beginning of the world's financial depression, set off by the Wall Street crash in America. The repercussions of this event, though not exactly or directly concentrating themselves on 28 Cobden Road, did nevertheless probably have some bearing on the fact that Father was having increasingly longer periods of unemployment, and Mother a bigger tussle providing something for the table.

These adverse conditions, strangely enough, brought me some measure of relief from my own troubles. For after long discussion between ourselves to find ways of reducing the worries of financial insufficiency and the agonies of being skint, it was decided that the quarterly money order sent to pay my fares would be used to buy a bicycle on the never-never. As the size of the money order was greater than the instalments, this would create a few extra pennies for Mother, the family's financial wizard, to play with.

A catalogue from W. Graves of Sheffield was borrowed from Mrs Pilcher across the way. Then with delight and excitement I selected a 22 inch framed three speed 'Speed King', with chrome handlebars, a pump, and a saddle bag complete with tools. Then for weeks, when at home, I was anchored in the front room watching and praying for the horse drawn van from the South Eastern Railway to arrive. It took an endless 33 days before what I considered to be my scholarship prize arrived.

It was a Saturday morning and everyone helped to rip off what seemed like miles of protective wrappings. I was so excited I couldn't talk, being so full of pride and too near to tears. Finally I had the saddle and handlebars adjusted and then took off on my first ride. I got onto the Dymchurch Road and pedalled and pedalled, through to Dymchurch, New Romney, Rye, and on to Hastings, hardly believing that the gleaming reflection from each shop window *en route* was in fact imaging the truth. Arriving on the sea front I finally stopped, leant my sparkling new possession against a bench, sat down and spent more than a while just admiring, thinking, "It's mine, it's mine."

Suddenly, I began to feel tired. I had in fact covered about thirty miles, using up all my breakfast energy and a fair percentage of any built-in natural reserves I might have had. I was hungry and thirsty, and moneyless. So it was simply a matter of on my bike, and get back home. It was a long, sad journey, uphill out of Hastings to start with, taking toll of what little energy I had left. The hard leather of the new saddle almost took the skin off my tender bottom, and my legs seemed to be in a state of rebellious conflict with my mind, as I agonisingly covered the miles I had so happily and thoughtlessly travelled earlier on.

Eventually I arrived home late in the afternoon, feeling not only wobbly kneed and knackered, but half dead into the bargain. I had no trouble lying down for a couple of days, it was the sitting that hurt; which meant, sadly, that the first instalment on the bike was a dead loss, for I had to take the bus to school. But as there were only twenty one weeks at three shillings a week to be paid, Mother did eventually reap some benefit from the enterprise.

My benefits came in other ways, as a muscle builder, fighting the south westerly gales along Sandgate sea front and also conquering the hefty gradients of Sandgate Hill and Coolinge Lane. My sense of independence was also boosted as I could now time my arrival at school to coincide with the general exodus from the assembly hall, after the morning's religious five minutes, thus escaping the attention of the prefects detailed to catch and report late arrivals. The old bus always got us there in time to enjoy the miseries of early morning Hall.

I also now had, for the first time in my life, a possession which evoked the admiration and maybe jealousy of a few of my school mates. A little ego boosting which, at the time, did me no harm at all. What did do me harm, however, was my first real fight. It was with Kenny, the second son of 'Buller' Griggs, who was the coxswain of the Hythe lifeboat. Kenny, a year older than I and bigger by a couple of inches, had borrowed my brand new bike by telling Mother that I needed it, and he had come to fetch it. He then enjoyed himself by riding it up and down the stone steps between the beach and the promenade. When I spotted him my glittering prize had already suffered scratches and broken spokes.

The attack was immediate. Uncontrolled anger and resentment sent the adrenaline rushing through my veins as I grabbed him around the neck in a two armed strangle hold, and I struggled down the beach to get him into the sea. I think my intention was to drown him. At that point I certainly couldn't see reason, only scratched enamel and buckled wheels. Fortunately his physical superiority frustrated my murderous ambitions, for after some ten minutes or so the adrenaline petered out and the whole thing deteriorated into a shouting match, using newly acquired swear words at tannoy level. Uncharacteristically, Ken gave in completely and slowly left the scene, giving the bike a final kick as he went. It took four or five days for our scratches and bruises to heal, two days for a dozen or so spokes to be replaced by Mr Capon, the little sad faced owner of the lovely smelling wooden cycle shop in Prospect Road, and a couple of weeks before we shook hands and became friends again.

Some two months later, to while away a Saturday afternoon, we decided to try out the joys of smoking. Poverty and hygienic ignorance allowed us to go on a fag-end finding jaunt around the local streets with another pal and, after collecting enough butt ends, we took ourselves out onto the 'ranges' to hide amongst the gorse bushes to savour the joys of Lady Nic. Ken, being the biggest and the eldest, kept and smoked the longer ends. After sampling two short ones I gave up, I was feeling sick and dizzy.

Alan mastered a few more then he too retired, looking pale and decidedly unhappy. So we left Ken stoically puffing out clouds of blue smoke, and we staggered home to our respective Mums to be, in my case, sympathetically chastised back to health.

Much later in the day Kenny's Dad called in to ask if I knew where Kenny was and I took him to the spot where I had last seen him. He was still there, flat on his back, breathing spasmodically and as yellow as a Chinaman, reeking of fag smoke and surrounded by a soggy mess of pin-holed dog-ends. We managed to stagger home with him, although it was no mean task

A SHILLINGSWORTH OF PROMISES

across half a mile of loose shingle. It took a week or more, with medical attention, to put him back on his feet again, and nearly as long for my strained muscles to stop aching.

Smoking is said to retard growth, both physically and mentally, but I hardly think a couple of illicit dog-ends were responsible for my indifferent academic performance at this time. Nothing would seem to motivate me, not even the genuine concern of some of the staff, who were a mixture of ex-wartime servicemen and young inexperienced teachers straight from the universities with their newly acquired degrees. They all in turn, after a period of blandishments and cajoling, gave up, to let me drift along, hoping that maybe somewhere a hidden thirst for knowledge would eventually reassert itself.

To break the monotony of classroom routine in which the taking of copious notes seemed to be the sole method of dispensing facts, I would condense or shorten the text in order to keep up. At the same time abiding by the association of ideas theory I would use what I deemed to be acceptable *aide memoir*. For example calling William the Conqueror, Bill the Conk, and turning Henry VIII into Hal ate. All of which was of course totally unappreciated by the young history master who, when meandering round the class at dictation speed, came up behind me, read my notes, gave a bellow of disbelief and promptly rapped me over the nut. It didn't change my style or attitude, but I proved a point by taking the Form 4B prize for history at the end of term exam.

But I was not so successful with other deviations made during the English Literature lesson. Poor Mr Halford, the English teacher, who was totally absorbed in, and master of, his subject, was flogging a dead horse when he so conscientiously tried to convince me that William Shakespeare, i.e., Bill Shakes, was the greatest of all writers.

"I come to bury Caesar, not to praise him..." I had to learn the speech word perfect and could repeat it parrot fashion at the nod of a head.

During class, 'Hamlet', 'The Merchant of Venice', 'Romeo and Juliet' all had to be read and struggled through, with each boy forced to participate by being allocated a part. Each and every reading necessitated detailed explanations and interpretations of what the great Bard had said and meant. To my youthful and unclassical mind the unravelling of these convoluted speeches and conversations was just a little too much, and if my allotted part was a small one with only a few words some seven or eight pages further on in the play, then I would have a very strong tendency to drop off to sleep.

Awaking from one of these nodding off spells, I realised I was in some sort of trouble, for Mr Halford's face was as black as thunder as he glared at me. I had slept right through my four word part, and the play had come to a sudden halt. However, as I dumbly stared back at that accusing face, expecting the lightning to follow the thunder, the clouds lifted and that tortured face slowly became wreathed in a lovely self satisfied smile. Then this Master of Arts regaled us with his pun of the year "Ah, I see there's been a Hitch in the proceedings." I got away with it that time but not the next, which happened some months later.

The class had been set the task of learning an extract by heart. This I did to my satisfaction and then set about amusing myself by re-writing the balcony scene from Romeo and Juliet. Juliet, red-faced with passion;

"Romeo, Romeo, wherefore art thou Romeo?"

Romeo, squinting upwards; "A'm darn 'ere."

Juliet, cocking a deaf 'un, loudly; "Romeo, Romeo, wherefore art thou Romeo?"

Romeo, remonstratingly; "I just bleedin' told yer, A'm darn 'ere."

Juliet, still cocking a deaf 'un, calls; "Romeo, Romeo..."

Romeo, exasperated; "You gorn Mutt an' Jeff or summink? A'm darn 'ere, wiv me fing in me 'and."

Juliet, realising her luck was in; "Git up 'ere den, quick. Wot yer doin' darn there, wastin' time."

This re-write was never presented to dear Mr Halford for approval. I don't think his sensitive classical soul would have survived the shock. I was of course unable to recite the set task to his satisfaction and duly received his acid admonitions. It was Mr Halford who had marked my entrance exam English paper, and he found it hard to believe how a child could have reached a peak at the age of ten and then have deteriorated to such an abysmal level by the age of thirteen. I suppose, as with every one of us, it was simply a matter of timing between potential and accomplishment, both of which are infinitely variable factors anyway.

It was somewhere around this time that I experienced my first encounter with death. Nothing at all dramatic, it happened when the granny of one of my home town pals passed away. Alby Curd was my pal's name and we were whiling away a Saturday morning when he suddenly asked if I had ever seen a dead body. On my saying no, he invited me in to see his granny who was lying at rest in the front room of a tiny terraced house in Chapel Street.

The room seemed stagnant and dark and a faint beam of light penetrated the drawn blinds, illuminating the fine old wrinkled face, now a frozen mask of what, for a lifetime, had reflected unerringly all her human emotions.

I felt sad, but not unduly upset, and while making my way home I fell to pondering on, strangely enough not death, but life.

This short experience really convinced me that death was simply a quick transfer into complete and total nothingness. Whatever that dear old granny had been, had done, had learnt, had known, was now completely lost. Except for what she may have passed on to others in the form of knowledge. This led me on to the assumption that there is no such thing as original thought, only a variation of or improvement on acquired knowledge; and knowledge is only an appreciation and understanding of something which already exists, this something having been produced by those that have gone before.

I rejected the thought of Granny's soul being heaven or hell bound. An indeterminate journey in either case. I came to the conclusion that death was finite, and it was the infinite variety of actually living that really mattered.

Later in the day I tried to talk to Dad about the day's experience, telling him I didn't think I'd mind dying as long as I'd enjoyed living. He made a typical comment that at times he found it hard to enjoy life, but he would no doubt find it harder to enjoy dying.

And in any case, for a lot of people, sadly, life was simply a matter of going to work, to get money, to buy food, to get energy, to go to work, to get money, to buy food, to get energy, to go to... "OK Dad, OK Dad," I said, getting the message. He smiled and carried on trimming the rolls of wallpaper for his current late night moonlighting job. The whole month's proceeds from one of these jobs in Blackhouse Hill, where I had to take his supper of hot tea and sandwiches, was used to pay for Mum's false teeth. They fitted beautifully, making her look years younger, a suitable reward and outcome for a month's work.

Unfortunately for Dad the long walk each evening to Blackhouse Hill brought on an acute attack of aching feet, which caused him to walk Chaplin-like in an exaggerated effort to avoid aggravating the tenderest spots. I remember him on some evenings spending hours paring huge slices of hardened skin from the soles of his feet using a murderous looking little corn razor, and then sighing with relief as he went on a trial trip around the kitchen, with his feet now pointing more or less in the direction he was going.

September 1929 and I progressed into the Remove and the mysteries of physics in the form of magnetism, heat, light and sound. And mathematics advanced to Algebra and geometric riders. These subjects had great appeal which meant that history, geography, French and English all suffered a balancing lack of interest, reflected of course in poor test and examination results.

Near the end of one of these exams, with the woodwork master as invigilator, I was accused by him of talking during the exam and reported to the headmaster. I had finished my own answer papers and was sitting watching the clock, when I was hissed by the lad behind who had faulty vision and couldn't see the clock. Then I corner-mouthed the answer to his request for the time. This was my crime and the headmaster duly gave me my second six strokes across the arse, for he believed not a word of my explanation. Which was, simply, how could I have been cheating when in fact my answer papers had already been finished and handed in?

I was seething with anger and totally frustrated because I could see no way of righting the injustice. I could have accepted punishment for talking, if hissing 'twenty past three' was actually talking, but the accusation of cheating was absurd. I was on the point of making a few mind boggling suggestions as to what he might do with his Grammar school, but the thought of being expelled strangled the escaping words somewhere in the region of my epiglottis. But I did slam the door on leaving, as a rebellious 'thank you'. Sadly, this brought no alleviation for the pain in my arse but it was some slight relief for my injured pride.

To finish the saga of these unwarranted attacks on my rear end, a third beating was given as a result of a report from the school caretaker that I had blocked up the WC with orange peel. Untrue, of course, and I could never work out how the accusation could ever have been made, mistaken identity being the only explanation. Anyhow, I assured the Head that the only time our family ever had oranges was at Christmas. This explanation was deemed to be frivolous at best, and a lie at worst. So the school penalty for lying was duly administered. This time a few tears welled up and trickled down my distorted face, and for the first time a look of concern, and maybe doubt, flickered across the old man's face. However, I quickly recovered enough *sang froid* to reassure him it was not the pain that caused the tears, only the injustice. Whether this remark touched his soul or not, I'll never know, but I suffered no further humiliations for the rest of my years at the Harvey Grammar, even thoroughly enjoying my final year in 5A, where the beak himself presided over the mathematics classes.

The Easter holidays of 1930 brought me a temporary release from the seat of punishment and learning, and my Aunt May financed a few days break at Wimbledon. There I had a cousin, Fred Beadle, who was some eight years older than I. The depression was now making life difficult for all, but cousin Fred was enjoying the fruits of a well paid but miserably filthy and smelly job at a leather tanning works by the river Wandle. As compensation for the dirt and suffering during the week, there was always enough wherewithal to enjoy a few pleasures at the weekends, when a visit to the Dog and Dirt track in Plough Lane was a must. Not forgetting the football at Craven Cottage for Fulham's home games.

It was to a Fulham versus Portsmouth game that cousin Fred took me, and the journey to the match in the crowded underground was unexpectedly disturbing. Just the proximity and pressure of all those bodies, with their heavy mixture of friendly and unfriendly smells, filled me with a desire to escape, and a yearning for clean, fresh air. But relief came on entering the Fulham football ground, a green oasis which, although surrounded by crowded terraces, seemed vastly less oppressive. There were maybe ten thousand spectators and I had never before seen so many people in one place. Glancing around me in amazement I suddenly thought, "Where did they all come from?" Imagination answering, told me, "They all started way back, from a little tickle in the end of someone's dick, aided and abetted by the activities of a determined spermatozoa, encouraged by a welcoming glint in the eye of a loving partner."

Anyway, what I was looking at was only the result of successful tickles, and adding in all the unsuccessful ones, then there must be a pastime more popular even than football amongst the workers of the world, giving a new twist to Marx's advice, "Workers of the world, unite."

Now, looking intently at all these results of bygone activities standing around me, I suddenly felt a little puzzled. The human race, what were we? These people and me. What do we all do? Nobodies, trying to be somebodies, all in a relentless search for some sort of fulfilment. But succeeding only in enjoying the banalities of life and doing nothing much more than just turning food into faeces. Emotional and animated 'shit machines' sustained by a lifetime of expected and supposedly better tomorrows.

My convoluted cogitations were suddenly interrupted by cousin Fred pounding my earhole with a long dissertation on the reasons why Fulham could not possibly be beaten. Looking at me he said, "You ain't even been listening, 'ave yer?" I think Portsmouth won three nil.

The journey home was uneventful and quiet. The evening came, bringing with it an unforgettable visit to the Dirt Track. And it was all the noise, the multi-coloured gear of the riders, the rasping exhausts of the busy little engines, the flying ashes, the skidding crashes and the final winning burst of speed at the end of the last laps that maybe convinced me that the combination of racing machine and shit machine was maybe something that could question the logic of my earlier thoughts. Jim Kempster and Vic Huxley became my immediate heroes, they of course being S.M.'s of a very high order, respected, accomplished, fearless and brave.

Around this time a famous four legged machine was ruling the greyhound world, Mick the Miller, who won the Greyhound Derby twice, once in 1929 and then again in 1930. He also held the record of nineteen consecutive wins. So cousin Fred felt obliged to take me to see this wonder dog in action. Of course around Wimbledon way Mick was king, and an anti-depressant in those dreary days for the doggy *cognoscenti*. The bookies would quote no odds for an outright win for Mick the Miller, just varying odds for a combination of Mick as winner and one of the other five to take second place. One bookie, however, gave no odds for Mick but virtually anything you liked for the others, starting at twelve to one for a dog called Loughnagare. I liked the name, and sixpence to win would give me six shillings and my tanner back.

I must mention that at this time the only thing I knew about Mick the Miller was cousin Fred's, and everyone else's, advice that he couldn't be beaten. But Loughnagare was such a lovely big dog and surely worth a little bet. So I took my tanner and my impudence down to the row of bookies to lay my bet. The recipient of my considered wager, smirking at his mates, said, "Got a right one 'ere."

To me he said, "What yer doin' son, risking your life's savings? Nuffin' ain't goin' to beat the Miller."

I think he was genuinely concerned about me losing my tanner but he took the bet just the same.

The race became due and the dogs were paraded and then put into their respective traps. The electric hare buzzed and rattled around the track on its preliminary circuit. The lights dimmed as the hare flashed past the opening traps, releasing the whining dogs in a multi coloured flash to chase the always winning hare. Some ten or fifteen yards out Mick was badly bumped. He stumbled and fell then recovered and raced on, but too late. The big and beautiful Loughnagare romped home, making me, I'm sure, the only punter to be paid out in the whole of the stadium. Ignorance indeed became bliss. It was probably the sequence breaker for Mick the Miller, and I wasn't old enough, or involved enough, to feel sorry. A shame.

The Easter holiday was wearing out but I still had time for a quick visit to see Aunt Sis and cousins Jim and Rose at 41 Sellincourt Road, Tooting. A longish road of terraced houses, some spotlessly clean with their whitewashed

A SHILLINGSWORTH OF PROMISES

front steps, others equally were neglected and dirty. But all the occupants on sunny days, so it seemed, would be out front leaning on their gates, some cheerful some chesty, but all chatty. The rattling of the trams up Merton High Street at the end of the road intermittently interfering with the tales of fearful pregnancies and sufferings from unheard of illnesses with obscure and indescribable symptoms. All unerringly recounted in minute detail, maybe lacking aspirates but not ingenuity. The colourful cockney vocabulary at its best or worst. Troubles involving dustbin lids, or troubles and strife, puzzled me for a long time, until unravelled by cousin Jim.

Aunt Sis' upstairs flat at number 41 was always intriguing to me, with its highly polished brass door knob and knocker, and its remote controlled, mechanically operated door catch. The entrance door led to a shiny lino covered stairway, smelling richly of freshly applied Ronuk, lavender scented. The small living room had a tiny kitchen at the rear with a scrubbed white wooden working top situated immediately in front of a sash window, ivy surrounded and looking out onto a miniscule back yard. Access to which was gained from the living room through a light wooden door giving straight onto a narrow, well scrubbed wooden stairway, with the only WC at the bottom. A tiny affair with a very low seat, very claustrophobic and giving the impression it had been installed as an afterthought. Dark and chilly, maybe a place where one would not spend an awful lot of time contemplating the future in the atmosphere of the past. And if ever it had been required to be used in a case of emergency, I imagine the point of no return would have been reached with uncontrolled relief on or about the fourth step down.

Cousin Jim was older than I and worked as a compositor in Fleet Street. A self assured London lad with a safe job, good looks, a liking for the ladies and an interest in all things technical. At my age of some fourteen years, only the last of these assets stimulated any sense of envy. Thus it was that I was introduced to, and astounded by, the intricacies of the art of 'crystal tickling' with a cat's whisker. The resulting whistles and squeaks coming through the earphones finally resolved themselves into recognisable music. Cousin Jim enthusiastically informed me that I had fine tuned the 'wireless' and was listening to an orchestra playing far away in London and being broadcast by 2 L.O. To me it was inexplicable magic, a phenomenon that was part of the future, and therefore it would have to be gone into when I was a little older.

Sadly, not so long after, cousin Jim contracted tuberculosis and died. In a later era, antibiotics would have saved him. How he would have enjoyed the scientific and technical advances his hobby went through in subsequent years.

On returning to Hythe I had a long fight with my conscience, trying to decide in which direction my literary tastes should take me. As an antidote to *Silas Marner, A Tale of two Cities, The Conquest of Granada* etc. etc. I had been sharing the weekly worries, joys and excitement of Harry Wharton and Co. of Greyfriars. Acquiring a sneaky liking for Vernon Smith, the Bounder, a high regard for Harry of course, a hatred of Quelch (how the name fitted) and sometimes sympathy, but mostly contempt for Billy Bunter, the fat owl of the Remove. Now, under the recently acquired interest in things technical or mechanical, I decided to change to the magazine 'Modern Boy', reading avidly but assimilating little. After a few months of struggling, lacking the very basic know how to really comprehend what I was reading, I disappointed dear old Dad and came home with 'The Thriller' stuffed into my coat pocket. Simon Templar, alias 'The Saint' was much more fun, applying his particular brand of technical perfection to solve impossibly complicated crimes, during the process of which he endlessly escaped from certain death into the arms of adoring, and always beautiful, girls. This was the literature for me. Bill Shakespeare had no chance, it was Leslie Charteris for me. Pure excitement in lieu of pure boredom.

September 1930 and I moved upwards into form 5B. This scholastic year of 1930/31 would bring the realisation that I had final examinations to take in the form of the Matriculation exam of London University. Unfortunately, this realisation came too late, for burgeoning manhood interfered with my powers of concentration, taking my thoughts a long way from trigonometry, logarithms, mechanics or calculus. These distractions, linked with the complexities of irregular verbs, French and otherwise, all seemed a little too complicated for a brain already struggling to cope with and understand the social and physical aspects of just living.

In the event I failed the exam, though only in two compulsory subjects, French language and English Literature. Really not surprising. However, I partially succeeded in my alternative tests. These being set by the University of Life and based on a very different and undefined syllabus.

Now it was early summertime in 1931 and, at the age of 15, an interest in my own personal appearance seemed to dominate my life. It was an effort, I suppose, to try to outdo the attractions that other lads might have on offer. I managed to control my unruly mop with lashings of Brilliantine. Those threepenny tins were quickly used and, much to Mother's disgust, finished up as an oily dark patch on her beautifully white and ironed pillow cases.

My features were beyond any attempt at improvement. After all, what can one do with an overly protrusive hooter? There was some consolation; at

A SHILLINGSWORTH OF PROMISES

least it was in, and proportional to, a rather large head, size seven and a half. So there was a certain degree of natural camouflage, making it look as if it were part of, but not an addition to, a general symmetry of design.

The town was, at this time of year, always alive with attractive girls on holiday and looking for fun. So, as in all seaside resorts, why shouldn't the local lads benefit? The local girls too. Why not? Fresh faces and new accents, it added a little zest to life. Out of season the local lads and lasses had each other, and happily a lot of them eventually married, enjoying, or maybe not enjoying, a lifetime together, some spending the whole of their lives in the same area, and sometimes the same house.

Mother would, during the holiday weeks let off the two front rooms, giving full board and lodging, it seemed to me, to the same couples year in and year out. It provided a bit of extra cash, and enabled us all to enjoy a few of life's little luxuries. Ranging from things like a swivel-headed potato peeler to a long narrow zinc bath for the family to relax in on bath nights. And what bliss that was, washing everything all in one go. But the cold from the concrete kitchen floor, would, unless thickly insulated with Wednesday's and Thursday's Daily Herald, penetrate the bottom of the bath and the bather, reducing any luxuriating to a minimum.

I was particularly enjoying this summer for I had found a soul mate. A Leeds lass, friendly, with a fine sense of humour, and beautifully busted and bottomed. A great temptation to the most controlled of wandering hands. A lovely warm smile and very pretty, with her dark straight hair parted in the middle, curtaining her large, beckoning and exciting hazel eyes. How she was dressed I can't remember but every detail of her face and figure remain with me yet, and her walk could only be described by a fifteen year old as pure temptation.

It was my first big emotional tumble, sadly to end in something less than a fortnight. But those few days took me to heaven and back. We would stroll along the sea front, arms around each other's waists, chatting and laughing and gripping more tightly as each day passed. Now it was a Saturday afternoon and we had arrived at the fishing boat end of the promenade and Griggs' small trawlers were anchored out to sea some thirty to fifty yards beyond low water mark. A beautifully calm day, the Channel crystal clear, the surface softly undulating, silky smooth and beckoning. As we continued our walk along the water's edge, the tiny darting whitebait could be seen in the miniscule waves that unwound themselves along the shore, gently massaging the tiny stones of the shingle beach and creating a cadence of sound that caressed us both as we clung ever closer to each other.

The tumbled ruins of a Martello tower, whose eight foot thick walls, now broken and scattered, provided us with a heavenly privacy. Here we could cuddle, kiss and roll together unleashing what were previously only dreamt of sensations and feelings. Happily discarding our few lightweight bits of clothing we were soon naked, laughing and excited. It was high tide, and the sea was within ten feet of the entrance to our sanctuary. With one mind we both ran and plunged into the invitingly clear water. Swimming, floating, diving, splashing and contriving all the time to make ever more intimate contact. But the chill waters of the Channel eventually forced us ashore and we scuttled back into our retreat to dry and warm our goose-fleshed bodies in the sun.

Still naked and choosing a sun warmed patch of light sandy shingle we lay together and softly caressed each other. It was the first joy of physical love for both of us, requiring no instruction for nature surely, had built male and female in such a way that what should come naturally, really did.

Now satiated and happy and with no sense of shame or regret, we slowly made our way back along the shore, still armed together but not so tightly or urgently as on the outward trip. There was even time, on reaching the area where the fishing boats were beached, to stop and talk to Wilby Lee who was busy installing an old car engine into one of his small boats. The smell of oil, tar and nets assailed my nostrils and I suddenly wanted to be an inshore fisherman. A momentary urge for a sharp tug at my elbow reminded me that other urges were dominating life at the moment. The slight flicker of boredom that showed in her eyes was enough to instantly quell any budding ambition.

But, like all holiday romances, there had to be an end, and on the last day of her holiday we vowed steadfast and lifelong devotion before making our tearful and tender farewells. But then, after a few intense letters swearing undying love, we were both reduced to writing disjointedly about the more mundane things of life. Love could not be sustained on a diet of weather reports and tales of family ills, and it died an inevitable death. And naturally, we both encountered other emotional storms, and never met again. But the memory of first love, as with everyone surely, remains deep and unforgettable.

The Autumn of 1931 came and with it the realisation that my last school year had started, bringing a final chance to Matriculate. This would demand of me hours of swotting and a degree of concentration that I was not sure I possessed. I tried, not always successfully, to divorce myself from the distractions of the evening activities of my non-scholarship contemporaries. One of their lesser evils being to spend hours sitting and nattering away the evening in Ma Crump's shop on the sea front, eating coconut squares and drinking hot cordials. My share being paid for by my ever generous working mates. Names like Kenny and Leslie Griggs, Eric Marsh and Alan Wrigglesworth spring to mind. Another unavoidable distraction on any rain free Wednesday afternoon would be to go beach fishing using a hand slung line with four hooks baited with herring strips or lug-worm, if I could cadge the necessary threepence from Mum to buy them from Twiggy Blackman's shop in the Red Lion Square.

Hythe beach required long casting to reach fish of any size but Dungeness point to the west provided easily reachable deep water and larger fish. So I would cycle to Littlestone and thence onto the hard sand and along to the point. There the sands petered out and the steep shingle beach began. In those days there was no road approach as exists today so quite often I would be the only person fishing there. A contrast to today when the point gives hardly casting room there are so many enthusiasts.

The stretch of coastal sand and dunes between Greatstone and Dungeness was always empty and eerie. Real Doctor Syn country. History and rumour has it that it was a smuggler's paradise and I duly relived their activities as I cycled along. Picturing the revenue men and the smugglers in full combat on a misty dawn, with the smugglers always getting the better of the struggle and finishing up spending the proceeds from their contraband celebrating in the nearby fleshpots and inns of New Romney, Lydd and Dymchurch.

The winters of this era were often very severe and I recall one occasion when a force nine or ten south west gale blew up. The sea became frightening, with huge waves thundering and rolling with a wash of some fifty yards up the beach, spray and spume flying high and far in the howling wind. The lifeboat siren had sounded and the volunteer crew had mustered. The boat itself had been man-handled out of its shed and was resting on the greased sleepers waiting to be crewed and launched. A sailing barge was in distress somewhere off Dungeness and the situation and weather were somewhat reminiscent of the time when the Rye lifeboat disaster occurred, when the boat and the whole crew of gallant volunteers perished in the angry breakers.

The usual crowd had gathered on the promenade, my Dad and I amongst them, leaning on the steel rails totally unconcerned by the drenching elements, to watch the launch of the Hythe boat. This was always a heart pounding event to watch. The boat seemed so small and fragile. A tiny thing with flailing oars and straining oarsmen trying to power their way through the breakers to the comparative safety of the open sea. Sometimes the boat seemed to be at an impossible angle, almost totally upended on the largest of the huge waves before crashing down into the depths between, to reappear magically and safely again on the crest of the following wave.

On this particular day the launch had, for some reason, been delayed before finally getting off to stand by the distressed vessel. During the waiting period a big gangling oaf of a man, a stranger witnessing his first launch, made some offensive remarks, suggesting that the crew were too frightened to go to sea. Father's face showed exactly his disgust and contempt and his answering comment was, fortunately or unfortunately, carried away in the wind. However, his chance came very soon, for Buller Griggs, the boat's coxswain, came along the beach under the rails and shouted something to someone in the crowd. The howling wind made it impossible to hear exactly what had been said and the big visitor enquired patronisingly, "What's he shouting about?"

Father, winking at me, replied, shouting, "Oh, that's the skipper and he's a man short in the crew. He's asking for a volunteer, preferably a big bloke, like you."

The big man's face reddened and then paled, his jaw dropped and his legs suddenly worked overtime, taking him away from the crowd as quick as he could go, followed by echoes of derisive laughter.

Now it was well into 1932 and the great depression continued. With some three million out of work, the majority of them being the bread winners of their families. With nothing to do the men would gather in bunches on street corners to discuss, curse or laugh at their problems. All shabbily dressed but sharp of mind, sharing their fag-ends and fantasies. From 1931 the government had been in such financial trouble that it had not even been able to pay unemployment benefits. The civil servants suffered a cut in pay and the armed forces were considered such a financial burden that there was even talk of disbanding the Royal Air Force altogether. The family too suffered in these hard times, for Father's spells of unemployment became more frequent and my younger brother's health problems became more critical, necessitating visits to the specialists at Great Ormond Street hospital in London. As there was no National Health Service in those days, these trips were all done on the 'panel' in conjunction with the Oddfellows Friendly Society.

My elder brother had started his working life as a door to door salesman on a commission only basis. This of course hardly paid his expenses let alone provide anything for the essentials or luxuries of life, and he was drawing on, instead of adding to, the family coffers. So when J. Sainsbury's advertised for counter assistants, he applied, and succeeded in being selected for training.

He finished up on the butter and bacon counter in their shop in Sandgate Road in Folkestone.

But then in 1932, sensing possible cut backs in staff, he pre-empted the possibility of being sacked by resigning and then joining the Royal Navy as a cook. This proved to be somewhat fortuitous for he succeeded in becoming a commissioned catering officer, surviving the war with all its hazards, including the slight fracas in the English Channel when the German battleships made their dash for the safety of the German port of Kiel.

Within the family it was now my future which became the critical issue. The choices were few, but one thing remained certain. I would stay at school in order to sit the London Matriculation exams. But in those days educational qualifications could not pre-suppose a good job, or any job for that matter. So as a possible safeguard I decided, with reluctant approval from Mum and Dad, to sit the Royal Air Force entrance examination for engineering apprentices. This exam would be taken at school several weeks before the turmoil of taking Matric.

My last six or so months at school were made more difficult by the wearing effects of cramming, also wondering and worrying about becoming suddenly one of the millions struggling to find a job, a near impossibility in those days. I remember one vacancy being advertised for an assistant at Baker's jewellery shop in the High Street, and some seventy kids applied. It was a young fourteen year old girl that got the job eventually, and became a legend almost.

The summer lunch time breaks at school did, however, bring one relaxing diversion, for it was possible to get an almost unobstructed view of the Cheriton Road cricket ground from the window at the end of the first floor corridor. And when the County games were played one could be lucky enough to catch sight of some of the Kent and England heroes. Frank Woolly, Tich Freeman, Leslie Ames (an ex Harvey Grammar boy), A.P.F. Chapman and of course others from the opposition such as Patsy Hendren and Wally Hammond.

But more serious things were looming up, for inevitably and inexorably the week for the examination approached, when all nine subjects would have to be taken in one nerve wracking week. Examination rooms always seemed the same to me. Inquisition chambers, almost sepulchral and overly intimidating with their neat rows of desks, each carrying a little pile of neatly arranged blank answering papers resting on virgin blotting paper. Challenging you to empty a fact-swollen brain by putting into some form of logical presentation, the asked for details. Not always easy, and sometimes impossible. As each candidate arrived there would be no talk or welcome as he scanned the room before nervously sitting at his allotted desk to arrange, and then rearrange, his pen, pencil and instruments. The deadline would bring the silent issuing of the question papers which, when quickly read, would bring confident smiles to some and furrowed brows to others. Then for the duration of the exam the tick – tick of the clock would seem like a Chinese torture, challenging you to scribble away as quickly, and as accurately, as you knew how. Hoping for the best with maybe an intruding and dominating faint fear of failure.

However, in the event my results were not too bad – Curate's Eggish. General School Certificate standard in five subjects Matriculation standard in the remaining four, with a distinguished pass in one, namely mathematics.

The Royal Air Force entrance exam was taken in one day, with several other candidates from the school, but some thousands nation-wide, and I succeeded in taking a place in the first hundred, sufficiently high enough on the list to be called forward for a medical examination in September 1932. However, that's anticipating the event as I still had some three months to make up my mind as to whether I should join the Royal Air Force, find a home town job or join the unemployed.

Luck was with me, however, for I had a new-found pal who had recently moved into the area and was working at the International Stores in the High Street. He tipped me off that a store boy would soon be required there. I presented myself to the manager who eventually gave me the job, after what seemed to me to be endless and irrelevant enquiries concerning my background. I think the fact that I had once been a Senior Sixer in the Cubs and my brother had been in the church choir were deciding factors. Anyway, I was informed that the job was probably only temporary, and not even that if ever I thought about fiddling anything.

The job consisted of weighing up and packaging flour, raisins and sugar into thick, dark blue paper bags, eventually learning to fold and flick over the tops with effortless ease.

The actual workplace was located in the large warehouse behind the shop, where I was surrounded by half sides of bacon, huge blocks of red and white cheese and all sorts of other salivating goodies. These mixed and pungent aromas delighted my sense of smell but the sight of so much food in one spot seemed somehow to me, who all my life had been subjected to some sort of rationing or restriction, to be a little unfair.

Fortunately, as was my habit, I rationalised my tentative revolutionary thoughts by thinking that, "Well, the people who produced the stuff had to sell it, they couldn't give it away. The people that needed it had to buy it with money obtained from working. So that's why I was there." It was so simple, production with profit, distribution with profit, sales with profit and working for profit. And using the word benefit instead of the word profit it all seemed acceptable.

But eventually it became a suffocatingly boring job, and the fifteen shillings for some forty hours a week seemed to be hardly the right benefit for the job. But the job changed and the benefit seemed less relative. For I was promoted to be delivery boy, or more exactly, assistant to the van driver, a Mr Burvil.

Life became a little more exciting, even to achieving sixty miles an hour – a mile a minute! – along the Dymchurch straight. That put a little zip into things and made working more of an adventure. As also did the transient relationships encountered in my expanding world.

This seemingly menial job brought me into contact with a variety of people, from kitchen maids and house keepers, to haughty mistresses and harassed husbands. Some of the maids offered cheerfulness and chat, pleased to have someone to natter to. Some becoming loose tongued enough to tell sad stories of how they had to fight off the wandering hands of randy sons and ambitious fathers. With one giggling confessor admitting, with an inviting wink, that she hadn't struggled that hard. The admission being linked with the information that the whole family were away for the day. Mr Burvil's "Oi, how much longer you gonna be?" rumbled down the drive, and saved a young sixteen year old from certain seduction. A shame, for she was a dangerous and delightfully friendly girl.

Not so others, who were bad tempered or po-faced as they gave their peremptory orders to put the heavy grocery box up there, or over here or under there. With others, more experienced and wordly wise, the accidental closeness was a mutual pleasure as they pointed up, down or under, managing at the same time the softest of bodily contacts, almost heaven for a near virgin van boy. Mostly, however, the people were kind and sympathetic, offering cups of tea, soft drinks or back chat. And old Bill Burvil would tell me exactly what reaction could be expected from every one of his customers, depending on the time of day, the day of the week, the weather, or whatever crisis was in the news or family.

My evening or Sunday strolls around the town also became a little more interesting. For when seeing some character or other going about his or her daily business, I would have mental pictures of their private activities. That old military, be-sticked, red-faced ex Major prodding his way along the sea front would be totally unaware that I knew all about his boozing and betting failures and his occasional lascivious ambitions. Or the well groomed lady strutting along with that superior self-satisfied smile wouldn't know that I knew that she was up to her eyes in debt and was, according to her maid, madly in love with 'that bloke down the road, him with the short legs and big arse'.

Nearing the end of August 1932 and late one afternoon, we were driving the delivery van at a rattling twenty miles an hour along South Road, and about to cross the end of Lady's Walk, when a kid's Tate and Lyle box cart with roped front wheel steering, suddenly shot out from the little sloping side road which leads down from Moyle Tower. Mr Burvil pushed and stiffened on the brake pedal, the van coming to a stuttering halt. But not in time to avoid catching the back end of the cart, sending its youthful pusher, together with the cart's contents, sprawling across the road.

The cart's pusher was my younger brother and the cart's contents were a good half hundredweight of freshly laid and recently gathered horse manure. Fortunately no damage had been done so, after letting Bill Burvil have a few colourful words of advice on the rules of the road, we re-gathered the manure and its collector, and went our separate ways.

I finished the rounds and went home. My young brother went on to dump his load on the allotment before he too returned home, totally unconcerned and unconvinced that his last days had nearly overtaken him. No word was said to Mum and Dad. There was nothing to tell them, Tommy said. But Father had met Mr Burvil on his way home and later on in the evening, after supper, he simply asked, "Any trouble, Tommy, with the horse manure? Apart from having to shovel it up twice?" He heard Tom's version and made no comment.

One morning shortly after a long buff coloured envelope arrived bearing O.H.M.S. in large letters on the outside, and inside a somewhat impersonal invitation for me to report on 5th September to the Royal Air Force Technical School of training at Halton in Buckinghamshire. Also it contained the information that if medically fit I would be accepted for training as an Aircraft Apprentice, and if successful in passing the final examinations at the end of a three year course, I would then have to serve a twelve year term of service, starting from my eighteenth birthday. Also included were details of how to reach Baker Street station, London, where candidates from the southern counties would assemble to be entrained for the journey to Halton.

Suddenly the compact existence of a secure home life with its usually solvable daily problems seemed to be very, very attractive. I didn't want to go away. A van boy's job, menial as it was, suddenly appeared to be anything but dead ended. But seeing the world and becoming involved with aircraft, with a possibility of really flying in one, was finally an idea exciting enough for me to overcome any doubts, and I decided to take on the challenge. Little did I realise what a vital decision it really was, to commit myself for so long to such a disciplined way of life, or that the twelve years would encompass, among other things, a world war.

It had been decided that I would spend the evening of 4th September at Aunt May's home at Wimbledon. So early in the morning on that day Father gave me a very explicit warning of what to expect, based on his own experiences. I think he thought that after I had sniffed service life I would take advantage of the final option to change one's mind, given to everyone after completion of three weeks of initiation. He never knew how nearly right he was. His advice came with an uncharacteristic bear hug of affection and a quick tearless 'good-bye'. Then he went off to work, splay-footed as usual, and he walked up Cobden Road, there to turn into Park Road without even looking back.

Mother's good-bye was a little less controlled, and slightly wetter. She felt that she was being deserted. Why did both her grown sons have to leave home? She really knew the answer I think, for feeding five on Father's two pounds five shillings a week wage would be a little too much strain even for her capacity to make do and mend. Had we all been sure of finding full time employment, that would have been different. But in those days this was not a possibility.

Stebby, a pal whose family was connected with Stebbings hardware shop in the High Street, came to see me off from the railway station and to take my bicycle back to Cobden Road. He sat on the crossbar holding my lightly packed suitcase containing toiletries and one change of underwear, as instructed. The hill to the station had to be walked, and we spoke hardly a word. Stebby was no great chatterer and I was feeling anything but talkative. I began to realise I was leaving everything I loved, family, friends and a town which meant a great deal to me. Giving me an emotional setting on which I was to base many a nostalgic moment in the future.

A quick handshake and a funny grin from Stebby before he put his leg over to ride quickly away down the hill, giving a short wave as he went, left me with only a few short paces to take to reach the empty platform. There the three carriage train waited with steam up and ready to go. A few minutes wait, a tentative whistle, a few little puffs of hissing steam and I was on my way, clickety, clicketing to a maybe exciting, but uncertain future.

2 ▨ Newton Benoulli & Bullshit

Early morning of 5th September 1932, a spasmodically tearful Aunt May busied herself getting me breakfasted and ready for 'joining up' as she put it. She, I'm sure, felt the situation was the same as when, during the 1914–18 war, the boys had to leave home to do their bit. I did my best to convince her it was not so and that I was only going away to help solve the family's problems and not the world's.

The long walk with Aunt May up Hayden's Road, and then Merton High Street on the way to Wimbledon underground station, gave me once more that uncanny feeling of unreality that I suppose all country boys have when coming into close contact with the threatening activity of city streets. The clanging double decker trams and the big red London General omnibuses still seemed as fascinating to me as when I first saw them. And then came the delights of my second trip on that wonder of wonders, the underground, with its labyrinth of passages, its escalators and lifts, and the sudden draughts of air along the tunnelled platforms as the trains came in, coming to a stop with electric motors whining. The train itself with its sliding doors, face to face seating, straps hanging from the roof, destination strips and advertising panels, together with the strange smell of the place, gave me a disturbing and apprehensive feeling that life was indeed on the move.

The stations came and went from Collier's Wood, Tooting Broadway, Clapham South, Common and North and on to Charing Cross. There we uncertainly made the change along what seemed an endless conglomeration of corridors, passages, stairs and escalators to the Bakerloo line which took us on to Baker Street station, where we arrived about one and a half hours ahead of the allotted time.

"Would you like a nice cup of tea and a bun?" enquired Aunt May.

"Yes please" I agreed, thinking a nice cup of hot tea washing down a sugary doughnut would be just the thing, and a nice introduction to the sophistication of eating out.

A short lived hope. For the cafe was narrow and long, with fly-blown mirrors on dingy walls and stone topped tables so close that the customers either enjoyed or suffered a somewhat enforced intimacy. The tea arrived and was served without any trace of oriental ceremony. Dumped would be a better word. It was cold and insipid but not quite a total disaster. It was at least wet. And the bun was sweet and sticky enough to be almost enjoyed.

This allowed me to reassure Aunt May with a clear conscience when she remarked, "That was a nice cuppa, wasn't it?" by saying, "Yes, very enjoyable. Just the thing."

After a long silence she dolefully declared, "And now we'd better get over to the station, we don't want to be late, do we?"

Arriving there we found the entrance to the platform to be crowded with Mums and Dads and girlfriends, all enjoying the transient sadness of their good-byes. Once on the platform itself the faces of those about to depart reflected a multitude of emotions; some looking self confident; others, including myself, slightly bewildered; and not a few looking just plain scared.

I made my own farewells to Aunt May and then that dear little soul slowly left, holding a tear-filled hanky to her face and waving a hesitant good-bye as she went. Now surrounded by a mass of new faces I found myself for the first time in my life feeling a little lost and rootless, being pulled along and manipulated by events over which I had little control, and it was to be thus for the next twenty five years. But at this point in time I didn't realise it as a fact, just an emotion. It certainly didn't register with me that joining the Fighting Services really meant total dedication to a very particular way of life.

Had I been capable of foresight I certainly would, there and then, have made a bolt for it, to catch up with and console my loving and tearful Aunt. Now, with hindsight, I can say that, during the whole of my service life, it was not true dedication that triggered my allegiance, just a series of circumstances, private and eventually public, that kept me loyal.

A combination of self and national interest, one being voluntary, the other a bounden duty, but together acceptable to King, Country and me, with optimistically mutual benefit to all three.

However, at this moment I was part of the 'pick of the Nation' (Lord Trenchard's assessment, not mine). Some were thin and weedy and looking half starved, some pudgy and slack, others well built and muscular, all within the age group of fifteen and a half to sixteen and a half.

Tall ones, short ones, smartly dressed ones, poorly dressed ones, all spasmodically chatting in a variety of accents. And all unconsciously and tentatively taking their first steps towards one of the basic elements of service life – comradeship.

The sergeant and corporal escorts suddenly came to life and in gentle tones intimated that it was now time to 'entrain'.

"You, young lad over there, you in the black jacket, get in line, PLEASE with them others over here, and get yourselves seated in the first carriage. Now you bunch there, eight of you, into the next one please."

And so on, with very little audible back chat, except for a few macho murmurings when one bespectacled corporal, attempting a funny, suggested that, "Now Mummy isn't around, you'll have to cry on *my* shoulder."

The journey to Wendover was uneventful. Conversation being not as yet uninhibited and privacies were respected. Only small details, names, home towns and such like being talked about.

'Detraining' was smoothly accomplished, as was the 'embussing' onto the solid tyred three ton lorries waiting to take us on the final stage of the journey to Halton camp. But as we debussed there it became noticeable that the requests by the N.C.O.'s to do this and that, became just a little more staccato and peremptory. Naturally, I suppose, as they were now on home ground and the feeling of power was reasserting itself. But they were still moderately polite, the true reassertion would come in a few days, after medicals, swearing in, and kitting out had been completed. Then true discipline backed by the Air Force Act and the threat of being put on a '252' would be brought into play, if that's the right word.

By the second day I was beginning to question my decision to join and would have welcomed an honourable rejection on medical grounds, such as hammer toes. A condition which enabled a Folkestone compatriot, Billy Groves, to escape unscathed and return home, honour intact. I had no such luck, being referred to by the sick bay orderly as 'that ten stone monster' when being called into the examination room to be, it seemed to me, casually looked over and passed as 'fit A1'.

Swearing in was completed shortly afterwards. The text being droned out by a junior officer to small batches of recruits who together monotoned their responses to become either willingly, inexorably, incidentally or accidentally, totally dedicated to serving King and Country. The seriousness of it all did not come until later, years later in some cases. Next, all in line, we filed slowly past an N.C.O. who, seated at a trestle table, allocated to each of us in turn a numerical identification our official service numbers, mine being 566186. The only other numbers I can remember out of the some 200 members of the 26th entry to Halton are 566188, a George Ogle from Coventry and 566189, a Steward from Amble. Other names I certainly remember but not linked to any identifying number.

Within a day or so we were kitted out and, contrary to all preconceptions, a great deal of effort went into fitting bodies to sizes and not vice versa. Jackets, trousers and pantaloons being tailored to fit where considered necessary. One tentative concession here to preconceptions, the tailoring maybe could have been improved, seldom reaching a degree of perfection

A SHILLINGSWORTH OF PROMISES

that the name would seem to imply. Caps were no problem, being mostly six and seven eighths and seeming to fit all and sundry, ears in or out, except when some real big-head came along to upset the system. Shirts and underwear had a limited range of sizes but an unlimited capacity to irritate tender ex-civilian skins. The whole outfit was designed to withstand heavy wear and tear, especially the boots, and we tender and raw recruits suffered torture and agony getting our bodies fit enough to enjoy, and be proud of wearing, 'The Blue'. To avoid undue periods of painful breaking in of new clothes, our gear was always well looked after. This also had the benefit of conserving one's clothing allowance, the unused residue of which was credited to each individual and added to his pay packet at the end of each term.

'Service Uniform' could not be more precisely and exactly the right term. For whereas at Baker Street station we were all individuals, separated to a degree by how and in what we were dressed, it was now a matter of being peas in a pod. All starting from a common base, and it would be what was inside the uniform that would control the degree of non-conformity that would separate one from the other. Which poses the question, 'Where would our leaders come from?' The answer, I think, is from those that escape conformity but still remain one of us in the process.

My dedication to the Royal Air Force was not exactly gratuitous. Nearly, but not quite. For as well as being fed, clothed and accommodated for nothing, I was also being paid. One whole shilling a day (including Sundays). A magnificent seven shillings a week. Three shillings of this I actually got my hands on at each Friday's pay parade where we all joined a mammoth queue and snaked our way up and down a large dining hall in alphabetical order to eventually arrive in front of the paying officer. There to jerk to attention, salute, scream out the last three figures of our service number, scrape up the three bob, salute again, then turn smartly and march off. Not exactly a matter of getting rich quick but a painful way of staying poor slowly. And nattering in the queue would bring a sure reward of extra duties. Overtime without pay one might say.

The remaining four shillings of the week's wages would be credited to one's account to accumulate therein in order to cover the cost of buying a reduced return fare railway ticket, giving a trip home and a short breath of freedom at the end of each term. If, however, your clothing allowance had been overdrawn or some barrack room damages had to be paid for, then for the last six or seven weeks of term all the agonies and hazards of the pay parade had to be endured for just one piddling shilling. And out of this the necessities of life had to be bought, but luxuries first. Threepence for a

Duncan's chocolate bar, fourpence for ten Woodbines, threepence for the pictures and, avoiding temptations, the remaining twopence on Lux or McLeans or Cherry Blossom. These final items being provisioned for over a period of weeks and, in some cases, months.

Attempts to escape from life's financial problems led to many devious and questionable schemes being invented and perpetrated by those who, willingly or otherwise, readjusted their conceptions of personal morality to suit the changed circumstances. One of these dubious schemes, ingenious to a degree, was tentatively debated and rejected. The small band of schemers deciding reluctantly that it did not pass even a relaxed morality test. And in any case it might become too popular, creating an imbalance between potential gainers and certain losers, making it unworkable.

This rejected ploy was described technically and accurately as 'fractional reconstitution', but was in fact plain pinching, with little probability of being found out. As everyone's soap, toothpaste, blacking and Brasso were always on regimental display on the open shelf of a bedside locker, and the brands were mainly the same, all the miscreant would have to do would be to regularly and surreptitiously change his own item for a similar, minutely larger, one. The principle being, he always had soap, toothpaste etcetera of a constant size, thus requiring no replacement involving money, and the victim would never become suspicious. For a tube of toothpaste minus a couple of squeezes, or a bar of soap minutely more second hand, would never be noticed. To my knowledge the veracity of this conclusion was never put to the test. Fortunately, for I'm sure any discovered 'tealeaf' would have suffered rather more than just a culture shock, more likely a flogging.

A less contentious scheme, nicknamed 'the swindle', was more acceptable and worked quite smoothly, with a little threatening prodding required only very infrequently to some 'early receivers' seeking unacceptable payment deferments. Sob stories, by decree, were never listened to. This scheme was simple in the extreme eleven members being required to contribute a shilling a week and each member drawing his ten shillings in turn, usually coinciding with his long weekend for the term. This enabled him with luck, to afford the fare home and back.

The organisers of this scheme were usually the same ones who, during the soccer season, would also run a highest score sweep. Some hundred odd teams being involved at a penny a go. Whether the team with the highest score for a particular week had always been legitimately sold, I was never sure. An enquiry along these lines posed to the organisers was tersely answered in four words, two of which were 'Perks mate', a third being 'off'. This I

A SHILLINGSWORTH OF PROMISES

quickly accepted as legitimate belligerence, deciding at the same time to forego any future weekly investment.

The transformation from civil to service life was slowly and almost insidiously being accomplished. But the greatest shock, putting it very kindly was the absolute uncosiness of barrack room life. It was sparse and cold, a description which could also at times be applied to the food. Ninepence a day, I believe, was the allowance the catering officer had to spend per apprentice, and it must have been rather less than that, I'm sure, for the accommodation.

The beds were rigid steel framed monstrosities, designed primarily for long life and made to concertina to half size during the daytime, to provide extra space to a barrack room which housed some thirty or so individuals. Each having about six feet of width, three of which was taken up by the bed. Three square, horse hair filled 'biscuits' would then be arranged to form a mattress on which an old, well worn blanket was doubled and placed in position to ease the discomfort of the joins. Two coarse linen sheets with three blankets and a hard bolster completed one's resting place. Or in Air Force slang, one's 'charp', or 'pit'. I considered 'resting place' to be the more apt description for, after a full day's training, technical or physical, and usually both, one's nightly sleep seemed more like a short course in death.

To complete one's 'unit of accommodation' a scrubbed wooden locker was neatly fitted into the three foot space between oneself and, hopefully, a non-snoring neighbour. This locker contained all items in daily use, the rest being kept in a steel locker anchored to the wall above. Everything contained in these lockers had to be arranged or stored in regimental fashion, as was the bed when not in use. The whole being subjected to a daily inspection, together with the room itself, to ensure that uniformity and conformity had been maintained to the required standard.

Morning reveille would be at six thirty, when the duty N.C.O. would exercise his tonsils and his stereotyped inherited humour by bawling out,

"Come on now, get yer hands off yer joy sticks and git yer warm feet on the cold floor. Out of it! Out of it!"

Then the beds would be made up, bodies abluted and breakfasted, floor spaces cleaned and bumpered, buttons polished or breathed on, boots shined, trouser creases checked etcetera. A knackering hour and a half before being bugled onto a working parade at eight o'clock sharp to be inspected.

"Git your 'air cut! ... When did your boots last see blacking? ... Git that button done up!" A never ending barrage of sometimes fair and sometimes unfair criticisms. But all part and parcel of the theory of how to create a well disciplined and controllable fighting force, and not a rabble of 'go-it-aloners'.

The non-commissioned ranks of disciplinarians and drill instructors at this time contained many transferees from the army and they were ideally suited to their jobs. But training technicians as ceremonial fodder was I felt, even as a young apprentice, a fundamental mistake. It should have been appreciated, even in 1932, that a modern air force needed primarily to be superlatively technically trained, and that perfection in foot drill, and particularly rifle drill, was really an anachronism.

The subject of food, no doubt, took priority in most letters home, ensuring sympathy, parcels and well fed leaves. But it must be said that the menus were dietetically sound, if somewhat plain. Sometimes being indeterminate in taste, questionable in consistency, occasionally mysterious and always variable in smell and quantity. But almost always eaten, for the energy absorption level of apprenticeship life was large, making quantity and not quality a sad, and nearly always absolute, priority. A state of affairs enjoyed by the cookhouse staff if not by anyone else. But there were some meals enjoyed by all. 'Top of the sops' being fried fish and chips on a Friday. Even then some cook comedian would fry a well battered dish cloth to a golden brown to disappoint some greedy apprentice when grabbing what seemed to be the biggest. Eggs and bacon, sausage and mash, savaloy and peas, bacon and red lead (tomatoes). These were all appreciated dishes and uncomplicated enough to survive the hazards of both cooking and cooker.

All uneaten food was daily barrelled and sent to a local pig farmer and I suppose the whole system can be considered to be a success, for I think the health of both pigs and apprentices remained unsullied and disease free, at least during my three years of participation.

The real food problem came in the evenings, for only breakfast, dinner and tea were the recognised meals. Supper consisted of two hard tack biscuits, which I swear were relics from the 1914 war, taken with a mug of thick greasy soup which, if drunk when relatively hot, was accepted by the digestive system without undue fuss. The rock hard biscuits, however, had to be nibbled slowly and, strangely enough, were quite tasty, but a dire threat to anybody with ailing or tender teeth.

My acceptance of the disciplines of service life was equivocal. General discipline leading to self discipline was logical, but out and out bullshit administered in raucous tones just to cower one into submission, grated on my sensibilities and required a self control that, in my early days, sometimes gave way, resulting in angry verbal combat with not a few over enthusiastic and lesser striped disciplinarians.

A SHILLINGSWORTH OF PROMISES

On one particular occasion during the first month of square bashing I was constantly being picked on and bawled at.

"Swing your arms, 'itchcock." – I did.

"Git 'em up, git 'em back." – I did both.

"Throw your chest out." – I tried the impossible. After a couple of minutes, again it came.

"Come on, 'itchcock, lift, right, lift. Git 'em up boy, git 'em up."

By this time my arms were reaching for the sky, both fore and aft. Almost circling. I was putting maximum effort into it. And when the session was over I felt like a wanked out windmill. Then on being pulled aside to be told that I marched like a handcuffed hunchback, anger took over. I loudly retaliated, "You won't cure my flaming hunchback by bawling at me."

Net result, I was charged for the crime of insolence and awarded three days confinement to camp, with extra fatigue duties. This punishment being the judgement of Squadron Leader Hall and his dog, a lovely labrador which usually lay under the desk during any proceedings and never forgot to wag his tail on hearing the summing up and sentencing, for that meant that he, unlike the offender, would soon be free.

My second brush with authority came soon after. By this time our basic technical training had begun and, on returning to the barracks at the end of a day's work, I found a piece of paper on the top of my bedside locker. It was a note from the room corporal and it read: 'Aircraft Apprentice Edgecork will scrub the winder ledgers tonite.'

I was feeling tired and hungry and became resentful when I thought that I should have to do the bidding of someone who couldn't even spell. Thinking of the years of study I myself had spent at the Harvey Grammar, I thought I was entitled to some small degree of intellectual snobbery and I rebelled. I screwed up the note and threw it out of the window onto the grass.

Result – I was charged for refusing to obey a written order. Judgement day came and then, gloried up in my best blue uniform, escort fore and aft, I was marched to the C.O.'s office, there to be halted until being bawled at by the Flight Sergeant discip. An order loud, staccato and curtailed penetrated my uncapped head.

"Pris' and 'scort – shun! Quick mar' – rye turn – lef' turn! 'alt! Rye turn. A/A 'Itchcock saah!"

Squadron Leader Hall looked severe and his dog managed a side glance from one watery eye. The charge was read out and I was asked,

"Anything to say?"

I tried to explain that I had received no written order but I had indeed found a piece of paper on my locker with some sort of hieroglyphics on it, which I had screwed up and thrown out of the window.

The corporal was sent out to retrieve this vital bit of evidence. He returned and, with a self satisfied smirk, gave the unravelled scrap of paper to the C.O. As he read it his cheek muscles twitched as he barely controlled an erupting laugh. But finally, looking up stone faced and now hard of eye, he said, "Hieroglyphics maybe, but this is a rare example of a not yet extinct English version and, I would have thought, well within your intellectual capacity to decipher. And I'm awarding you three days confinement to camp with extra duties. March him out."

"Pris'and 'scort – lef turn quick mar' – rye turn –'alt!"

I was re-capped, dismissed and sent off to begin my three days of muscular misery, scrubbing the dining room floor, some hundred and fifty feet long by sixty feet wide. It was tough going, the secret being, however, never to look behind, for the unscrubbed acres would bring on a sensation of a sort of horizontal vertigo. Better to keep one's eyes focused on the bucket and its diminishing contents, refills notwithstanding, and never to make a race of it with one's compatriot confinees, for the quick 'uns always had to make up for the slow 'uns.

We were having a session of physical training on a grass plot behind the cookhouse and I was in the rear row close to the perimeter fence. I was in fact feeling happy and at ease and enjoying the effects of the simple body exercises being given to us by the corporal P.T. Instructor, or muscle mechanic as he was more accurately described. Soon the Wing Warrant Officer appeared on the scene. He watched for a while and then started to walk between the ranks and as we responded to the corporal's orders he started to criticise.

"Pull your stomach in, then" to one. "Get your knees up" to another. "The corporal said bend, not curtsy" to a third. And then to me, "Wipe that silly smile off your face, and stretch when you're told to".

I just stood still, ignoring any further instruction from the corporal and glared at him. He gave me a peculiar look and just marched off.

That, of course, was not the end of the affair. In less than half an hour I was taken to the Station Headquarters to be immediately presented to an adjutant who, to my total and utter surprise, invited me to sit down and relax, and to tell him exactly what was worrying me. He indicated, with concern, that all early reports on my attitude and behaviour gave the impression that I was becoming a problem apprentice and not likely to turn out to be a good reliable member of the Royal Air Force. At the same time I

A SHILLINGSWORTH OF PROMISES

was pointedly told that 'make your mind up time' had come and that I had to change my ways, or else.

The alternatives floated quickly through my mind. Having to return to home and family with certain unemployment, and hardship for all, or biting the bullet, swallowing my pride and accepting the ego-busting discipline of apprenticeship life.

After a few moments of silent cogitation I chose the latter and forwent the temptation of airing my views on life's indignities and then simply parodied an answer by saying that I had assumed my role in the Royal Air Force would be more that of an engineer than someone trained only for ceremonial exhibition.

The point and the sarcasm were well taken. The former being deemed invalid and the latter unnecessary. I was then given the fatherly advice to control my criticisms, change my attitude and accept things as they were, and take advantage of a last chance. There was also a tacit indication that no action would be taken concerning my latest misdemeanour.

It was virtually Hobson's choice and I promised to accept the proffered advice. An irretrievable decision to sell the next twenty five years of my life for a small pot of gold or, more accurately, the lack of it. Only the unfolding years would reveal who got the better of that bargain. But from there on I avoided any head on collisions and life became smoother. I also sensed that I was being picked on somewhat less frequently. So advice, surely, had been accurately targeted in other directions.

As time progressed deeper involvement in the engineering and academic side of apprenticeship life brought welcome compensations. The mental stimulation and the challenge of absorbing highly technical processes and theories, together with the application of theory into practice, all helped to overcome the hardships and moral insults of the domestic side of existence.

These two totally different aspects of life were made to seem even more remote one from the other by the fact that the workshops, school buildings and the aerodrome were all situated at the bottom of a hill and away from the barracks, parade square and domestic areas. Thus daily giving one a real sense of escape. Had it been the other way round it would have been even more appreciated for marching up that hill after an exhausting day was always a little bit of a strain. This daily march to and from the workshops, overalls neatly rolled up and carried under the left arm, with the right free to swing or salute was always supervised by a senior N.C.O. to ensure that we all managed the trip in an orderly lump, in rhythmic step, and silent.

One controlling genius was a certain Flight Sergeant Payne, a very small man with a loud voice, about five foot nothing in height including his hat. One couldn't see where the voice came from but it certainly reached you. Some wit had nicknamed him 'Twinge'. An overstatement I thought. Accompanying this daily trek was a small drum and pipe band, thumping and squealing out the necessary marching rhythm. At first I couldn't stand the screeching and wailing of those bag pipes but the rolling beat of the drums had an attraction and the two together eventually got through to me and I began to enjoy marching to the regular rhythms of all the well known bag pipe marches.

I have Irish blood from a grandmother but not a drop of anything from north of the border, so it says a lot for the power of the pipes and proves the theory why, in past battles, the sound of the bag pipes inspired the advancing troops whilst at the same time demoralising and puzzling a half-scared enemy.

Working in a large conglomeration of workshops was initially somewhat intimidating and awe inspiring. For they housed a host of demonstration and instructional 'mock-ups' consisting of sectioned engines and components, located amongst aircraft in various stages of assembly and repair. All steeped in an atmosphere that smelt enticingly of oil and dope, spiced with a myriad of other connected smells. The walls were a mass of complicated diagrams detailing and explaining the workings and mysteries of every control system ever evolved or used since the Wright brothers first unhooked their size eights from mother earth.

Intermingled amongst all this paraphernalia, in strategic positions, were small areas housing the necessary rows of desks and forms facing onto a blackboard and, of course, the instructor's podium. During each session the desks would be occupied by those nodding in agreement and understanding, countered by others nodding off in soporific incomprehension, with minds that had been paralysed and saturated with a seemingly endless glossary of technical terms and explanations. It was all rivettingly interesting, but hard.

The instructors, almost to a man, were capable and hand picked, with a variety of talents in disseminating the necessary knowledge. Some were humorous, others less so, but all were capable of anecdotal distortions of their previous exploits of before, during and after the Great War. One sad story concerned a well known Royal Flying Corps war-time ace whose aircraft had developed a mystery fault which resisted all attempts at correction. So in desperation his C.O. had sent for the finest engineer in the whole of the Royal Flying Corps. Our blond and straight faced instructor continued and

A SHILLINGSWORTH OF PROMISES

ended the story with, 'And when I arrived...' There were murmurs of 'Cor' and 'Big Head'. True or not, we never found out.

The Autumn term eventually came to an end, bringing the first break from voluntary imprisonment, for that is virtually what it was. On three shillings a week I could see no point in spending days or evenings off, pantalooned and putteed, pop-eyed and penniless, mooching about the streets of Wendover, Aylesbury or anywhere else. And it made end of term leave that much more attractive, and necessary.

The Christmas leave of 1932 saw the first home-coming of both sons. Brother Bert from the Royal Navy contributing his ration of cheap fags in the form of never before seen in our house, Flat Fifty tins of Gold Flake. These made our old Dad splutter, he preferred his own hand rolled, matchstick thin fags made from dark shag. The dog ends of which he stuck into his top right waistcoat pocket to be unravelled and used, before lashing out on a new ounce. A habit from his London days of absolute penury, and a habit he couldn't, or wouldn't, break.

On these festive occasions Mother permitted the front room to be used. Where the furniture and lino in their pristine condition, smelling of religiously applied polish, reflected the light from a large-ish curtain draped bay window, giving the little room an air of comparative opulence. A sort of refined poverty, proudly presented. A brightly burning fire made from freshly gathered coke from the local gas works, largely but not intrusively visible from the back yard, added warmth and cosiness to the scene, giving a comfortable feeling of intense family togetherness.

The Christmas dinner was seasonal in every respect except, in lieu of turkey, Father had managed to find a large home reared white rabbit. It roasted beautifully and, with fresh vegetables straight from the allotment and with Mum's faultless Yorkshire pudding, Air Force nosh suddenly seemed to be part of a far distant and faded past. Music was provided by a portable gramophone obtained by brother Bert with B.D.V. cigarette coupons. This enabled him to saturate the festive days with music from just two records. The length of both would strain the capacity of the spring so he had to sit within easy reach of the winder. Jack Buchanan fading out on 'Who', or Sophie Tucker giving up on some unremembered tune, was a little too much, even for my unmusical ear.

Fortunately, this restricted musical diet was augmented by some welcome seasonal tunes from a salvaged three valve home built wireless set. It was a set I had built from a simple layout and wiring diagram presented in the magazine 'Wireless World'. It had required no highly technical knowledge, just the ability to follow instructions, using recommended components, a hacksaw and a soldering iron. But on completion, and after connecting up the dry battery, wet accumulator, ariel and earth, nothing happened. And try as I might, checking and re-checking, all I achieved was a few faint clicks and squeals and whistles. I gave up, and its dialled face appeared to look at me in silent contempt as I sadly stored it away in the garden shed.

Mother, of course, knew absolutely nothing about the workings of a wireless set, but this did not stop her from having a fiddle with my discarded failure after I had left home. And apparently, on her first attempt, after connecting up all the terminals, the set burst into life with a strong French accent from Radio Toulouse. Mother had fiddled to good effect, connecting a black lead to a red terminal and vice versa. Something I, of course, with my profound knowledge of electrics, would never have done. There had been an error in the layout diagram and Mum had inadvertently corrected it, proving that two wrongs can sometimes make a right. And Mother merited her notoriety amongst family and friends for having outsmarted her clever-dick son.

These few brief happy days of my first leave quickly came to an end. The return journey to Halton followed a route that was to become all too well known, picking up returning companions at various stops until, at Baker Street station, there would be quite a sizeable gang, chatting and bragging of their good times and conquests. The former being probably fact, the latter largely fictional. 'You can't make love to three girls in half an hour, can you?' I thought about it enviously but round about Rickmansworth I decided that my mate was more likely to be a good liar than a good lover.

Back in barracks service life began to develop into its fixed routine. A mixture of technical and related academic schooling, poisoned by a surfeit of ceremonial drill, but with welcome sporting and recreational activities in the evenings and at weekends.

I took up, and dropped, quite a number of these activities and even tried boxing. I got involved in an eliminating bout with a certain broken nosed Jock Tanner, supposedly boxing at featherweight. He was an excellent player of the bagpipes but an even better boxer. About twenty five seconds into the first round he loosened two of my front teeth. I spat blood and a few white fragments then quickly retired hurt, preferring cowardice to toothlessness. My interest in boxing quickly evaporated, especially as the performance was unnecessary anyway, for neither of us were even approximately nine stone featherweights, but more like light welter weights.

I really did enthusiastically enjoy one of life's two main lying down sports. The one I mention here is rifle shooting, both .22 and .303. The other, I

A SHILLINGSWORTH OF PROMISES

hasten to add, I also learnt to enjoy but my silver spoon and medal were prizes for good performances at Kimble, and the rifle Mecca of Bisley. Both being team shoots and not personal performances.

A certain Jimmy Rose, a Featherstone Rovers fanatic, inveigled me into trying a game of Rugby. I had previously enticed him into playing football, saying that football was for really skilled ball players and that Rugby, well, that was just a legalised rough and tumble, and certainly not a spectator sport. He simply said, 'Try it.' I did, and after being handed off twice in as many minutes with a closed fist, I spent the rest of the game running where the ball wasn't, diving in the mud at moments of unavoidable involvement, finishing up out of breath and appropriately muddied. I feel certain that a good fifty per cent of all Rugby players do exactly the same. I stuck to football but Jimmy, though faithful to the egg-shaped ball, also enjoyed the artistry involved in playing with the round one. He said.

Our enthusiasm though led us on one occasion, when clean sports gear was not available, to use shorts from store that had endured the sweaty contamination of a previous game. And within a week Jimmy and I were in adjoining beds in the skin ward of Halton hospital suffering from rampant *Tinea Cruris*, or 'Crutch Disease' as we called it. The treatment prescribed entailed heavy applications of some evil smelling ointment under a thick layer of bandages, to be changed at three day intervals. On the sixth day the Medical Officer, making his rounds, came to Jimmy first. When he took off the bandages a terrible stench wafted across to me in a nauseating wave. I held my nose and leered at my embarrassed mate. The M.O. sniffed, sniffed again, looked puzzled and uncertain, cogitated a little, then gave his professional verdict. "Give this stinker a bath." I looked away, smirking, but not for long. It was soon my turn. The same stench, the same medical reaction, the same treatment. "And this smelly little so and so."

However, the medication changed to stinging applications of iodine at frequent intervals. It was painful but effective. We were released, deemed to be cured, in something like twelve days, never again to use anything other than the purest of white sports gear.

The domestic, or barrack room, side of life, though somewhat monotonous, certainly had its moments of relief and revelation. Living with the mixed and uncertain personalities of some twenty five other characters in the close confines of a barrack room was not always easy. Friendships came and went with mood largely affecting the choice of one's immediate company. The result was a general feeling of relaxed comradeship with here and there maybe a closer friendship developing.

However, the closeness of barrack room life certainly helped one to get rid of a number of inhibitions, which enabled us all to enjoy the bawdy, cryptic or black humour that endlessly flew back and forth. There was one fruity voiced character who would refer to farting as 'posterial burping', an event which would occasion a variety of responses or enquiries.

"What's crawled up your arse and died?" and "Phew, who's shit?" would invariably be answered by, "Yours if you want it." Or, more politely, "What's wrong, can't you stand a comrade's breath?" Or more accurately, "He has, he don't believe in having a good crap, he just likes to blow it out in dust!"

I'm afraid I earned myself a lifetime enemy when making what I thought to be an advisory but amusing put down. My bedside companion led an active night life resulting in the rhythmic rattling of his iron bed, and was fast becoming a focus of behind the hand comment. So one morning I sought to give him some advice. Either to join Wankers Anonymous for help, or to get his bloody bed fixed. He did the latter using bent up fag packets, and never spoke to me again. Another lad though was less sensitive, accepting combined criticism quite light heartedly. He had the type of figure, character and features which, in spite of all his efforts, would never prevent him from looking anything other than just plain scruffy. He was inevitably nicknamed 'Dirty Dick'. This he smilingly accepted but insisted that on Sundays he be referred to less disparagingly as 'Filthy Richard'.

Sundays, of course, were our days of total relaxation, but only after having undergone the rigours of a full ceremonial church parade. And being agnostic I personally took it as a blatant excuse for the perpetration of a bit of arm swinging bullshit. To be dressed immaculately in one's best blue, to parade on the barrack square, to be minutely inspected for the slightest deviation of dress or comportment, and then to be marched about half a mile to the camp church behind a full pipe and drum band, was not my idea of the good Lord's advice that on the seventh day thou shalt rest.

But thank heaven there were occasions when, due to bad weather, the whole miserable performance would be cancelled. The cancellation being announced in a sequence of well remembered trumpet blasts which would evoke a howl of appreciation from every throat in every room in every block. For then a whole day of total freedom was there to be enjoyed.

The use of free time presented very little difficulty. The dedicated would swot a bit, the non-dedicated would play cards or simply go back to bed to rot until lunch time. Some, including myself, would lash out and buy a Sunday newspaper. The popular choices being the *News of the World*, or the *Empire News*. We would first read the back pages, then the spicy bits (the vicar of Stiffkey springs to mind) and lastly the serious articles on the economy, the government and the world in general. And it was about this time, very early in 1933, that a certain Adolf Hitler made the front pages by becoming the new chancellor of Germany. An item of news I read in about five minutes and forgot in about five seconds, except to remember how stupid he looked with his funny quiff and his circumcised moustache.

Unceasing rain on a Sunday would result in virtually the whole strength of the station being confined to camp. And that would put a strain on our ingenuity on how to pass the time, resulting in many unconventional and foolhardy escapades.

The one I love to recall is when a swimming pool was made of the ablution block. We started by wetting and soaping the shiny concrete floor with issue soap and then, when fully naked, to slide on a bare arse from one end to the other by giving a take-off shove on the wall with one's feet. The velocity and joy of the ride had to be experienced to be believed. Balls held high, of course, well out of harm's way. Bums, not surprisingly, finished up clean, polished and pimple free. Then someone hit on the idea of sealing all the doors with soap and turning on all the taps, flooding the place to a depth of some two or three feet, thus making a unique private swimming pool. All went well until some fully dressed nut, attracted by the noise, had to satisfy his curiosity by summoning more fully dressed help to force the door open. Wet and woeful poetic justice was quickly administered.

And so would pass the seemingly interminable weeks between leaves, when a return to one's home and roots would bring sanity and a sense of normality to what was really a sort of monastic existence, albeit of a very unreligious nature.

Since joining the Royal Air force my love life had naturally suffered a set back, but it was intermittently pursued during most spells of leave with varying degrees of success and failure. One of these spells enlightened my immature soul as to the vagaries of female emotions and devotion. For Leslie, my bosom pal, was rocketing around town on his newly acquired Velocette 250 with a certain Kathy as a close clinging pillion passenger. And she had been a soul mate of mine. It was a bit of a shock but I revenged myself by taking up with his ex girl friend, Kirsty.

The good news about this interchange was that Leslie and his Kathy eventually married and brought up a family, living happily in Hythe all their lives. And are still supporting each other in their advancing years, maybe less cuddly, but just as clinging, and they are an enjoyable source of nattering nostalgia whenever we meet at their home in Old London Road.

Sadly, Kirsty lost her father soon after, and her mother, together with the rest of the family, Barbara and baby Billy, left Hythe, eventually settling in the small village of Twyford near Winchester.

I continued to be affected by the enduring spell of my birthplace. The canal in the summer months being always a source of serene pleasure. In those days the water would be kept clear and free of weed by being regularly swept by a flat-bottomed chugging dredger. And the overhanging trees would provide welcome shade to cool a body which had become overheated and sweaty after a two mile feathering row in one of those beautifully sleek, sliding seat boats that were really a pleasure to row in. Most unlike the horrible tub things that wallow along the canal today.

A typical afternoon's pleasure would be to take one of these boats on a leisurely row as far as the Carpenter's Arms public house, where the landing stage gave access to a shady garden, and a small light beer or shandy to revive one for the return row back to Hythe. There to pay a shilling for the hour's trip to an ever smiling boatman before taking a few steps across the road to have three penn'orth of the nine hole putting green at the side of the cricket pavilion. It was my ambition to conquer this green in eighteen shots but the nearest I ever got to that was a round of twenty one. It was more usually between twenty five and thirty, nothing to urge me on to contemplate taking an interest in playing on the beautiful two level golf course up on the hill near to the railway station, or on the smooth, attractive wind swept links adjoining the Hotel Imperial.

After the putting I would take a gentle stroll down the delightful Lady's Walk to the sea front to have a twopenny ice cream at Ma Crump's little shop before returning to 28 Cobden Road in time to see what delights Mother had prepared for tea. Shrimps, or home made brawn or even some crisply cooked leftovers. A bubble and squeak which would make any semi-cooked modern 'nouveau cuisine' appear and taste just a little insipid.

After a repetitive journey back to Halton the training and straining of apprenticeship life would be resumed. Becoming less irksome as one learnt to accept the inanities and to take advantage of what was, after all, probably the best aeronautical training in the country. The theories of flight and control, and the internal combustion engine in all its forms, together with the study of fuels were all highly technical and absorbingly interesting subjects.

The school master mainly involved here was A.C. Kermode. He was credited, I think, with having written some of the first text books on all these subjects. In fact it was he who told every new entrant that there were two ways of becoming famous in the aircraft engineering world. One being to design a jet engine, the other to discover a method of obtaining an infinitely variable wing section. The first, as the world now knows, was accomplished by Sir Frank Wittle, an ex RAF apprentice and no doubt inspired by A.C. Kermode. But the second still defies the combined ingenuity of all experts, professional and otherwise.

Mr Prior was the mathematics and mechanics master who had a tendency to insist rather too strongly on a lot of homework, to be done in the evenings. An infringement on one's spare time and not to be taken too seriously (I decided). Especially if it meant repetitive exercises in a subject item that had been totally absorbed during class. And when I had no homework or prep to present for checking I explained that I saw no reason why I should waste my precious spare time going over something I already knew. I was, not surprisingly I suppose, considered to be a big head and left to look after my own progress from there on. This I did with added effort and to good effect, for in the final examination a near maximum score was achieved. The odd points being lost for, I like to hazard, using the wrong coloured ink.

As a point of interest, I held on to the actual question paper for some fifty years before eventually presenting it to the RAF Museum at Hendon. However, the examining authorities had the last word and marked me down, due to lack of zeal and attainment during my three years of training. A considered judgement no doubt, but a trifle vengeful I thought.

One typical evening with no homework or extra room jobs to do and with the necessary threepence, I joined the inevitable queue for the presentation at the camp cinema of a recently released and recommended film.

I remember this showing, not for the attraction or quality of the film, but for the immediate and mass reaction to what seemed an insensitive miss-portrayal of the story. An opening scene was of a very young girl, a child, getting out of bed to run to the door of her room, and then along a cold, narrow corridor to enter another room. There to run to a bed to hug and greet her mother before running to a blazing log fire to lift her tiny nightdress sky high to warm herself, revealing a delightful little rounded bottom.

Later in the film, and reflecting the passage of years, the child, now played by a pulchritudinous twenty year old, repeated the sequence of events. As the scene progressed one could sense the anticipation of the enthused audience. But when it all devolved into a simple hand warming – disappointing all expectations of a more erotic happening – a mighty roar went up, followed by a repetitive chant of 'swindle, swindle' which slowly subsided into appreciative laughter and then silent enjoyment of the rest of the performance...

The final year's syllabus contained an extensive period of training on the aerodrome which brought with it the very first exciting contact with aircraft that really flew. Proving that all the theory and simulated practical work so far undertaken was in fact related to actuality. These airborne marvels were AVRO 504 K trainers, fitted with Lynx radial engines. String and fabric bi-planes that looked untidy, cumbersome and ill at ease on the ground, but in the air a magical change would take place. They came into their own, not exactly birdlike, there were too many wings, but proving beyond doubt that the air was their natural element.

To stimulate our enthusiasm the pilots of these aircraft would, from time to time and quite randomly, select an apprentice to be taken up on a trip. These trips would last for some fifteen to twenty minutes and were highly prized. On being asked if I would care for a trip my reactions were a mixture of surprise, delight and trepidation. The last feeling dominating when it came to putting on a parachute, receiving the briefest of instruction on how to operate it if the necessity arose. However, when fully harnessed and parachuted, and consequently bum heavy, I waddled to the aircraft to struggle through the slipstream to the rear cockpit, there to be strapped in and asked if I was comfortable. A lying 'yes' was the almost breathless and inaudible reply.

I was thinking that I had been brought into the world at ground level by a thoroughly conventional process designed by nature, and here I was about to be taken off it by a softly vibrating, fragile string and fabric contraption that seemed anything but natural. I suddenly realised it was man made, and vulnerable.

Now, out on the airfield and head to wind, the pilot opened up the throttle. The engine roared and the aromatic smell of burnt fuel assailed my nostrils. The plane moved forward, slowly increasing speed and the tailskid shuddered madly as it slid over the not too smooth surface of the airfield. Then the tail lifted, leaving the aircraft to move more or less smoothly on its wheels, before the increasing speed provided sufficient airflow over the wings to give the lift for take off.

The squeaks, whines, rattles and wheezes experienced during the take off ameliorated and amalgamated into a noisy, pulsating rhythm, giving a strange feeling of security, which was tempered slightly on realising that the only things between me and mother earth were the bottom members of the fuselage frame, covered only by a now fluttering skin of doped fabric. My first real impression was the lack of any sense of height, due I concluded, to the fact that there was no physical link with the ground. A circumstance, I

A SHILLINGSWORTH OF PROMISES

suddenly thought, that would rapidly change if anything went wrong. Dicing with death on a single take off, two circuits and a landing? It was time to come down to earth, both mentally and actually.

The landing was perfect and the pilot taxied back to our starting point where I unclobbered myself from the harness and 'chute to give it to the next lad due to experience his first sensations of being airborne. Although I thoroughly enjoyed the initiation and the excitement, I had no overwhelming or intense desire to become a second Lindberg or a Captain Ball.

Now my apprenticeship days were nearing an end and life in the Royal Air Force proper, as one of 'Trenchard's brats', was fast approaching. This expression was hardly a term of endearment and was used, I suspect, in the early days, in a contemptuous sense. But hundreds of ex-apprentices quickly and easily proved the innuendo to be false and unwarranted.

The tetchy days, weeks and maybe months before the final examination were filled with intense periods of revision and anxious moments of doubt. The vastness of the whole three year syllabus provided ample scope for misgivings, some subjects having been easily absorbed and others being still shrouded in mystery. So, as usual with all exams, there was going to be a high element of luck. If you knew the subject matter of the question, all would be well. If not – hard luck!

The written element of this particular inquisition proved to be no great burden. But in the oral examination, direct confrontation with those supposedly experienced and knowledgeable old Flight Sergeants, filled me with a sense of awe and intimidation. And my natural instincts let me down once more for I reacted with an attitude of seeming aggression – with of course, dire results. I passed out from Halton as a middle of the road Aircraftsman first class, still mentally arguing the pros and cons of the effects of longitudinal dihedral angles with an unconvinced and puzzled examiner.

The passing out parade was, as anticipated, an immaculate spectacle, reflecting success for the massive number of hours we had spent practising the rifle drill and manoeuvres required for this ceremonial ritual. High ranking officers and some families witnessed the event, the former approving, the latter applauding. We participants were just simply glad when it was all over. The presentation of prizes and cadetships followed, being enjoyed by only a limited, and well selected and maybe preordained, few.

Escape from the years of penury was now near at hand, for even as a lowly A.C. lst class I would have all of twenty eight shillings a week to spend. It seemed a fortune and I could hardly wait to know to which unit I would be posted. It was to be to 9 squadron at Boscombe Down in Wiltshire.

So the village of Amesbury and the city of Salisbury were to be the beneficiaries of my new and immense spending power.

The great day came and, all armed with free travel warrants, we happily departed, regaled in full best blue uniform and heavily laden with over stuffed kit bags, to enjoy a well earned three week summer break before reporting to our various units to start life as full blown members of the real Royal Air Force.

August and September of 1935 had a high quota of sunny days and Mother had a full five to six weeks of bookings for the two front rooms. And now, with the two grown sons of the family fully financially independent, an unusual affluence assailed the old home, which then had to suffer the impact and indignity of a few minor renovations and replacements. Sad, but inevitable.

The old copper in the scullery cum kitchen was the first to suffer. It was attacked by just Mum and I one Saturday morning. By midday it had been completely demolished, but it took slightly longer to get rid of the brick and cement dust. It had penetrated every uncovered nook and cranny, infiltrating into the larder to do likewise to our unprotected leftovers. Now, with the old chimney bricked up, and all patches of bare wall re-plastered and artistically touched up with whitewash, all was ready for the installation of a brand new gas cooker. This transformation took but a few days, covering a period between two of Mother's lets. An Ascot gas water heater was then added over the sink, bringing to an end this particular frantic spell of modernisation.

There was still no bathroom in the house and the downstairs outside loo was still fully utilised, storing the precious long zinc bath and the produce from the allotment, together with Father's other odds and ends. Occasionally, and maybe anticipating a dire emergency, he would tentatively pull the chain to check the plumbing. Why? I don't know, for the only time I ever saw the thing in use was when, with the door wide open and in full view, he would sit open legged on the seat, preparing his seed potatoes. Halving the big ones and pruning the shoots of the smaller ones.

My young brother Tom was now twelve years old and, due to his indifferent health, had been the main worry for Mother. And naturally a very strong emotional attachment had developed between them. His education had been intermittent and sparse but this disadvantage was countered to a degree by his natural desire for social contact with all and everyone, particularly with those who were even more disadvantaged than he was. He learnt from life more than he could possibly have learnt from any formal schooling. And now, with hindsight, there had been nothing for

A SHILLINGSWORTH OF PROMISES

Mother to worry about, for at the age of 69 and still going strong, he is equally as well off as either of his two, supposedly more fortunate, brothers.

The Romney, Hythe and Dymchurch railway, innovated by a certain Captain Howey, had been an attraction for Hythe and its visitors since 1927, and it was about time the joys of this miniature masterpiece were sampled by the family. Who so far, to say the least, had been a little indifferent to the whole thing. However, with some four pounds of leave pay now burning a hole in my jacket, I took brother Tom on a day's outing, which included a trip on this new and unique public service.

A small railway system as a big hobby, hopefully making big (or small) profits, ensuring its continuing existence, was thought by nearly everyone to be a very good idea. The small engines were magnificent, beautiful scaled down models, and perfect replicas of their big brothers, gleamingly seductive to any grown up with half an eye for beauty, mechanical, aesthetic or otherwise. And to children of all ages they were an entrancing, large and fully working toy, to be wondered at, dazzled by and maybe tentatively touched.

The carriages, however, were a slight disappointment, there being no attempt to miniaturise the real thing. They were designed specifically, I would guess, to carry grown ups and children in conditions which were assumed to be tolerably comfortable. But the open-sided, hard seated, four passenger compartments were successful only in providing a draughty viewing cab where each couple, sitting side by side and facing each other, had great difficulty, when swivelling to enjoy the views, in avoiding knees and thighs locking together. A rather enjoyable disappointment, depending entirely on the nature of the opposition. The journey to Dymchurch was interesting to us inasmuch as we now saw familiar sights from a slightly different angle. And as we crossed the flat, sheep filled marshes, we re-recognised the old landmarks of Port Lympne on the roughs, and the Grand Redoubt sky-lined on the coast at West Hythe. Of more immediate passing interest were the little bridges under or over which the small train travelled, and the level crossings with their queues of held up traffic, also the arrival at Dymchurch station. Here we were welcomed by tiny skyward pointing signals and a series of little piercing whistles which maintained the illusions of scale.

It was a short walk into Dymchurch itself which, at this time of the year, was always crowded with holiday makers, mainly from inland Kent and London. All milling around the centre of the town where harassed but happy Mums and Dads could be seen guiding, cajoling or maybe cuffing their ice-creamed progeny in and out of the arcade, around the cockle and whelk stalls and onto the sands. There they would wander along virtually miles of rippled golden sands where, if the tide was out, stranded pools could be probed for tiny crabs, shrimps, starfish and sometimes barely covered little flat fish. With, hopefully, no sign of the beastly little poisonous weaver fish. This foreshore scene was delightfully new to us, for Hythe had only shingle beaches, sand being visible only when tides were very long, revealing what were known as the 'bar sands'.

Tom and I joined the throng and lashed out on a stand up lunch, scoffing plates of cockles followed by cucumber and cheese sandwiches. Then wandering onto the immense expanse of sand we made our way to the sea, taking off shoes and socks *en route*. And, with our sock-stuffed shoes laced together and slung round our necks, we joined other happy paddlers in a scuffling walk along the water's edge. Mums being ankle deep, Dads knee deep and the younger, more adventurous ones paddling, and maybe piddling, in deeper waters. We soon regretted that we hadn't thought to bring our bathing costumes with us. We could have escaped to less crowded, or maybe less polluted, depths.

Suddenly Tom elbowed me, bringing my attention to two girls bearing down on us on their bicycles. The leader, screaming, giggling and pedalling hard, was the cause of the elbowing. Apparently she was one of the avant-garde of the topless brigade, revealing her beautiful and bouncing assets to all who cared to look. Unfortunately, at this point, a patch of soft sand caused calamity. She catapulted over the handlebars, slowly sliding to a halt on the welcoming sand. Standing up, she revealed to the world what now looked like two little sand dunes and both, though well sanded, were somewhat less tanned than the rest of her body. The second cyclist, fully costumed and apparently a slightly elder sister, reassured herself that no great damage had been done before seizing the chance to scold her daring sister on the dangers of being topless.

Her answer was simple. "But Sis, I'm not hurt, and two big white spots looks daft." She appeared to look in our direction for confirmation. All I could do was to enjoy a studied glance in both directions and utter a hopefully helpful, "Oh yes – Oh yes". With a smile from the younger one and a glare from the other, they cycled off to firmer ground, no doubt to happier and fully sun-tanned holidays to come.

Tom and I slowly made our way back along the sands having thoroughly enjoyed our leisurely afternoon. The tide was now racing in, causing frantic rescuing of half submerged deck chairs, bicycles, push chairs, buckets and spades where the unwary and unwise had nearly been caught out by the unexpected speed of the returning water.

A SHILLINGSWORTH OF PROMISES

Back in the town itself the Punch and Judy show was closing down but the fish and chip shops were opening for the evening session. So we both had a threepenny piece with two penn'orth of chips. It was local caught cod, cooked beautifully in a crisp dry batter, with chips firm to the bite, flavoured to perfection in good clean fat. The flavour enhanced of course, as tradition dictated, by being wrapped in newspaper of uncertain vintage. This meal lasted the walk to the station where we took a draughty, happy and knee free return journey to Hythe. It was the one and only time that I ever used the Romney, Hythe and Dymchurch railway but I'm thankful just the same to Captain Howey for having chosen the right locality to indulge his unique hobby. A sentiment, I'm sure, which is shared by the hundreds and thousands who have travelled the line over the years.

The remaining few days of this leave were spent just idling on the beach close to home, taking a cooling dip every so often in the clear, sand free waters. The choice between sand or shingle beaches depends, I suppose, on one's liking or distaste of sand-filled crevices and sandwiches, as opposed to semi bruised bums and tender, tortured feet. It is sad to relate that, in spite of the many hours I spent in the sea, I never mastered the art of swimming the crawl; being forced to breast or side stroke my miserable 150 yards or so. But all my contemporaries could swim like fish for hours on end with supreme confidence and total nonchalance. Gaining and enjoying looks of jealous appreciation from some of our beach bound visitors. The specific gravity of my carcase, however, was such that I could sink like a stone. So with a deep breath and a dive from the breakwater, I was able to outswim, under water, any of my mates. But who was watching?

The penultimate day of my leave, a Saturday, was spent with Fred Jenkinson, the milkman's son, loafing on the beach in the shade of the sea wall. Suddenly, the noise of an aeroplane engine penetrated our dozing brains. Everyone on the crowded beach stopped in their tracks and waved at what I quickly recognised to be an AVRO 504 K, roaring along at about seventy miles an hour at a height of some three hundred feet, hugging the tideline as it went. The pilot and passenger enthusiastically waving in return to the appreciative and excited holiday makers.

I felt a strange sort of pride, wondering how many amongst the crowd would, like me, know how to adjust the incidence and dihedral angles of a 504 K, or how to service its Lynx engine. I found myself bragging to my pal in a somewhat unnaturally loud voice. But who was listening? Life can be very unfair.

On returning home I learnt that Mother had just received a letter from her sister Beattie in Canada, giving the sad news that her husband, Bob, had died. He was a brother of Father, two sisters having married two brothers. I could not remember either my aunt or my uncle, and Mother gave me a short history of their life together, starting from shortly after the war early in 1919.

After demobilisation uncle Bob had found it impossible to find a decent job in London and, out of work and penniless he had walked from Tooting to Hythe, arriving in Cobden Road after four foot weary days, not having eaten for the last two of them. Hythe proved to be no more fruitful than London. So, after some ten days he took off again 'a pied' westwards along the coast road, lightly equipped and even more lightly financed, on a journey which took him eventually to Southampton. Here his sea legs took over, for he joined the crew of a cargo boat and worked his passage to Quebec.

Now apparently in a state of perpetual motion he hiked and bummed his way across Canada, finally arriving in Vancouver. But from Vancouver there was no way to go except backwards. He had run out of English speaking countries, and he didn't fancy crossing the Pacific to China or Japan, so he made Vancouver his home.

My Mother's sister eventually joined him some eighteen months later. She made a more conventional Atlantic crossing but then had to make a piecemeal journey from Quebec, having to stop off at Winnipeg and Calgary to 'odd job' some money to pay for each subsequent stage of the journey. Bob, meanwhile, had found a series of jobs requiring very diverse talents, from road sweeping, to handling dog sleighs, to paper hanging, to being finally a game warden. This last job he kept, and enjoyed, for the rest of his life. This couple had no children and we three brothers often wondered what similarities there might have been between the families had it been otherwise. Now uncle Bob's relatively short life of adventure had come to an end. The first death in the family during my lifetime so far, and it made me aware that each generation itself has a lifespan; and that no particular generation has a monopoly of eternal youth. Although each generation seems to think it has, and behaves accordingly.

My leave was now over and the final Sunday morning saw me sadly saying my temporary farewells before climbing into the rear door of Newman's station bus, which took me in luxurious ease, with kit bag as foot rest, up the hill to Hythe station. That little stage of the journey indicated a growing affluence and it was worth the tanner fare, for after all, I had a free warrant for the rest of the trip.

A SHILLINGSWORTH OF PROMISES

After arriving at Charing Cross station I negotiated the hazards of a one stop journey on the underground to Waterloo. There to search out the well known and well named 'Union Jack' servicemen's club where one could have a room, a bath or a meal at any time of the day or week at a reasonable price, and always more than good value for money. I lashed out on two sausages and mash, apple pie and custard, washed down with a mug of sweet tea.

After this welcome repast I wandered back across the road to the station, scanned the departure board, then trickled through the main line station crowd to my train, which was already waiting at the platform. Station crowds always intrigue me, for they present a marvellous cross section of the human race. Some rushing, anxious faced and over laden, others blasé and self confident, some superior, others tentative. Some well dressed in quality clothes, others well dressed in somewhat less expensive gear. The shabby, the untidy and then the unfortunates – drunks and drifters, loafing and skulking in odd corners. The drunks would always appear to have a self-effacing, happy grin on their faces as they shared their bottled booze with each other. Caressing the bottle tenderly as they carefully replaced it in a concealed pocket, or openly on the floor, between well spaced gulps, which would keep their minds at the right level of hazy happiness.

On leaving London and its suburbs, the panorama of terraced houses and a thousand shed-bespattered back yards, mingled with larger buildings and factories, slowly petered out as the green fields and woods of the real world took over; bringing a welcome sense of peacefulness and detachment. Some three hours and five Woodbines later, I was changing trains at Salisbury to make the final stage of the journey to Porton Down.

It seemed to be a totally lifeless spot, isolated and remote, and was apparently some sort of experimental base, and the nearest railway link to the RAF station at Boscombe Down.

On arrival at Porton I was met by a somewhat morose and untalkative MT driver and his 15 cwt. van, in which he silently took me and my kit bag on the last few miles to Boscombe. There I was unloaded at the guard room and taken over by a corporal who conducted me to a pre-allocated barrack room. And still not a word of prolonged conversation. I was beginning to think that maybe they spoke a different language on the great plains of Salisbury.

I reported to the corporal in charge who authoritatively pointed to an empty bed and curtly said, "That one there, the seventh on the left."

He disappeared into his own private little bunk at the end of the room, muttering something about Sunday being Sunday. That, I supposed, accounted for the general antipathetic attitude, and the MT driver's moribund sadness at having to spend his time collecting an intermittent flow of new arrivals.

Some half dozen of these turned up during the next couple of hours. Amongst them were two ex 26th entry Halton apprentices, Pip Wright and Punch Hanson. Both were wearing the insignia of a Leading Aircraftsman, which indicated to me that I was only one step off being the lowest of the low in the technical hierarchy of the Royal Air Force. But these two received the same peremptory introduction to the real Air Force that I had had, being directed to the eighth and ninth beds on the right, by the corporal's unwavering and rigid digit.

We had all arrived in time for the evening meal and, borrowing some eating irons (knife, fork and spoon) and a mug from some obliging old hands, we sauntered off to the Airmen's mess to sample our first ex-Halton meal. The menu of egg and mash was not strange to us but the atmosphere at table and the subtle differences in the cooking were. The eggs, I would say, had spent much less time in transit from pen to pan, and the mash, if not exactly creamy, was certainly not the glutinous, lumpy splodge that we had all enjoyed over the previous three years. And the tea, I swear, had been made with real milk, and was even adequately sugared. And, miracle of miracles, a second helping was on offer due, it seemed, to the difficulty of accurately forecasting catering requirements at weekends.

Back in the barrack room we could light up our after meal fags without fear of being nicked by some over zealous corporal or sergeant. The transition from the boys' Air Force to the mans' Air Force suddenly seemed absolute and complete, but as yet we were still very green, albeit with an appetite to change colour as quickly as experience would allow.

The author, aged 21 in 1936, a single lad and usually skint...

A SHILLINGSWORTH OF PROMISES

3   An Erk in Baghdad & Beyond

Eight thirty on the morning of the first working day saw all new arrivals reporting to the station Orderly Room. There to be officially included on all relevant lists and records, including rosters for what seemed at the time such oddly named duties as 'fire picquet', 'weekend guard', 'duty crews' and 'Airman of the watch'. All these duties had to be carried out during non working hours. When this requirement was tentatively questioned, we were loudly and tersely informed, "You joined the RAF for twenty four hours a day, my lads, no more and no less."

One had to admit the answer was stupifyingly logical and absurdly correct.

However, in the event and in the queue, I was asked by an immaculately turned out administrative corporal, "When did you last see a barber?"

Four weeks of unhampered growth was the cause of his concern and the reason for his order, "Get round to the station barber now and report to me immediately after."

This I did but, having registered only on the roster for 'Airman of the watch' before this enforced tonsorial intervention, I escaped inclusion on the other rosters. A fact I didn't fully realise until tackled by my mates, who asked suspiciously, "How come you never seem to get nobbled for guard or picquet duties?"

A sort of self induced honesty tempted me to answer, "I think I'm excused on medical grounds – growth glands are over active or something."

On the second morning 'B' Flight of number 9 Squadron experienced the influx of three well trained, but totally inexperienced, ground staff, reporting to a Flight Sergeant McClaren. It was a sunny morning and, after an initial morale boosting chat we were conducted around the hangar, each to be introduced to and paired off with an experienced old hand, to crew a particular aircraft. My new mate's name was 'Tweet' Allcorn and the aircraft was a Vickers Virginia night bomber, affectionately known throughout the RAF as a 'Ginny'. A huge bi-plane with two Napier Lion liquid-cooled engines and three open cockpits. One for the pilot and navigator sitting side by side, one air gunner's position right forward, and a rear gunner's cockpit aft and virtually out of sight behind a box plane tail section. The Ginny had a top speed of approximately a hundred miles an hour, that is if it had the advantage of a following wind. With a head wind the ground speed could be negligible, or even less.

Our initial introductions were suddenly interrupted when the persistent hooting of a car horn coming from the airfield side of the hangar announced the arrival of the N.A.A.F.I. van for the ten minute morning break. An orderly queue was quickly formed, no pushing and shoving as in the old apprentice days. Then, sitting on an upturned wheel chock and leisurely nibbling a jam fritter and sipping a mug of real tea, and being gently caressed by the warm autumn sun, I began to feel at home with myself and the ambience of my new surroundings. The familiar smell of hangared aircraft now topped up with the sight of live aircraft lined up on the tarmac, seduced me into thinking that maybe the course of my, so far, depression directed life was not, after all, such a calamity.

This consoling reverie ended when my new technical corporal, a corporal Gwyther, called out, "Come on then back to work, you two there, Allcock and Hitchcorn."

It was difficult to decide whether to feel flattered or insulted. Preferring the former I accepted the temporary aberration as a somewhat exaggerated compliment, and willingly joined the returning throng.

The geography of the hangar was quickly learnt, together with a rapid familiarisation with all safety procedures and records. Amongst these the most important would be the individual maintenance record for each aircraft, known then as a Form 535. A number easily remembered at the time as it had had a fair amount of press coverage; it being the number allocated to Cunard's great new liner before it became known as the Queen Mary. The F 535 eventually became the F 700, and the Queen Mary a floating hotel in California.

The first week passed rapidly enough and its ending brought with it the magnificent wage of twenty eight shillings. What on earth was I going to do with so much money? Thinking that the end of each subsequent week would bring similar windfalls. One whole tanner was quickly invested in the station football sweep. And then, on the first Friday evening in barracks I was inveigled into learning how to play three card brag, depleting my capital by some seven bob at one stage, and recuperating five of them before the orderly sergeant on his rounds almost politely insisted on someone 'putting those bloody lights out'. Service life was becoming progressively more tolerable.

Saturday mornings were usually taken up by the unavoidable intrusion of such things as kit inspections or barrack inspections, or some other atrocity conjured up by our disciplinarian and administrative friends. But Saturday afternoons and Sundays were free, unless of course one had been nobbled or selected for some odd weekend duty. So, this Saturday being free, Punch

A SHILLINGSWORTH OF PROMISES

Hanson and I, sports jacketed and flannelled, caught the afternoon bus from Amesbury to Salisbury to sample life as it was intended.

This joint initiation started with an investigative amble around the town centre, followed by the luxury of a quick beans on toast in a small and smelly cafe, followed by a dive into the hoped for girl infested local cinema. But we had no luck and our subsequent aimless wander suddenly turned into a pub crawl which, to Punch, had been the whole object of the exercise from the beginning. As he was a misogynistic non-smoker he was only interested in the first of a hedonist's three basic requirements of beer, bints and baccy, supplemented maybe by a game of darts.

All the pubs seemed to be oak beamed and cosy, particularly the private and saloon bars, but even our new found affluence only permitted the use of the public bars. Here the pleasant rumble of voices as the evening wore on became somewhat raucous and finally discordantly tuneful. Our dart playing suffered the same sort of regression, doubles and trebles being difficult at first, then somewhat easier as the first drinks enlarged the slots and steadied the hand, but deteriorating sadly later as hand, body and mind became uncoordinated strangers. Our pleasures came to a sudden end when a large red-faced and punctured bystander suggested we pack it in. My world was beginning to go round and round but Punch was still largely unimpaired and he offered the lad a pint and sympathy, all timed to perfection, for before the offer could even be considered the landlord's 'Time, gentlemen please' echoed around and off those friendly oak beams.

The cold night air turned a slightly unsteady walk into a positive stagger. But, supported by a true pal, and after a long, ill directed piddle and a learner's rendering of the Shaibah Blues, the bus station was reached in time to catch the last bus back to Amesbury. The hour long limp, alcoholic snooze on the journey revived us sufficiently to realise we were hungry. So we partook of one of life's sublime offerings and floated a gourmand's helping of fish and chips on a lake of stale beer. The digestive capacity of a young and healthy stomach is to be wondered at. What a shame it has to deteriorate over a lifetime into such a tetchy organ, eventually becoming a gurgling cauldron of evil discontent.

Now, to all intents and purposes, perfectly sober and eighty per cent articulate, we presented ourselves at the station guard room to sign in before making a short, controlled saunter to our barrack room before, as all well trained airmen do, we undressed, cleaned our teeth and donned pyjamas to go, semi-mindless, to bed. Incapable of appreciating the supreme banality of the past twelve hours or so.

On waking next morning a man's size headache, a full bladder and some colonic irritation necessitated an urgent visit to the loo, where physical relief was replaced by a degree of mental discomfort. For thinking of buying a Sunday paper, I suddenly realised that the previous evening's outgoings had been somewhat haphazard and uncontrolled. So a quick dash to investigate the pockets of my twenty one inch bottomed flannel bags, neatly folded in a lump on the floor, told me that I now had exactly ten shillings and twopence ha'penny to last the rest of the week. The change from the embarrassing wealth of Friday evening to the relative poverty of Monday morning was quick and salutary, to say the least, and turned out to be peculiarly repetitive. The poor will always be with us someone once said. But I thought the remark should be qualified. It's true as regards the condition but not the collective noun, for the poor can get rich, and vice versa, with of course a long list of reservations.

It was on the working parade of the following Monday morning that I was told that a sergeant Peters was looking for me. He was an admin sergeant so I naturally assumed I had contravened some rule or regulation and was due for some sort of admonition, or worse. And for three weeks I successfully avoided him, diving out of sight whenever I saw him coming. I needn't have bothered for he had never spoken to me so he would not have recognised me anyway. But on Friday's pay parade he was within earshot of the paying officer and, on hearing my name called, he looked up and then followed me. Quickly catching up with me and in a semi irate voice he demanded, "Where the hell have you been lately? I've been looking for you for weeks."

Fearing the worst and automatically looking guilty I said, "Round about, sergeant, round about."

He looked almost affable and, with a funny sort of grin on his face, he asked, "Have you still got your ticket, blue, number one-o-eight, for the football sweep three weeks ago?"

Scrabbling in my top breast pocket I retrieved the hastily folded and forgotten bit of paper. It was blue and it was number one-o-eight. Sergeant Peters gently took it from me, replacing it with seven one-pound notes, a few odd shillings, and a bit of advice. "Next time, don't play so bloody hard to get."

Now I had a problem. What to do with this windfall? Wealth too could bring its problems. After a little doubt and reflection I decided that I would apply for a long weekend, go to Winchester, and then search out my old Hythe girlfriend, Kirsty, in her new home at Twyford. It would be the first time I had seen her for some three years.

A SHILLINGSWORTH OF PROMISES

The necessary application for the weekend pass was granted and an early escape was made on the Friday, enabling me to reach Winchester around six o'clock in the evening. Then a stroll to the bus station by King Alfred's statue took but a few minutes and, within the hour, I caught a Southampton bound bus which took me direct to Twyford. I remember only three things about this journey, one being how easy it turned out to be, two, how shallow and clear the river Itchen looked, and three, how brilliantly yellow the ends of my twenty Gold Flake looked.

Arriving in Twyford I began to feel just a little nervous, for I had been unable to give any warning to the Price family of my proposed visit, and as yet I had no idea of their actual address. The village was small and seemingly deserted. However, a shouted 'Hallo there' to a little old lady drooped over an ancient and protesting bicycle brought her, not unwillingly, to a stuttering two-footed halt. She was pleased, able and volubly willing to answer my enquiry as to where I could find the Prices. She was one of the world's chatterers and it took her close on ten minutes to tell me that they lived in the middle house of 'those three over there'. They were all of a hundred feet away, so that worked out at about ten feet a minute. If passing the time of day was her ambition, then she was certainly a very quick thinker. I thanked her kindly, smiled and waved her good-bye as she restraddled her bike to make a slow and wobbly departure.

It was now about seven thirty and getting almost too late for surprise visits, but having come so far I persevered, and the first rattle on the knocker brought Ma Price to the door. After a first look of questioning doubt, a huge smile of welcome spread across her face as she grasped me in a big cheek to cheek hug, before pulling me into a cosy but unlit living room. There a glowing fire sent flickering rays of light around a small room, and I did not immediately see Kirsty dozing in a big arm chair by the fire.

Ma nudged me and pointed. I looked, and there she was, the girl that had been romantically and erotically in my thoughts for the past few hours. I tip-toed over to her with all the old feelings rising within me, and kissed her gently on the cheek. She didn't move and I transferred the kiss to her lips. Her eyes opened and a flicker from the fire brought instant recognition, and a cry. "Good God, what are you doing here?"

Fearing a rebuff, an insipid grin crossed my features and I blurted, "What do you think? I've come for some of Mum's cooking, ain't I?"

Seeing the look of almost belief on her face, and before she could reply, I added hopefully, and threateningly, "And you, and you!" She laughed and pulled me close, and eventually we changed places and she made herself tantalisingly comfortable on my lap, unknowingly following a basic tenet of engineering practice, i.e., before you start work, get everything at a convenient working height.

Ma quizzically enquired if we were comfortable and then disappeared into the kitchen, saying, "I'm sure you're hungry, Fred. I'll fix you some eggs and bacon, and don't make a noise, Billy and Babs are asleep upstairs."

But Barbara, now aged eleven, had heard enough to excite her curiosity and she came downstairs to see what was going on. The eggs and bacon appeared on the table at that moment, and three pairs of male-starved female eyes watched my every move as I ate. It was, I remember, pleasantly disconcerting. During the nostalgic chatter which accompanied the meal, Ma hinted more than a couple of times that I should visit more often. I felt my freedom being threatened, but a rising feeling of belonging killed any thought of resistance. I said that I would.

Kirsty and Ma were delighted and the chat became increasingly animated, and before bedtime arrived, there even seemed to be a tacit feeling that an engagement might quickly transpire. The only puzzling thing at the time was that young Babs' face reflected some sort of hostility, and she suddenly stood up and hurried off to bed. Having only had two brothers, the moods of pubescent eleven year old girls were a complete mystery to me, and I thought no more about it.

As usual, the weekend passed all too quickly. On the Saturday I was cajoled into doing a bit of digging in the back garden, with a compensating bit of snogging in the afternoon. The cinema in Winchester was the evening attraction, with a cuddly trip on the bus back to Twyford followed by a slow fanny fiddling walk back to the cottage. All was well with Ma, for we had brought back some fish and chips, stone cold of course. but succulent enough after ten minutes in the oven.

I left around eleven o'clock on the Sunday morning, not wishing to impose on Ma the extra cost of feeding a healthy and virile young twenty year old any longer than was necessary. It was obvious that the family were living through difficult times but in spite of that, when I slipped a portion of my football winnings into Ma's unwilling hand, I think I felt happier than she did. But her eyes and her parting kiss reflected her affection and appreciation. Kirsty's parting kiss was, as I had hoped, loving and moist, and Babs', though short and shy, was flatteringly enthusiastic.

During the journey back to Boscombe Down I became extremely pensive. Chain smoking my way through at least a dozen fags, wondering how things would turn out. Permutations of certainties with possibilities were endless

A SHILLINGSWORTH OF PROMISES

and I was unable to picture any clear pattern for either the near or distant future. But it did not really matter, for the Royal Air Force, fate and world events were to signpost the direction, not only of my future but also that of many others.

In a mental haze and harking back to earlier conclusions, it seemed one's life on earth could be summarised simply as 'A tickle and then what?' The 'and then what?' being as unpredictable as the tickle is predictable. So what could one do about it? Sweet FA except to try to avoid all hazards and pitfalls, and they, by definition, would usually come without any sort of health warning. And there's only one way to avoid the final catastrophe of death and that is not to be born. Those flaming tickles have a lot to answer for.

However, back to the here and now. My allocated task of maintaining a Squadron's aircraft soon became a comfortable and even fulfilling one. The daily inspections, the marshalling and refuelling, the carrying out of cyclical servicings, even the cleaning and polishing instilled a sense of pride and pleasure. Squadron spirit it was called, and it was potent stuff.

Test flights after any critical item of servicing were frequent and it was policy to allow any personnel involved to volunteer to take part. This I did, and quickly learnt to enjoy floating around over the local counties, pinpointing the towns, places and roads that I knew. This I found intriguing, so much so that I decided to volunteer to be a part time air gunner. The strength of this decision, I must admit, was augmented by the fact that I would receive an extra one and six a day 'flying pay' plus a brass 'Flying Bullet' insignia to wear on my arm. And that would impress Kirsty and the family, wouldn't it? I made an official application, passed the required medical exam and was accepted for training.

Sessions in the station armoury quickly followed, where the mysteries of the Lewis gun were revealed to me. There was not a lot to learn mechanically, but the variety of faults and stoppages it could have appeared to be endless, and not always easily corrected. Each particular gun and magazine seeming to have its own peculiar form of bloody-mindedness. In the light of the sophistication of modern 1990s sighting techniques, those of 1935 would appear to have been only a shade better than hit or miss, with the estimation of relative velocity, wind speed and direction being only as good as human judgement could make them. Bringing to mind the classic bomb-aiming joke of the time when the aimer's directions to the pilot coming up to the target were, 'right a bit, left a bit, right a bit, back a bit.'

Back to earth and to my first great technical success when, through my dedicated endeavours every 'Ginny' in the RAF was grounded, and at the time I found it hard to discern whether I had done something praiseworthy or blameworthy. It happened thus.

I was religiously going through the items detailed in the inspection schedule for a simple twenty hour servicing check, and when following the item annotated 'check the longerons for cracks, corrosion or damage', I disappeared up the back end of the fuselage armed with a torch. For I had decided that the inspection could not be done externally, the fuselage being completely covered with doped fabric. Inside it was a major struggle to crawl between all the bracing wires and struts to get into a good viewing position for each section. But the struggle brought its reward for, when flashing the torch onto the top port side attachment fitting for the tail section, I found that the longeron had a total circumferential crack. This meant that the whole rear section was only being held in position by the remaining three attachments, plus a healthy factor of safety in design.

I wriggled my way out of the fuselage and was immediately confronted by the corporal.

"What the hell have you been doing up there? Having a nap?" Ignoring the sarcasm I told him what I had found. He looked at me in disbelief and said, 'Now come on show me from the outside exactly where you think this crack is.'

This I did. Then, with a grin, he said, Now let's make a nice big cut in the fabric, and seeing as how you'll have to repair it. we'll make it a big one."

He did, and then his look of superior disbelief disappeared like a fart in a wind tunnel. His amazement exploded and found words. "Well I'm buggered!" Augmented after a thoughtful pause by "Well I'm fucked!"

Then he disappeared to pass on the bad news to the technical Flight Sergeant who after making his own inspection, immediately took action to report the defect to Group HQ. Within a very short period of time all similar aircraft throughout the RAF were grounded, so that they too could be checked for the same fault.

I received not the slightest word of congratulation from anyone except from my mate Pip Wright. He had flown in the rear cockpit for a couple of hours the day before, and was now safe from what might have been all undiscovered hazard of the future. (Carrying no health warning!)

Christmas 1935 came and went and the early months of the new year brought my first experience of night flying. It was a long round trip with Wing Commander Lucking as pilot, from Boscombe northwards to Oxford, Northampton and King's Lynn and returning via Colchester across the Thames estuary, and then westwards back to Boscombe Down. Take-off

A SHILLINGSWORTH OF PROMISES

was at seven o'clock in the evening and, with a trip of approximately four hundred miles, we were expecting to return to base before midnight.

Then the hour arrived and, in full winter flying kit, I left the warm crew room to waddle open-legged to the waiting 'Ginny' and to clamber into the open rear cockpit, only to discover that the ground crew had used it as a temporary storage place for the canvas engine covers. Thereby robbing me of some ten or twelve inches of cockpit height, and this meant that even my meagre five foot six left a goodly proportion exposed to the elements. Fortunately I was able to extricate the monkey chain to latch it to the harness ring, thus preventing any possibility of an unplanned ejection. An unplanned erection, now that would have caused other problems, for the flying suit was very, very tight and all embracing.

We took off and after some two hours of flying, and with a following wind, the outward leg of the trip was completed and we turned for home. By now the wintry night and the height had reduced the temperature to a disagreeable minus quantity, and at this point the primitive intercom system failed, leaving me alone and cold in a little world of my own. This in turn affected my bladder, but now squatting on the covers below the level of the cockpit, I was loathe to stand up and expose myself (and it!) to the icy blast of a hundred mile an hour slip stream, augmented by an increasing head wind. But, as nature cannot be denied, I had to make the effort. A simple process it would seem, but after unbuttoning the outside flap I found the hole in the suit to be some six inches too high and only an insulting one inch in diameter. But, after a frantic ten minutes or so of finger and thumb searching and manoeuvre, I managed to grab hold of a (fortunately) not totally circumcised dick to wriggle it out just far enough to use the rubber receptacle provided.

By this time I was almost sweating from the effort and gladly subsided onto the engine covers, listening to the drone of the engine and the hissing of the slip stream, and my own thoughts questioning the so called glamour of flying.

I was now getting progressively colder, and impatient for the end of this trip. I felt very lonely and a bit left out of things. But, on looking over the side, my spirits rose. The great glare of London clearly outlined the Thames estuary which was now right underneath us, so I calculated that within an hour we should be landing, and I sank down again to get as much protection as I could.

After a further ten minutes or so I looked down again and I swear we had not moved. We had been airborne for some four and a half hours and we were now having to struggle against a gusting force five to seven head wind, making the aircraft suddenly lift or drop or roll in a very disconcerting manner, taking on and playing 'silly buggers' with the elements, testing its inherent stability to the limit. And mine too, for we were crabbing along at a ground speed of about forty or fifty miles an hour, ensuring an estimated two more hours of this rock and roll. I stood up some twenty minutes later to see the lights of London disappear in the distance, and to have a second piddle. Rather more skilfully this time for there's no substitute for experience, and I agree and so does John Thomas, for he suffered less in the extraction process the second time around.

I settled down again and slipped into a half frozen doze, only to be awakened about an hour later by the sudden change in engine note as the aircraft touched down to make a perfect landing.

As soon as we taxied to a halt I jumped to the ground and made a bee-line for the crew room to warm up by the fire. But the first thing the pilot did was to rush round to the rear cockpit to see if I was all right, for he of course had not heard anything from me for some four hours. On finding the cockpit empty, consternation and speculation were rife. I think I had already been written off, assumed to have been left in mid air when hitting a hefty air pocket, and that I must now be a gory, well spread mess in some distant part of Norfolk, Suffolk, Essex or nearer in Kent, Surrey, Hertfordshire or Wiltshire. So imagine the disbelief and relief when the crew came into the crew room to see me in good, glowing health, standing by a nearly red hot combustion stove, grinning from ear to ear. Relief and recognition were expressed quite succinctly. "There he is. It is him, isn't it? Yes, it is. You little nutter, you had us all scared to death."

I had the feeling I had done something wrong but what, I couldn't imagine. Maybe I should have left a note.

About this time the activities within Hitler's Germany, such as the occupation of the Rhineland and the formation of the Hitler-Mussolini axis, together with the fact that Hitler was already the Commander in Chief of the Wehrmacht, prodded our political and military leaders into contemplating the aggressive intentions of the new born Nazi Germany. And the general public were becoming increasingly aware that the so called civilian flying and yachting clubs were being used to train pilots and crews for more sinister functions in Germany's burgeoning Navy and Air Force. These were sure signs of Germany's clear intention to circumvent the conditions laid down in the 1919 Treaty of Versailles.

A SHILLINGSWORTH OF PROMISES

The undercover production of war materials and the building of a first class road and rail system put the German economy into gear. And it succeeded. Full time production and an assured military market ensured that the wages and salaries paid created a demand in the domestic market, and a suitable sense of prosperity grew nationwide. No wonder Hitler and his 'Heil' prevailed, and the indoctrinated German masses screeched their support.

So it was no surprise to learn that the Royal Air Force itself was to be expanded. 'B' Flight of number 9 Squadron, including me, was hived off to become number 214 Squadron and was transferred to RAF Station, Andover.

Being now a little nearer to London it was much easier at weekends to nip up to the smoke to sample the delights of the great metropolis. The famous theatres and opera houses held no attraction for my uncultured soul, except maybe those operating at a somewhat lower level such as Ben Travers farces at the Aldwych and Maskelyn and Devants Theatre of Magic. The cinema, the football grounds, Lords and the Oval, Wembley and Wimbledon dog tracks, these were the venues I headed for, but only when events of some major interest were taking place. Such as Chelsea versus Arsenal at Stanford Bridge, or Arsenal versus Chelsea at Highbury. Or Dennis Compton at Lords, who twice sent me home disappointed, having gotten himself out in the nineties when I dearly wanted to see him let rip after having made a century.

A rather odd attraction that a pal introduced me to was to go to the Old Bailey to enjoy half a day of some major trial, watching events from the public gallery. But it bored me to death and I went only the once. Hours were spent coming to some conclusion as to whether the witness became pregnant before or after the meeting with so and so. I nearly bawled out 'During!' But being shy and circumspect I said nothing, except to tell my mate 'I'm off.' And I went.

One never to be forgotten weekend was when, having drawn my pay of thirty eight and sixpence on a Friday, I sat in on a game of Napoleon with three others and went to bed some four pounds to the good. The following morning I caught an early train to London and made my way to Wimbledon to see my Uncle Fred and Aunt May. In the afternoon a visit to Plough Lane dog track brought its reward and I now had six pounds and a few odd bob in cash. So now, feeling lucky and carefree, and suffering from gambler's flu, I went off to Wembley dog track for the evening meeting.

My first bet was a six to four winner, bringing my cash in hand to seven pound ten. An even money bet to a pound stake on the second race came off and now I had eight pound ten, and that, in 1936, was a lot of money. But a good looking two to one chance in the third race tempted me to go big and I wagered eight pounds. The result was a heart-stopping dead heat, but the feel of the sixteen pound notes that I now had was exhilarating. So much so that I had a rush of blood to the head and thought I was invincible. Thankfully, I had the sense to leave a ten shilling saver in my waistcoat pocket before wagering the whole sixteen pounds on a six to four chance in the fourth race; having visions meanwhile of what I would do with the forty odd quid that I was sure was coming my way. In my mind I was already the possessor of an immaculate second hand Ford Eight. But it was not to be. The excitement of actual possession was denied me by an eight to one outsider that led from start to finish, so I didn't even get a thrill out of losing my lolly.

Chastened and despondent I made my way back to Wimbledon and to Uncle Fred's sympathy and Aunt May's disbelief. She couldn't imagine how I could have been so daft as to lose such a huge amount. Me neither, and I haven't bet on a dog or a horse from that day to this. But playing cards, that's another matter, for on returning to Andover and reaching my barrack room about seven o'clock in the evening, I immediately sat in on a game of solo whist, starting with the ten shillings I had wisely put out of harm's way in my waistcoat pocket at Wembley. Luck waxed and waned during the evening, waxing to just thirty eight and sixpence at the finish, around one o'clock in the morning. A suitable coincidence one might say, for I had had an exciting and educational weekend, and it had cost me exactly nothing, except maybe the contemplative ownership, if only for a few moments, of my first car.

But the corporal rigger, he did have a real car, an open MG, and most weekends he would go home to Southampton to see his wife and child. My interest in the corporal's car was stimulated by the fact that he had to pass through Winchester *en route*, so there was a strong personal element triggering my technical interest in his pride and joy. And when I offered to help with the petrol money for a weekly lift to Winchester, he saw it as a good deal, and accepted. So now my trips to Twyford and Kirsty became more regular and more convenient. But sometimes, when the weather was wet and windy, I thought maybe I should have insisted on a spontaneous opt-out clause. However, the little MG motored well, taking the sharp downhill hairpin bend in Wherwell in its stride, straining and rattling its windy way safely and at a fair speed, to Winchester and Southampton. But I swore I would never own an open car of any sort, they are worse than any open cockpit, and I always had to suffer the ribaldry of the family each time I arrived, looking and feeling like an over used bog brush.

But the rewards made it all worthwhile for I saw a lot more of Kirsty and St Catherine's Hill. One memorable bright and sunny Saturday afternoon, the long grass, passion and a condom ordained that I should adopt a trousers down and bum in the air position, with Kirsty looking at the sky and the hedge further up the hill. Suddenly, and almost timed with the glory strokes, she sat up and screamed, "You filthy little sod!"

With my three piece strained to the limit and with my brain working overtime wondering what I had done wrong, I managed a high pitched "What the hell?"

Looking flushed and angry she pointed to the hedge and yelled, "There's a bloody little Peeping Tom up there. Go and sort him out!"

By the time I was de-erected and re-trousered the 'little sod' was scuttling off at a rate of knots half way down the hill. Kirsty and I returned to our pleasures with unabated zeal but with very little attainment; eventually making our slow way home to Twyford to enjoy the evening with plenty of exercise but with no Peeping Tom, for Mum had gone early to bed.

Round about April 1936 we were serving under a new King, for George V had died in January and the Prince of Wales had become King Edward VIII. And it was just about this time that I was detailed to go to North Coates Fitties in Lincolnshire to undergo a full air gunner's course. This entailed having an air crew medical exam which I passed, but only just survived. For the corporal medical orderly, when giving me a preliminary hearing test, asked me to repeat a whispered sequence of numbers. I immediately recognised them as being the telephone number I had been asked to ring when explaining away a double date mix-up for a pal. So instead of repeating the sequence, I foolishly gave him the girl's name. The rest of the test was at a somewhat higher decibel level and aggressively confrontational, starting with, "What the hell do you know about Jennie?" The green eyed monster was at work so, sensing a full frontal attack, I hastily declared a nil interest, saying that I was engaged to a girl in Winchester anyway. A fiction that ultimately became fact. The trip to North Coates was on a Sunday and all buffets were closed, but I remember that I was able to fend off starvation when a village pub opened as I was waiting for the bus to take me on the final leg. A simple meal of a chunk of hard cheese, two thick slices of white bread and a generous helping of pickled onions, all washed down with two halves of draught bitter, saved the day. A repast I can taste to this day, in spite of the many so called gourmet meals that have attacked my taste buds in the intervening years.

The following day my initiation into the mysteries of air gunnery soon got under way. The aircraft were two seater Westland Wallaces, and they were highly manoeuvrable. Flying in them was vastly different from lumbering along in a friendly old Vickers Virginia. The objects of the training were simple enough. Firstly, air to ground practice on fixed targets along the coast at Donna Nook using Norman Vane sights, and then air to air combat. That was a different story entirely, using, of course, Scarff ring mounted camera guns with two aircraft at a time going through all the manoeuvres of a simulated dog fight.

The only concrete conclusion I came to after these mock fights was that, if a gunner ever hit an opponent it would be by pure luck only, for the centrifugal and G-forces acting on a standing gunner in any manoeuvre were such that he must spend most of his time with collapsed knees, hanging on for dear life to the spade grip of his gun for some sort of unattainable stability.

Once, when in a loop and collapsed on the floor of the cockpit with the gun pointing directly out into the skies, I opened my eyes and found the attacking aircraft to be beautifully within my sights. I took four quick camera shots, and they turned out to be the only scoring shots I ever made. I soon realised that the functions of an air gunner would only pay some sort of dividend if he were able to perform from a stable base, such as in defence or attack from a bomber. A fighter needed fixed forward firing guns and a pilot of extreme skill. These were my simple conclusions at the time, leaving me feeling pleased that 214 Squadron was uniquely a bomber unit.

Summer leave in 1936 was taken rather late, about mid September time, but Hythe still worked its magic for me, the beauty and the tranquillity of the place recapturing my soul. It made me feel somewhat resentful that the lack of any chance of decent local employment had forced me to leave this delightful corner of England's green and pleasant land. But it was a consolation to meet up with others who were in the same boat, revisiting old haunts and old friends. That was how I met up with my old chum George Hilton, the swearing postman's son. He had left Hythe to join the Metropolitan Police force and was currently stationed at Elliott House in London.

I spent many hours reminiscing with him, his dear little old Mum and his irascible old father. But the highlight of that leave was when George and I took a double sculler on the canal for a nice comfortable row out to the Carpenter's Arms in West Hythe, and whilst refreshing ourselves on the lawn there, being challenged to race the motor driven pleasure boat, crowded with holiday makers, back to Hythe. George, now a real six foot giant, made a quick, unsupported, decision to accept, leaving me stunned and open mouthed in disbelief.

The race duly started and, although cheered on by all the passengers and egged on by George, my tortured five-foot-six and ten stone frame gave up just short of the Duke's Head bridge, and we lost by a distance, to disembark quietly and unapplauded some five minutes later at the landing stage, with aching backs and at least one busted ego.

Mum and Dad, now with only young brother Tom at home, and with the country pulling out of recession, were beginning to enjoy a somewhat less arduous life. Elder brother Bert had by now married and was living with his mother-in-law at Southsea. He had married early and, being under twenty six years of age, he received no marriage allowance from the Navy and was living on his basic wages, feeling financially deprived but emotionally fulfilled. But this state of bliss quickly came to an end as Naval exigencies, aided and abetted by H.M.S. Courageous, separated him from his family for long periods at a time, sometimes running into years, and his married life became typically that of a sailor, a matter of touch and go, resulting eventually in a family of four. Mum and Dad, a daughter, and then a long delayed son. The family, complete with grandchildren, now live in Tasmania except the daughter that is, she got side-tracked somewhere along the line, becoming a dedicated political pundit, and is now living somewhere in Brixton.

My visits home were erratic and the family ties naturally became looser, but there always remained the feeling that there would be a safe haven of love and affection to return to in case of any dire emergency, emotional, physical or otherwise.

Soon after returning to Andover I learnt, with very mixed emotions, that I had been detailed, selected, or just picked on, to serve overseas. This inconvenience we all experienced sooner or later but I thought it could really have been delayed a while, having only just escaped from three years of restrictive existence at Halton. And overseas service in those days meant a tour of some five years, a long time to be away from home, family and friends.

Iraq, still referred to then as 'Mespot', was the preferred destination for the first two years, and it was a men only posting. A sad outlook for any raunchy youngster, or oldster for that matter. The departure, scheduled for the beginning of November, gave me the golden opportunity to spend my twenty first birthday whilst on embarkation leave, at home.

I remember the newspapers at the time were all concerned with a Mrs Simpson and King Edward, and a possible abdication. But my concerns were nearer to home and, after a sadly happy twenty first birthday cum farewell party, a tearful good-bye saw me on my way back to Andover. With again that awful feeling that I was no longer master of my own fate or actions, and I was doing something I really didn't want to do. Much the same as most people do for about eighty per cent of their lives. A useless but somehow consoling thought. There followed a final quietly hectic weekend at Twyford with Kirsty. We spent the Saturday morning window shopping in Winchester and, as we looked at the jewellery on display at Samuel's, we just looked at each other and I simply asked, "Shall we?"

And she, just as simply, replied, "Yes."

And we did. She chose her ring and it left me with just seven bob and a few odd clods, but who was counting? I was, I suppose.

We spent the evening as usual at the cinema and then dawdled our way along the bus route to Twyford, to an outlying stop to save a few pennies. But we stopped for a kiss and a cuddle and nature took over, directing us to a nearby churchyard. And between an 'At Rest' and a 'Not forgotten', we did, without even a 'Shall we?' or a 'Yes'. Memorable, certainly, but not to be recommended, it makes your knees ache and tends to strain one's respect for the departed.

The following Saturday of this fateful November of 1936 saw me fully kitted out for overseas service and assembled on the dock side at Southampton with the rest of the draft ready to be embarked on the troopship 'Dorsetshire'. A ship of some considerable size, all white with a single blue stripe, looking not exactly like a luxury liner, but seductive enough to give me and others quite the wrong impression of the cruising Joys to come.

We had known beforehand that we could, if we wished, spend the final Saturday evening ashore, so Kirsty and I had arranged to meet at the bus station. It was an emotionally erratic evening. We had the usual quick cafe meal of baked beans on toast before going on to enjoy the magic and fantasy of Fred Astaire and Ginger Rogers in the film 'Top Hat', both of us becoming temporarily oblivious to our immediate worries. After the film we found a park to spend the final few hours, cuddled together but doing nothing but talk about the future. Both of us, I think, realised that, although we had known each other for some time and felt strongly attached, the engagement had been rather more spontaneous than planned. But we didn't break it, and our final good-bye at the bus station was a tearful one, made all the wetter by thinking of the frustration of an expected five years of separation. She grumbled, "It's a long time, isn't it?" And, wiping away the suspicion of a tear from her eye, I replied, "Yes, it bloody is!"

A SHILLINGSWORTH OF PROMISES

She turned away quickly and climbed the steps onto the bus, just as the conductor dinged the bell to start, and I couldn't even see her hanky covered face as I waved good-bye, before disconsolately mooching my way down to the docks.

Back on board the Dorsetshire I met up with quite a number of my contemporaries from Halton, all putting a brave face on things and chatting away, joking positively about the past and wonderingly about the future. Some names which come to mind are Jimmy Rose, Punch Hanson, Lofty Mee, George Ogle, Primrose Vickery and Charlie Lark. We shared the same mess deck, which was simply one long table with two long forms arranged parallel with others on each side of the upper troop deck, all being stowable and allowing room to assemble that masterpiece of fiendish ingenuity, the hammock. A thing which takes ten minutes to climb into and ten seconds to fall out of, and requiring a knowledge of all the variables involved to position it satisfactorily. Such things as weight, height, length and distance from one's immediate neighbour. The last being necessary to counteract the effect of any possible sonorous, or odorous, by products of a deep sleeping comrade. The principle of the hammock is sound enough, the ship should roll and pitch, leaving the sleeper hanging motionless, but somehow weather and sea conditions always seemed to defeat the objective.

On the first day a quick look at the orders posted on the notice board disclosed a list of duties to be performed. Mess deck duties, guard duties, fire picquet duties and others. Also we had the first of many practice calls to take up 'boat stations', preparing one for emergency take off in one of the ship's lifeboats in case of disaster and a call to abandon ship. All rather disconcerting and taking the edge off any feeling of having a nice peaceful cruise to foreign parts.

But it was a long journey and some peaceful days were enjoyed. However, a few basic facts of troopship life had first to be learnt, such as appreciating the difference between leeward and windward. Getting one's own back is not always such a good thing. It was advisable to keep well clear of the stern regions of the boat when the Lascar crew were enjoying their ghee cooked meals, otherwise some permanent damage might result to one's sense of smell. Also never to get involved in any illicit Crown and Anchor game organised by nimble fingered sailors. That's entertainment alright but with a high degree of intrinsic robbery involved. And always squat near the tannoy during sessions of housy-housy, for a missed number might mean a missed fortune. And always be early in the queue for the morning and afternoon tea and biscuits provided by the crew and not the ship's galley. It was private enterprise at its best, and good stuff.

The first day at sea brought all the enjoyments of being seaborne and of being off on one of life's great adventures. Hectic, romantic, exhilarating but, unfortunately for some, also sick making.

The Solent slipped away behind us, and then the Needles, a green and white remnant of the United Kingdom, floated past on the port side and, as we progressed out into the English Channel, dear old England gradually diminished and disappeared into the distance. We were now really on our way and a sudden mood change descended on me, making the thought of the next five years seem something definitely akin to a life sentence.

One quickly became unaware of the dull, vibrating pulse of the ship's engines, in fact at times it would act as a welcome soporific. Which was just as well for, during the first night, the western approaches became decidedly rough and the Dorsetshire reacted accordingly, rolling and pitching with enough abandon to make the early morning activities of rising, washing and stowing of hammocks more than a little chaotic.

I remember that the breakfast that morning must have been chosen by some cook with a very vicious sense of humour – kippers. The sight of a steel serving tray filled with hot oily fish quickly sent the majority of the lads hurrying off to the bogs, leaving but two of us, Punch Hanson and myself, to help ourselves. We managed to see off three each and were contemplating a fourth when a duty officer in search of the hale and hearty, nobbled us for guard duties in that part of the ship housing wives and their children going out to join their husbands in Egypt.

We were detailed for the four to eight p.m. shift and the duties involved were simple enough. To control the entrance to the quarters and, in case of emergency, to close and secure the hefty bulkhead doors if ordered to do so.

By midday we were well past the French port of Brest with the Bay of Biscay looming ahead. The weather had continued to deteriorate and now a full gale was blowing. All hatches had been closed and all open decks put out of bounds as the Dorsetshire began to roll and pitch between the enormous waves that rolled in from the Atlantic. The height of these waves must have been forty feet or so, for large cargo vessels going in the opposite direction would suddenly sink right out of sight, to reappear reluctantly on the crest of a following wave, only to disappear again almost immediately, leaving one's gaze hypnotically focused for the reappearance.

I had seen force ten gales sending huge waves up the beach at Hythe and wondered then at the frightening aspects of the forces of nature. These same

A SHILLINGSWORTH OF PROMISES

forces were now attacking the Dorsetshire causing it to shudder in protest as it plunged its way through each great wave, and my thoughts disturbingly focused on the unsinkable Titanic – which wasn't.

Our particular battle with the elements was less ominous but the ship's motions became threateningly monotonous, and all the passengers reacted in their own fashion; some becoming horribly sea-sick, others just queasy, and a few proudly unaffected. All, either sitting or lying down, struggling with their own personal misery or moving around like uncontrollable drunks without having had the causal pleasure, grabbing at anything and anybody for temporary support. The poor children and wives were having the worst of everything and there was little one could do. The feeling of helplessness gave little substance to any attempt at reassurance. So the trauma and the misery and the penetrating smell of a hundred and one heave-ho's, continued until the sea conditions decided otherwise. Which was somewhere a few miles off Cape Finisterre. The Bay of Biscay had lived up to its worst reputation.

Our journey continued with the sea becoming increasingly more friendly, with everyone appreciating and enjoying the relative calm and the exercise of repetitive circuits of the open deck, interrupted by lengthy leans on the port side rails to watch and wonder at the beauty of the Spanish and Portuguese coastlines as they intermittently appeared on the horizon.

Then eventually turning left a bit, then a bit more, we thankfully slipped through the Straits of Gibraltar, leaving the unfriendly Atlantic behind, and passing the famous rock and its Apes, with the Moorish coastline of North West Africa well in view on the starboard side. Later, looking north towards the Spanish coast and seeing all the dazzling white houses with their red tiled roofs nestling on the green and brown hillside, romantic notions took me back to the Harvey Grammar at Folkestone, where 'The Conquest of Granada' had been studied and dissected in preparation for matriculation. The Moors, Malaga, the plains of Andalusia and Granada itself were now transmuted in my mind from fiction to fact, and I became momentarily part of the invading hoards.

As we progressed into the Mediterranean, the routine on board became firmly established. Meals were somewhat repetitive in a dietary sense, and exercise was also repetitive in as much as there was nowhere to go except around in circles, pausing at times to lounge on the ship's rails and just watch the water. To parody an old quotation this could be done either leaning and thinking, or just leaning. Sometimes, however, we would be delightfully entertained by a school of dolphins, following the bow waves, dipping and diving and changing formation, even surfacing at times, appearing to look up for some sort of appreciative applause.

The delight and monotony breaker of each day was of course when the morning and afternoon mug of tea with biscuits arrived. It was then that everyone found a favourite spot on deck to squat down, relax, chat, reminisce, discuss or argue. The only time silence reigned was during the calling of numbers for the housy-housy sessions. But somewhere between Sardinia and Tunisia someone either coughed or farted and I missed number seventy four being called, and a full house of some twenty odd quid. And to this day number seventy four is to me what number thirteen is to others, even refusing, in 1979, a car number plate with a seven and a four in it.

Some time later, snoozing after the midday meal in a hastily slung hammock, I was suddenly brought to life by the change in rhythm of the engines and strange noises echoing from the upper deck. We had slipped into Valetta harbour in Malta, and the ship's anchor chains were rattling noisily as the anchor dropped, bringing the first stage of our journey to an end.

But after off loading a handful of airmen and a few wives and children, and with, I suppose, a bit of re-provisioning of fuel and water, we were again on our way, cruising into the eastern Mediterranean with ever improving weather, and with the sun warming our backs, the thought of more distant places now began to fill our minds.

When a few miles out from Port Said, all airmen due to disembark were ordered to assemble on number one troop deck to undergo an F.F.I. (Freedom from Infection medical inspection). Then, all duly stripped off and completely naked, they formed three ranks of some hundred or so men waiting for the medical officer, torch in hand, to search for whatever he had to. However, at the same time all the wives due to disembark had been asked to go down to the luggage hold to identify their particular possessions, and the leading lady, mistaking her directions, inadvertently led her contingent down the wrong ladder and came face to face with a hundred and one droopy diggery-do's. There were screams of protest, or appreciation, and never were so many seen by so few, so unprepared for any sort of action, military or otherwise. Some lads turned discreetly, some turned full frontal, some tried cross handed concealment. But all roared appreciation as the advance guard tried desperately to reverse the descent, fighting a rear guard who were unaware and unappreciative of what was confronting them. Sadly, the rearguard lost.

A few hours later we entered the harbour at Port Said, anchoring in deep water some-distance from the quay, where we were immediately attacked by

A SHILLINGSWORTH OF PROMISES

a small fleet of bum boats. The occupants of these boats, galabiehed Egyptians and half naked boy divers quickly got to work selling anything from soap to sandals, belts, ties, watches, plus an endless variety of locally hand made brass and copper ware. The shouting and haggling in broken English, interspersed now and then with a tirade of high speed and, to us, incomprehensible Arabic, resulted in a fair amount of mutually satisfying trading being done. This was carried out at a height of some fifteen feet by means of accurately thrown ropes attached to straw bags. A high degree of trust between seller and buyer was essential and was achieved without fuss, as the goods were always hoisted on board first before payment was made, then checked and usually accepted. A disdainful look directed at a potential short-changer by the floating 'merchant' was invariably enough to shame the culprit into paying the haggled contract price.

The lively boy divers too were soon at work, retrieving unerringly any silver coin thrown in their direction. Brown coins would tend to be ignored, not meriting a display of their unique diving skills, and indicating a true perception of the rate for the job. A distinguishing choice that I thoroughly endorsed.

Port Said of course gave me my first sight and smell of the real Middle East, and nothing mystic assailed my senses, just a feeling of something totally different, a mixture of repulsion and attraction, of things and smells identifiable and unidentifiable. And in 1936 it was the evidence of real poverty that made the biggest impact. The unusual sounds, smells and customs would also affect me in due course, but they would be assimilated slowly and be accepted as part and parcel of everyday life overseas.

After days on the open seas the journey through the Suez Canal provided a totally different scene. Watching sand instead of water. There was very little activity on the banks, just a monotonous expanse of sand stretching far to the horizon on both port and starboard sides, a thin ribbon of residual canal separating us from dry land. Camel country at its best but with no sign of any tented nomadic Arabs to satisfy romantic notions acquired at home. A potted resume of things learnt at school flitted through my mind, from the Pharoan attempts B.C. to link lakes and sea, and intermittent attempts thereafter, through to de Lesseps, the French lad that actually got the thing built. And subsequently Khedive Ismail's financial troubles that led to the sale of shares to Great Britain, organised by Disraeli, to gain control of the canal.

The journey through the canal was slow, relieved by a slight acceleration on reaching the Bitter Lakes. It was here that a compatriot complained of being constipated, not having performed since leaving Southampton. On being advised to consult the medical officer, he declared it wasn't necessary because, as yet, he couldn't taste anything! Foolhardy, to say the least. But a day and a half in the Red Sea plus an enema, eventually solved his problems.

Some four days after leaving Port Said we entered the harbour at Aden and had all the ship side comings and goings to watch, and with added interest, for ship board life by now was beginning to pall, and any contact with land, however transient, was taken as a sign of coming deliverance.

The harbour at Aden was then still a major refuelling and provisioning stop for all vessels involved with the maintenance and trade of the British Empire. My particular generation has seen this Empire go from being great to being non-existent, and it depends on the politics of particular historians as to whether that could be considered a privilege or not. My own feelings are somewhat ambivalent, but there are more than residual benefits on both sides.

The hinterland of Aden being slightly mountainous created a somewhat unexpected Arabian backdrop to the waterfront activities of the port. Where people with their carts, bicycles and donkeys lethargically hurried about their business. Their chattering and shouting echoing across the hot and humid bay to reach the receptive ears of hundreds of critical, rail-loafing onlookers, who were all unconsciously feeding their memory banks.

On leaving Aden our journey continued eastwards, and the Yemen coastline disappeared to port as we cruised to the Gulf of Oman, to resight land as we curved through the Straits of Ormuz to enter the Persian Gulf and eventually the Shat-el-Arab to anchor at the quayside in Basra on 18th November 1936. Some three weeks after leaving Southampton, which now seemed so irretrievably remote.

Primitive and enclosed as life on board the Dorsetshire had been, a certain affinity for the old ship was felt, which was not diminished by the pleasures of having solid ground under one's feet once more. However, this pleasure was soon to be put to the test.

Fully kitted and in serge uniforms, we were marched to the railway siding. Under the hot sun we wilted visibly and rapidly, and then totally, on realising that the collection of dilapidated cattle trucks, relics from the Great War and labelled 'Four horses or eight men', were indeed there to provide transport for the final stage of our grand journey at His Majesty's Government's expense. Now, formed up in bunches of eight, we were allotted to our specific trucks and ordered to entrain and, after a lot of Hee-Hawing, we began to settle down. In the corner of our steel horse box we discovered a pile of forty

A SHILLINGSWORTH OF PROMISES

service blankets and a box of hard-tack provisions. The food occasioned no comment, but in our sweaty, over heated state no one could work out why so many blankets? But after concentrated consideration, and realising the steel floor was a patterned mass of well rounded mushroom headed steel rivets, we all concluded that they had been provided to make a thick floor covering, so that we could sleep comfortably and peacefully through the coming night.

We were wrong. From midnight onwards, as the temperature plummeted to zero and beyond, the blankets were systematically transferred from under to over, and still we shivered. Awaking the next morning with aching and dented backs, painfully realising all those blankets had been just a basic, and not a luxury, provision. We also took note that desert nights could be bloody cold.

At last, arriving in Baghdad, which in 1936 was a somewhat nondescript and over romanticised city, we were met by a convoy of ten hundredweight vans, supervised by several Flight Sergeants, one of whom was a former sergeant Tresize, last seen and heard of at Halton, and an unwelcome reminder of former hardships. But this feeling quickly dissipated as he gave us all a quizzical grin of welcome. It would seem boy service and man service were not only years apart but poles apart as well, particularly overseas.

The arrival of a new draft at RAF Hinaidi, just outside Baghdad, caused no great stir, except for a few cryptically spurious enquiries from long term residents as to 'Who was King now?' For they had already served overseas under three monarchs, from George V to George VI via Edward VIII in something under twelve months.

Hardly had we been watered and fed and almost before we could return to our allotted accommodation, the skies suddenly darkened as a strong wind blew up, and with it an all embracing and choking dust storm. An alarm signal sounded and all hands were immediately mustered to picquet down and cover all aircraft parked in the open. It was an initiation I didn't appreciate. The heavy work caused heavy breathing, which caused heavy contamination of the respiratory system, and irritation of every orifice and crevice known to man, or women if there had been any. It took two showers and hours of coughing to recover and to really take stock of the new surroundings. I had been posted to a non-flying maintenance unit. This I thought strange, for had I not been trained as a part time Air Gunner? I immediately applied for transfer to number 55 Squadron which had recently been re-equipped with single engined Vincent light bombers and was under the command of a Squadron Leader Guy Hayes.

The application was granted and the aircraft that became my particular responsibility was piloted by a Sergeant Pilot Hilton, nicknamed 'Tubby'. This name was familiar to me, but he turned out to be not the swearing postman's son but, almost as surprising, he was an ex Harvey Grammar school boy and came from Tanner's Hill Gardens in Hythe. He was also twice my size and was then the current heavy weight boxing champion of the Royal Air Force. However, his tour of duty in Iraq was soon to finish, but not before he gave me the first big scare of my life.

We were flying at about five thousand feet, carrying out a test flight on a newly installed long range belly tank when the engine suddenly stopped. I couldn't see Tubby's head, he was bent down in his cockpit fiddling with the petrol cocks, and the aircraft went nose down into a glide, and deathly silent except for the hissing of the wind in the wires. The ground seemed to be coming up very rapidly and there was still no sign of Tubby's head, so I slipped on my parachute and was frantically debating the choice between a desert landing with a dead engine and a disappeared pilot, or a quick nip over the side at an assumed safe height. Then the angle of glide suddenly steepened, windmilling the propeller as the speed increased, and thankfully the engine spluttered and burst into life and we regained level flight at something under two hundred feet. Tubby's head reappeared. He looked back and gave me a thumbs up grin. I ran a hand around the inside of my shorts and gave him a reassuring sickly leer.

He had quite simply turned the cocks on and off in the wrong sequence, turning off the gravity tank before turning on the newly installed belly tank, causing an air lock in the pipe line, which fortunately cleared before the ground arrived.

Christmas 1936 came and went. It brought no presents, except an enjoyable three day alcoholic break. Each barrack room having an improvised and realistic replica of an English pub bar, adequately stocked with communally paid for drinks; with each individual trying hard to make a capital gain on his contribution. There were winners and losers and revelations. There was one wee Glaswegian whose idea of Christmastide bliss was to lie in an empty bath, totally nude, with eight bottles of Younger's milk stout lined up within easy reach, to be dealt with in systematic regimental order. The empties being lined up on the opposite side, in reverse order. The bath plug had been removed so a well directed piddle, with knees raised, was all that was necessary to ensure his undisturbed and continuing bliss.

With this first Christmas over it didn't take long to settle into the routine and changed requirements of service life overseas. Although, in contemplative

A SHILLINGSWORTH OF PROMISES

moments, one did wonder why the hell one was there, enduring all the monotonies and monastic miseries of this arid and sex starved land.

Furthermore, on the rare occasions that I visited Baghdad, I seemed to sense that there was a burgeoning resentment to a British presence there, mainly amongst the younger Iraqis. However, the merchants and the elderly were more amenable and welcoming, enjoying the traditional happy haggling, back chat and hand slapping of a completed purchase. But the town itself held no great attraction for me, with its flies and smells, and its seething crowds hustling and bustling along the narrow streets, which were overhung by dilapidated and dissimilar buildings, mostly of primitive construction, interspersed with a few more substantially built offices or shop looking totally out of place and pretentious. And on any trip through this labyrinth, one's conscience would be constantly assailed by the small army of beggars, some grotesquely handicapped and others with pitifully glaucoma'd eyes, all sadly pleading for bucksheesh. And young pick pockets abounded, catching the unwary. Ali Baba may have disappeared into history but his forty mates had surely remained and proliferated; operating with a crafty and improved efficiency.

Nineteen thirty seven, can be remembered only for the impact of the minor happenings of every day life. Rainy periods in the early months of the year would bring the threat of flooding from the Tigris, and concern as to whether the bund walls protecting the base would be breached. They remained unbreached, but even a moderate rainfall would turn the hard 'mutti' into cloying mud, turning one's boots into high lift stilts, with a high risk of sprained ankles even on the shortest of walks. This being only a temporary hazard as the eternal sunshine soon returned all to dryness and dust.

The outside latrines were more than somewhat primitive, consisting of wooden seats arranged in bench fashion with closely fitted, decapitated, four gallon petrol tins placed underneath as receptacles. These tins, or thunder boxes as they were called, were regularly emptied by the 'bog wallah' from a trap door at the rear of each cubicle, with a high pitched warning of 'No tin, Sahib' if a bum appeared over the hole as he was doing it.

On one occasion I remember, the timing was a little tight, for as I squatted down I heard the tin scrape and I sprang to attention, but not before the ragged edge of the tin had tickled my testicles. I couldn't help but spend the next few minutes in prayer and wonder. I broke into a cold sweat as I realised that had I been a fraction of a second earlier I would probably have seen the productive half of my low slung wedding tackle (it was a hot day) disappearing into the turd tin, and ultimately the Tigris. Not a pleasant thought and I uttered thankfully a low pitched sigh of relief.

As the months passed the long evenings became increasingly tiresome. Sometimes a boozy session in the NAAFI would ease the pain. However, as the frequency of this pastime increased, so did one's capacity, and with it the expense of alcoholic sublimation. But the full throttled rendering of 'Fuck 'em all' or the 'Shaibah Blues' would lift one's spirits, if only momentarily.

Long hours were also spent playing cards, mainly solo whist, for moderate stakes, acquiring an expertise which was later to be put to good use in playing bridge. A game which enthrals me to this day, but I still feel the 'open misere' hand in solo whist presents the biggest challenge to any dedicated card player.

Reading of course was the most popular of pastimes, and the two most dog eared books were, not surprisingly, the unabridged version of Lady Chatterley's Lover and Doctor Marie Stopes' comprehensive and beautifully illustrated Psychology of Sex. I read and studied the latter first, with the illustrations making more impact than the text. I must admit I had to learn a whole new glossary of terms for bits and pieces of the male and female body and their functions which had so far been adequately dealt with by mainly four letter words. Education is such a wonderful thing but I thought expressing oneself in such involved terms could make one's love life more an academic than an emotional performance, requiring a score out of ten or twenty just to make it more interesting.

But I was soon to be reassured for, on reading D.H. Lawrence's contribution, the game keeper restored my faith in the benefit of using my earlier vocabulary. 'Urinate off' or 'Copulate off' didn't seem to have quite the right directional emphasis.

Writing, naturally, took up a lot of one's time. Kirsty had a weekly letter. I wrote home to Mum less frequently but the letter would be longer. Everyone was sustained by news from 'Blighty' and the recently inaugurated Imperial Airways service with its new four engined Handley Page 'Hannibal' aircraft ensured delivery of mail either way in just three days, and that was an unimaginable boost to morale.

But it brought me bad news a bit quicker, for very soon after I got my 'Dear John' letter, telling me that five years was a long time and that people can change, and that I might not find her attractive any more when I got back. So she had married someone else, and did I want my ring back? I had a subsequent, and longer letter from her Mum. Kirsty had married the postman, and was pregnant. In the right order so I wasn't to worry. I didn't.

　　　　　　　　　　　A SHILLINGSWORTH OF PROMISES

RAF Station Hinaidi was soon to be closed down as a brand new base was nearing completion some miles west of Baghdad, across the Falluja plain, and located where the Tigris and the Euphrates converge. The base was originally named Dhibban but this was quickly changed to Habbaniyah, for apparently the word Dhibban had some peculiar and derogatory connotation in arabic. Our Technical Flight Sergeant at this time was a certain Flight Sergeant Etteridge and he boasted that he had joined the Royal Air Force when the Air Ministry was a tent, and I had no great difficulty in believing him. He also, apparently, had had the pleasure of meeting Lawrence of Arabia in the form of a general duties Aircraftsman second class, but when questioned about him he would become very uninformative, stifling any enquiry with a grimace and a shrug, which I suppose was as good as a ten page dissertation.

All Flight Sergeants were known as Chiefies, and this one was one of the best, with a fair sense of humour. He knew that there were those amongst us that had an intense dislike of all the desert creepy crawlies, centipedes, scorpions and the like. He also knew that the earthenware chargal that provided cool water during the summer months also provided a nice comfortable home for the scorpions during the winter. So, having detailed Charlie Lark and myself to check, clean and prepare the chargal for the coming hot season, he stood by awaiting our reaction. And when we lifted the wooden lid he wasn't disappointed. There must have been half a dozen or so of the beasts inside and they started scuttling around, tails up, startled and angry and ready, it seemed, to attack at any moment.

We quickly slung the lid back on and retreated ignominiously and pale faced as the pre-warned audience laughed their silly bloody heads off. We were then patronisingly introduced to the traditional game of scorpion baiting. They were scooped out into an empty petrol can and deposited onto a prepared area on the mutti, surrounded by a small built up bank of petrol soaked sand, which was then ignited. The scorpions immediately put their tails up, committing hari-kari by stinging themselves to death. Nature is strange, both beast and man.

The final months of 1937 saw the Squadron's transfer to the new base at Habbaniyah. The new single storey barracks, or bungalows as they were called, were a great improvement, being purpose built with bathroom, shower and toilet facilities practically 'en suite'. And the new hangars, spacious and technically equipped to a high standard, made life a lot easier. But the verdant and well irrigated nature of the new location provided a lovely breeding ground for mosquitoes and sand flies, testing to the full our acquired expertise in dealing with this particular middle eastern menace.

Our bungalow boy, Sayad, had moved with us. He was a little, even tempered man who looked after the room and, for a small extra payment, provided an early morning mug of tea, as well as keeping one's buttons, boots and bed space in good military order. A room of some thirty occupants, each paying him 200 fils each which, with a 1000 fils to a dinar, and one dinar equal to a pound, gave Sayad the equivalent of six pounds a week, which was double the maximum received by any one of the room's inhabitants. But he had a very large family to support in Baghdad, so his commitments were no doubt onerous, which is why the canny lad insisted on being paid in advance. A wise move.

Even 'Old Ben' the Armenian fruit wallah, whose four inch Jaffa oranges were out of this world, had learnt not to give credit. An old-sweat corporal returning to Iraq for a second tour, had left some six years previously owing Old Ben sixty fils, and he was quietly refused any sale of fruit until this old debt had been paid. When the corporal coughed up the look on Old Ben's face was a delight, breaking into a wide grin as he reeled off a list from memory of some twenty names, together with the amounts owed and, more astonishingly, what for.

The first months of 1938 passed without anything unusual happening. Just the routine of Aircraft maintenance, such as engine changes and repairs mixed with minor and major servicings. Flying training as a part time Air Gunner lapsed into an occasional trip out on a lengthy 'emergency landing ground' inspection, when a report had to be made as to the state of the strip and the condition of the stock piled four gallon tins of petrol. The only excitement was one bad landing, ending with the aircraft nose down in the sand with a well bent propeller, which meant a night's camping out, hopefully without the attentions of any curious Arabs or scorpions. It was a hope fulfilled.

An open Leyland truck accompanied by a Rolls Royce engined armoured car turned up the next day, complete with a new engine and propeller. Luckily, a shock-load test on the engine's propeller shaft proved to be within limits, so a simple propeller change was all that was required. A quick refuelling, and an even quicker take off saw us on our way back to Habbaniyah and its now more appreciated comforts.

On waking up one morning some few months later my nearest bed mate was muttering murder under his breath. Someone, for the second night running, had emptied his tobacco tin and he was furious. The following night, in an attempt to trap the thief, he had placed a circle of empty fag tins around his kit box, on which he always kept his baccy. He waited and waited

A SHILLINGSWORTH OF PROMISES

but finally dropped off to sleep. Come the morning, the surrounding tins were untouched but his Three Nuns had disappeared for the third time. But a more vigilant fourth night resulted in him hearing a slight tinny rattle and, on quickly switching on his torch, the culprit was revealed. It was a little timid and wide eyed desert gazelle, which stood transfixed for a second or two before shooting off through the window and out into the night. We tried for some time afterwards to tempt him back but with no luck, not even by changing to a more fragrant, expensive and divine brand of temptation. Three Nuns to St. Julian's.

The news from the U.K. began to indicate that there was an increasing concern as to the precise ambitions of a certain Adolf Hitler and his belligerent dedication to the policy of Liebenstraum for ex-patriot German minorities.

Also causing concern were his violent anti-Semitic activities, linked with his attempts to create a master race, leading to the expelling of all Russian Jews, the destruction of synagogues and the creation of concentration camps. Other governments in Europe were beginning to doubt the policy of appeasing German ambitions, and signs of belated reinforcement and re-arming of their fighting forces began to appear.

One of these signs being a call for volunteers within the ground forces of the Royal Air Force to apply for training as Sergeant Pilots. I immediately volunteered, not for any altruistic reasons, for I was motivated mainly by a desire to escape from the heat, hardships, flies and sexual deprivation of life in this glorious land of Iraq. Several others also volunteered, no doubt for different, and probably better, reasons, guided by a spirit of adventure and a desire to serve their country in a different capacity.

In the event three lads passed the interviews and returned to England to undergo pilot training. I passed all the medical checks with flying colours, being congratulated by the hospital adjutant on being perfectly medically and physically fit. But that was the only immediate satisfaction I had for I failed finally. But on what grounds I never did find out.

But fate had dealt me a lose and win hand, for sadly, my three successful companions were all lost during the war. And, deservedly or not, I'm still fighting to enjoy life at the age of seventy six.

Nineteen thirty-eight saw the end of my football playing activities, for one Geordie Chesson saw fit to stop me in full flight by sticking out a long left leg, sending me sprawling and causing what appeared to be a minor swelling below my left knee. It became very painful, making any movement an agony, but an unsympathetic medical officer deemed that I was in full working order, so I excused myself from any further sporting activities involving bodily contact. Subsequently, and later in life, I underwent three minor operations rectifying circulatory problems in the affected leg.

But, as rifle shooting required no great degree of physical contact, except with the ground in the prone position, I haunted the practice range and was eventually selected for the Squadron team in an inter-unit competition. We won, and the winner's medal, together with all my other trophies, i.e., one silver spoon, are hoarded together in the back of a drawer somewhere, awaiting summary disposal on my demise.

Mid 1938 brought some stirrings of excitement, for 55 Squadron was scheduled to make a long distance round trip of the Middle East. Circling the Arabian peninsula, across north east Africa to Khartoum, on to Nairobi, back up the Nile to Cairo and then, via Amman, back to Iraq and Habbaniyah.

Twelve aircraft were duly serviced and fitted with long range belly tanks, and the accompanying ground crews were selected from volunteers and I had the good luck to be included. The Squadron would be under the command of Squadron Leader Howe, and I was to fly with a Sergeant Pilot Richardson.

In early August the great day came and the Squadron took off, formed up and headed south. It was difficult to realise that these arid areas over which we were flying were considered to be the fertile lands of modern Iraq and the 'lands of promise' of many ancient civilisations, Ctesiphon Arch being some sort of relic and proof of their existence. And there was nothing to indicate the exact location of 'Ur of the Chaldees' or of Babylon, and it was left entirely to the imagination to realise that the Hanging Gardens and maybe the Garden of Eden used to be down there somewhere. It seemed like Paradise, well and truly, lost.

After some two and a half hours flying we approached the Persian Gulf and then followed the coastline of Kuwait. It was a welcome change of scenery to have the blue sea on the port side, but the dreary khaki of endless desert remained with us to starboard. And this was Kuwait in 1938 when it was only just being realised that oil was there in undiscovered millions of tons. And this would not start to be produced in any quantity until some eight to ten years later. Until then the main source of income for Kuwait's tiny population would continue to be the traditional fishing and pearl diving. There was absolutely nothing to indicate the incidental and fortuitous opulence that was to befall this small protectorate. In fact, within an hour we had flown over it, not even vaguely appreciating the future political and geographical significance of this small desert buffer state.

A SHILLINGSWORTH OF PROMISES

After another two hours or so of thinking and talking and singing to myself, we landed at Bahrain island. There to rejoin the other crews for a natter and a smoke before refuelling, checking and picketing down the aircraft for the night. Bahrain was still within the orbit of British influence and this devolved itself to my advantage in as much as the Royal Navy had established a canteen on the island. And on visiting it I was pleased and astonished to see, lined up on the shelves, bottle after bottle of Mackeson's milk stout with their labels proudly announcing 'Brewed in Hythe'. A hefty thirst was nostalgically quenched. Unlike Kuwait, Bahrain had already been exploiting its oil reserves for some years but it was early days and modern developments had not yet ruined the true Arabic nature of the place. And there were still literally thousands of small fishing and pearl diving boats whose crews gleaned a healthy living from the seas, gladly preferring and enjoying life on the water, as opposed to suffering the heat and humidity of working ashore.

The following day, after enjoying an unexpected luxury of filleted fish cooked with egg and breadcrumbs for breakfast (the texture was strange but the taste was excellent) we took off and headed for Sharjah and Muscat. It took two and a half hours across the water to reach Sharjah where we refuelled from the stock pile of four gallon cans that had been off loaded there by the Royal Navy for just that purpose. Then taking off again and skirting the western end of the Djebel Akhdar mountains, we entered the Gulf of Oman and followed the coastline to the twin towns of Matrah and Muscat.

As we lost height to land at Matrah the reflected heat from a ground temperature of 132 degrees Fahrenheit could be felt at about two thousand feet, and at one thousand feet an unmistakable stench of fish caused our nostrils to dilate and twitch in disgust and disbelief. On looking down the source of this acrid ammonia smell could be plainly seen – row after row of dead fish, ripening in the sun.

Muscat had a small harbour, the architecture and layout of which reflected the early Portuguese influence in the area. And one old windowless stone building, standing high on a rocky promontory, was currently being used as a prison. The sight of the poor wretches incarcerated there, pleading and scratching through a three inch gap at the bottom of a heavy wooden door for some sort of attention, filled one with a feeling of helplessness, also a feeling of shame that such imposed degradation could exist.

We were accommodated for our stay at Muscat in the residence of the British Political Agent who gave us no hint at all that it was known that the whole area was virtually floating on a lake of oil. The town itself was encircled by a wall and a nightly curfew prevailed. It being only possible to make a night time sortie accompanied and led by an approved guide with an old flickering oil lamp. So we didn't bother. But a daytime wander amongst the primitive houses and shops, and along the narrow mutti streets of this ancient port, gave us a very good insight into life in this inhabited corner of Oman.

Once, when meandering through one of those narrow streets, I remember hearing a high pitched buzzing noise and immediately concluded that some sort of electrical apparatus had found its way to this unlikely spot. But it turned out to be just a happy half inch layer of flies swarming over some displayed dates, and each time a sale was made, the penetrating hand of the vendor caused an angry buzz from a million flies as they lifted off for a second or two before settling back onto what appeared to be their natural and undisputed home.

A really sad memory of the town was the extent to which the population appeared to suffer from various forms of eye disease. The total resignation of these sightless people to their misfortune and poverty was hard to believe, and caused one to wonder at their incredible forbearance. But no doubt the technical and medical advances of the sophisticated and rich Oman of the 1990's has surely solved this problem, together with the elimination of the small colony of unacceptables that lived, outside the walls of the town at that time.

I thought that finding Mackeson's milk stout at Bahrain was a nice coincidence but, when taking a bathe in the harbour on the morning of the second day here in Muscat, who should surface right next to me but one Ernie Linden. He was an old Harvey Grammar school pal and a towny, living virtually opposite number twenty eight Cobden Road at number one Theresa Road.

At the age of six or seven I used to nick his fairy cycle, almost treating it as my own, until collared by his Dad who happened to be a retired Regimental Sergeant Major. It was a sad day. Ernie was now a Corporal Wireless Operator and one of a two man team manning a radio out station from the Political Agent's house. I don't know what the odds are against popping up out of the sea in the Gulf of Oman to find oneself next to one's Blighty neighbour, but it must be a few million to one.

Later, relaxing in the comparative cool of the evening, we enjoyed a return to schoolboy days, a few beers and a few laughs before I went early to bed to be well rested for an early take off the next day. The aircraft were behaving well so far, giving no technical troubles whatsoever, which was very reassuring as the trip from here-on to Aden would be over land not overpopulated by units of the RAF. In fact there were none at all. The first

A SHILLINGSWORTH OF PROMISES

leg of this stage of the trip, over the eastern end of the Djebel Akhdar range, was uneventful. Flying high in clear skies, I tried to lessen the incipient boredom by singing to myself through my own speaking tube, trying to out-Bing the old groaner himself. A bathroom occupation, taken up at the time by millions of fans throughout the world. After less than a short while I gave up and reverted to staring at the dry, arid and empty groundscape passing endlessly rearwards beneath us. Just watching the world go by, feeling detached and uninvolved.

We were heading for Mazira island off the southern coast of Oman and, on reaching the coastal strip, all that one could see was the cotton wool top of uninterrupted cloud tucked into the mountains and stretching right to the horizon. And somewhere under there was Mazira.

Squadron Leader Howe disappeared down into the mass of cloud and the rest of us remained circling above. Fifteen minutes or so later he reappeared, wagging his wings; then we formed up line astern and descended through this all embracing blanket that, fortunately, bottomed out at about five hundred feet. And there we were, right over Mazira. Navigation had been pin point perfect but the look of the boulder strewn coastal landing strip seemed to be far from perfect but luckily it provided all that was necessary for the whole Squadron to make a successful landing.

After refuelling from the stock piled cans and carrying out routine inspections, a meal was enthusiastically prepared. This simply involved opening enough tins of McConachie's beef stew to fill a large cooking pot, to be heated up, served out and eaten with the appreciative relish of deprived but hungry gourmets.

This activity had been watched intensely by the only Arabs we saw on the island, just one man and his son peering over a ridge of sand. They eventually made tentative and shy contact, making signs that they wanted to take away the empty stew cans. A prize beyond measure it would seem, and an unbelievable starting point from just fifty four years ago to the air conditioned modern Mazira of today.

That night we slept under the wings within sight and sound of the sea, too tired to think of any unwanted sleeping partners, such as centipedes or scorpions. I slept soundly until being nudged awake by my immediate neighbour. "Can you hear anything?" he whispered.

I listened, but all I could hear was the gentle rustle in the distance of waves breaking on the shore. "No, nothing," I said, and dropped off again. But another nudge and a curt injunction to 'listen' woke me once more. This time I could hear the irregular scraping sounds that were disturbing him. We scrambled out of our bags and stood up. The scraping noises suddenly increased and as suddenly stopped. We had been surrounded by a small army of land crabs that had quickly disappeared down their individual holes on being disturbed. We disappeared back into our sacks and slept erratically, and somewhat warily, until dawn.

The following morning the low cloud was still with us and, after the sparsest of toilets and a quick breakfast, we took off to fly some three hundred and fifty miles along the coast to arrive at Merbat in time for another McConachie's lunch.

The aircraft were refuelled, again from stock piled supplies. But this time we were helped by some local Arabs. Or, more precisely, by a few large and heavily muscled black Africans who were, for the want of a better word, supervised by their much smaller but vociferous masters. I had the impression that we were watching the diminished and dying embers of the results of what was once a flourishing slave trade, carried on between the Horn of Africa and Arabia by those old and famous ocean going dhows of piratical repute.

It had been deemed, for some reason unknown to the majority of us, that it would be more circumspect to stay over night at Salala, which was only a short fifty miles farther along the coast. So a half hour of virtually sea level flying saw us all safely landed in a broad V-shaped coastal inlet with three or four thousand foot mountains, heavily shrouded in low cloud, hemming us in on three sides.

Whilst brewing up the evening meal some dozen or so Arabs appeared from virtually nowhere and squatted on their haunches to watch our every move. They were passive but curious, and I felt convinced that it was the first time any of them had actually seen aircraft on the ground. Their galabiehs were thick with some sort of black powder, and their eyes too were darkly rimmed with the same stuff. We presumed it was some sort of fly repellent. In any case the eye shadow made their gaze intimidatingly intense. And they all sported a repellent of a somewhat different nature in the form of either a dagger or a sword, the blades of which were a dull grey-black colour and coated with rancid mutton fat.

Later, when seeing one of our crew cleaning a sparking plug with a small wire brush and a piece of emery cloth, they were quick to make contact, making it known that they would like some of the same to clean and polish their weapons. Not wishing to appear uncooperative or antagonistic, and as screwdrivers versus daggers would appear to be something of a mismatch, we assumed an attitude of total non aggression and gave a couple of square

A SHILLINGSWORTH OF PROMISES

inches to each of them. They then happily resumed their squatting positions and polished away vigorously, stopping every now and then to admire their handiwork. Leaving us meanwhile to quietly finish off our meal with a mug of tea.

Not unnaturally, I suppose, they assumed our generosity and hospitality to be not unlike their own and, when we put down our emptied mugs, they stopped their dagger work and came over to accept or, looked at differently, purloin, a mug each, causing us neither anger nor amusement, just wonderment tinged with almost disbelief. Come nightfall our friends melted away, leaving us to enjoy a night out, sleeping peacefully under the guardian wings of our Vincents.

Dawn came and with it a load of problems and concerns, for the low cloud was still with us. This meant that take off had to be directly seawards to avoid any danger of flying into the mountains that lurked around us. After take off and some fifteen minutes of climbing through the cloud, I imagined that the aircraft suddenly hit an updraught, and glancing down I felt sure I saw a black mass glide past just feet below, and to this day I am convinced we missed hitting the top of those mountains by the merest fraction. But the pilot, Sergeant Richardson, would have none of it, denying any possibility of having been in any sort of danger. However, and whatever, the truth, within minutes we had broken cloud to turn right to fly in clear skies over a carpet of cotton wool, heading towards Mukalla.

In less than an hour the cloud cover thinned and eventually disappeared altogether, giving a clear view of the coast line to allow us a trouble free trip for the rest of the journey to Mukalla. On landing there the Squadron was hospitably welcomed by the son of the sheik of Mukalla who, having had a university education in England, spoke English with an impeccable accent. This was something we did not quite expect in such a remote and desolate part of the globe. Also unexpected was the gift of a mutton stew lunch for all to share. This was received thankfully but with varying degrees of appreciation, with some searching in vain for the sheep's eyes, which every schoolboy knows, or imagines, the Arabs love to eat.

We had been one aircraft short at Mukalla for Sergeant Day had had difficulty getting airborne at Salala. However, he had taken off early the next day to appear as a burgeoning dot along the coast, just in time to prevent a one crew search party taking off. I would have been part of this crew and I remember being irritated at having been selected; for uncharacteristically, my digestive system was beginning to give trouble and I had been keenly anticipating reaching the sanctuary and medical care that was available at the permanent RAF base at Aden. And this was now, thanks to Sergeant Day's arrival, only some three hours flying away.

When we arrived at number Eight Squadron's base at Khor Maksa near Aden, the marshalling, refuelling and servicing of the aircraft seemed to take an exceptional toll of my energies. And I shall never forget the oppressive and humid heat of that day and I drank glass after glass of ice cold fresh lime juice, which then came out of every pore of my body as fast as I drank it. It was a stupid thing to do for it was, albeit unknown to me at the time, the root cause of a subsequent long bout of digestive disorder.

However, it was near heaven to enjoy the luxuries of a permanent base again after the restrictions of the trip when, having only the use of water that we carried with us, we had drunk and washed sparingly. And then only the parts that showed, the remainder now virtually required decoking and disinfecting, as did our clothing. Ah the bliss of a freshly washed carcase, clothed in newly laundered clothes, sand free, oil free, sweat free and smelling beautifully of just nothing. However, my bliss was short lived for I enjoyed, or more correctly, took part in, the sampling of the fleshpots of Aden for one evening only. When the atmosphere and animation of the waterfront bars, enhanced by an uncounted and irresponsible intake of alcohol, made me light headed enough to imagine that this was life as it should be, to be enjoyed with absolute abandon. It was only when I found myself crowded into a taxi with four other randy and raunchy airmen *en route* for the red light district of Shaykh Uthman that I began to have my doubts.

Once there, and surrounded by a choice of near naked and enticing prostitutes, beautified by an alcoholic haze, my doubts began to disappear, and a rising anticipation became paramount. And visible! But then a tiny thought penetrated my befuddled mind, asking me,

"How many others had been there already today?" And my revulsion to batting on a sticky wicket saved me. My wick remained undipped. But alas, the more randy and uncontrolled still went in to bat, but none, I'm sure, reached double figures, brewer's droop probably limiting their ambitions.

The following morning I felt like hell on earth, with a throbbing head, stomach pains and diarrhoea. The medical officer ordered me to be detained in the sick bay, diagnosing gastro-enteritis, or worse. However, after sympathetic and careful nursing over three days I was feeling sufficiently recovered to assume that I would be able to carry on with the Squadron when it continued its journey the next morning. The M.O. agreed, but prescribed a heavy dose of bismuth and opium tablets to be taken just before take off to ensure a more comfortable flight.

A SHILLINGSWORTH OF PROMISES

I took the tablets and powder and, for a while, I felt comfortable enough. But then, on landing at Perim island to refuel, I had an urge and wandered away some fifty yards to drop my shorts and deposit a neat little heap of bismuth, followed by a diarrhoeal gush.

Feeling now a little less in control of things I clambered back into the cockpit to settle down as best I could for the coming four and a half hour flight to Port Sudan. Within half an hour my troubles started and, as the aircraft was equipped only with facilities for 'peeing' relief, I had to use my working topee for the rest. And this, despite the size of my head, would only cope with about three pints.

My condition progressively deteriorated and I was soon lying shortless on the cockpit floor with legs apart and topee at the ready, getting paler and weaker with each successive spasm. After some two hours flying I began to feel desperately ill but just had the strength to stand up to throw a well filled topee over the side. We were flying close in to the coast line of Eritrea, which was then under Italian occupation, and by coincidence we were just off Massawa, the Italian air base, and the wind was in a favourable direction, putting it in some sort of danger. But no international complications followed so one must assume that no direct hit was actually achieved.

For my part, our landing at Port Sudan could not come soon enough, and by now I really didn't care what happened and I just lay prostrate on the floor, except for the spasmodic and automatic muscular reactions trying to evacuate an already dehydrated and empty bowel. Eventually, on landing, I was stretchered off to a small hospital in the town and can only remember waking the next morning to the comfort of white sheets, no pain and the quietness of an empty ward, having been skilfully seen to by the doctor and a nun dressed as a nurse, or vice versa, or probably both. The Squadron had continued on its way, leaving me to mend in luxury.

This in fact did not take so long, due to the resilience of youth, good luck and good care. The rate and quality of my recovery was checked daily by analysing a specimen of faeces, and I was able on the third day to present two beautifully sculptured and embracing turds, 'Rodinesque' in their perfection and sufficiently germ free to allow the doctor to certify me fit and functional enough for onward transmission to Khartoum by rail.

This journey took some sixteen hours. I had no money, no knowledge of the language, and no luggage. Just me and a package lunch launched on their way, and strangely my only reaction was a feeling of isolated freedom. But not for long for soon after I had ensconced myself in a corner seat in an empty carriage a family group of Sudanese arrived and I was squeezed first right into the corner and then right out of it. This performance was repeated in several more carriages before the family size diminished enough to leave me sufficient space and breathing room.

Despite all the inconveniences my overall impression of the Sudanese was that they were a friendly and proud race. Unusually tall and muscular, with beautiful white teeth which they kept in perfect condition by continuous rubbing with a short fibrous stick some four or five inches long. And as I watched the crowded platform just prior to departure I noticed that it was the men who held hands as they walked, or waited for the train to start, with the women discreetly in the background. Absorbing and appreciating the customs of other lands can sometimes be intriguingly puzzling.

Extra activity and a few prolonged whistle blasts indicated that the journey was about to start, and those passengers not already on board leisurely and one footedly hopped along as they got on board, spreading their good-byes along the length of the platform as the train slowly got under way.

The most tedious part of this journey was the first hour or so that it took to climb the gradient out of Port Sudan, almost reaching speeds of ten miles an hour at times. But after that it was just a matter of dozing, looking and wishing the time away, slowly getting thirstier and hungrier. But this time I steadfastly refused any temptation to drink or eat until I arrived at the RAF base at Khartoum.

I had some eight days to wait at Khartoum before the squadron returned from Nairobi. The heat was intense but dry, therefore bearable, but the mosquitoes were anything but, being vampire trained and voracious in their appetite for blood and expert at finding it. As I found out to my cost and discomfort when failing to arrange my mosquito net after more than a few beers had caused instant collapse as my head hit the pillow, leaving my bare arse temptingly exposed and totally undefended. But luck was with me for, in spite of the mass attack, no bite proved to be malarial, and no long lasting damage was done.

The reason for this slight alcoholic orgy was a meeting up with another ex 26th entry Halton boy, Billy Bond by name and a 500cc Duggie 'Flat Twin' enthusiast. He and his bike had been the envy of the rest of us, who constantly dreamed of getting our hands on enough folding money to compete.

But here in Khartoum he was bikeless, none too happy and bored, with little to do and not much to talk about. So when a small plague of locusts turned a beautiful green football pitch to bare earth in less than an hour it became a welcome talking point for days.

A SHILLINGSWORTH OF PROMISES

Soon the squadron returned and I was more than pleased and relieved to rejoin them, taking off the next day to follow the river Nile as far as Atbara, there to refuel and take off again, staying with the river for a further 150 miles or so before heading across the Nubian desert to land at Wadi Halfa. Thereby getting a ground level view of the river that we had been so faithfully following for most of the day.

Wadi Halfa was a very welcome and pleasant stopping place, it being close to the river Nile, on land made green and fertile by the annual flooding of this great river. Here we enjoyed excellent food and were remarkably well accommodated in a few railway coaches of the Egyptian State railways.

Continuing the flight the next day we again followed the river and were very soon flying over the great temple of Abou Simbel which, due to the advent years later of Abdul Nasser's great folly, the Aswan high dam, had to suffer the indignity of being removed to another site so as not to be lost forever in the waters of the newly formed and newly named Lake Nasser. Another hour's flying and some 110 miles further along the Nile saw us flying over Luxor with the ruined temples of Karnak looming into view soon after. The heartlands of ancient Egyptian civilisations were beneath us, but from the air I felt no emotion, just a lofty and very transient connection with those glorious and ancient cities of three thousand or more years ago.

As the sites of ancient history and the Valley of the Kings slowly drifted behind us, the green strip of the Nile valley became even more clearly defined, with eventually the sprawl of Cairo seeming to link river with desert, with the barren Moccatam hills forming a distant backdrop. Our approach to Cairo itself increased everyone's interest, as the symmetric perfection of the three pyramids of Giza appeared on the horizon and held our attention until we flew over the city itself, bringing our minds back to more recent times and reality. Very soon after, we landed at Heliopolis, a permanent RAF base, providing cool-ish beer, a soft-ish bed and up to date news of developing troubles in Europe. But after nearly two years of frustration in Iraq, more immediate troubles of our own took precedence in our minds. So the fleshpots of Cairo beckoned and, with our pay packets inflated with back pay, we went.

Pre-war Cairo, even on the brief visit that we were able to make, was impressionable. Looking both chaotic and purposeful at the same time, with seemingly no obvious rule of the road for hundreds of aggressive, independent and horn happy drivers. The heat, the hustle, the dust, the noise and the diverse smells of cooking and God knows what else, all being enjoyed, suffered and shared by the milling masses, and us. The galabiehed Cairean naturally predominated, but many were dressed European style, with a thousand red fezes giving a colourful topping to the whole scene. Pashas, Beys, City Arabs and Fellahin, with their cars, taxis, carts and donkeys, intermingling with porters carrying impossibly large loads, beggars, sightseers, all added to the seductive attraction of this large city.

Egyptians, it appeared, were either very rich or very poor and the city itself was likewise divided. With the modernity of the shops, offices and hotels of Sharia Soliman Pasha and Sharia Kasr-el-Nil and the surrounding streets contrasting vividly with the warren of dusty alleys that comprised outer Cairo.

The police at this time exercised control somewhat after the style of the British Bobby and this was not surprising for most of the main services, such as the police, railways, water and sewage, were operating under European influence. A state of affairs that was eventually resented and, among other things, triggered the troubles of 1952.

But at the moment we were seeking enjoyment and found it in absorbing the atmosphere of all that was going on around us. One source of amazement being the trams, draped as they were with a mass of white clothed Arabs, giving the impression that they had simply been scooped up from a large crowd, to be dumped elsewhere, clinging to each other, and it, in a hopeful attempt to arrive safely.

Late in the afternoon, tired and hungry, we found the American Long Bar, where cool beer, food and relaxation could be had. The 'mezee' served with the drinks was luscious. Great succulent prawns, the like of which I have seldom been able to find since. We also had a plate of spaghetti and salad. The salad was no problem but trying for the first time to stuff yards of slippery sauce-soaked spaghetti into one's mouth proved to be a messy failure, and a source of amusement to some big-gobbed local experts casually enjoying our embarrassment.

Now messily refreshed we wandered out into the cool of the evening to search out and find a bar particularly recommended by the old sweats of Heliopolis.

Then, after an hour or so of steady imbibing we left to explore the delights of Rue Ezbekieh, the focal point of the red light district. An area which proved to be somewhat less off-putting than that of Aden. The brothels were apparently controlled, and the 'Services', in their wisdom, had installed a medical treatment centre, where those who had succumbed to their urges and the attractions of the prostitutes, could obtain safety after treatment. And by all accounts this involved clearing one's willy with an internal scrape, accomplished by the insertion of a small umbrella-like instrument which

A SHILLINGSWORTH OF PROMISES

opened and cleaned on withdrawal. Fact or fiction, the mere idea brought tears to my eyes.

However, our tour of the district introduced us to the very basics of sex for sale. Apart from the controlled houses there was private enterprise in the form of little boys pimping freelance, with a very limited but precise vocabulary. "You wanna fuck my sister?"

A nil or negative reaction to this repetitive invitation would be followed by an insistent tugging of one's sleeve and a whispered enquiry. "You wanna buy feelthy pictures?"

These pictures proved that the only difference between ancient and modern pornography is that now it's done with better equipment. The subject matter is as old as history itself, and the variations on this single theme have certainly all been thought of and performed long ago, way back in history. Making the idea assumed by each successive generation that it alone has discovered sex, seem a little presumptuous to say the least.

Now, although sorely tempted, I had the same inhibitions that I had experienced at Aden. But one lad in particular insisted on having his oats so we all went in with him, some out of curiosity and some to test their resistance. The inside of this temple of lust was somewhat prosaic, looking almost like a doctor's waiting room. A longish room with half a dozen doors giving direct access to each individual 'bonkery'. There were also three open fronted, two footed Turkish toilets, strategically placed, where the girls, after each performance, would unconcernedly squat to wash and disinfect themselves with what looked like a solution of potassium permanganate. These girls were a surprisingly international bunch, coming mainly from Greece, France or Italy, but it was not unknown for a Blighty accent to be heard giving a giggling welcome.

Our uncontrolled and randy companion had already made his choice and we all sat bemused and intrigued on the bench, watching the comings and goings, waiting for the right door to open, when the girl would simply look out, smile and crook a finger for the next client.

Soon the door of the 'chosen one' opened and out marched not one, not two but three army privates, fully booted and spurred, with collars firmly done up and fit for any Regimental Sergeant Major's inspection. Then the girl came out, wearing nothing but a smile and a wedge of cotton wool firmly implanted in the target area as she walked over to the open toilet to prepare herself for our still randy mate.

She went back to her room, to reappear almost immediately to crook her finger in our direction. And in went our pal, to bat on the stickiest of wickets.

The thought of which again reinforced my safeguarding inhibitions. Our now satiated friend came out with a blissful smile on his face, which turned to a look of 'was it all worth while?' when he came out of the medical control room a little later, having received the full treatment.

A few days later, towards the end of September, rumour had it that the shadows of war were spreading over Europe. Caused by the aggressive activities of Germany in having already annexed Austria in March, and was now threatening to take possession of the Sudetenland of Czechoslovakia.

However, our Prime Minister, Neville Chamberlain, flew to Germany and had a chat with Hitler at Godesberg and then, together with Daladier of France and Mussolini of Italy, approved the ignoble Treaty of Munich on the 29th of September. He then flew back to London to wave the famous piece of paper signed by both himself and Hitler certifying the desire of our two countries never to go to war again, and at the same time recognising Germany's right to occupy the coveted Sudetenland.

It was anticipated that we would have 'peace in our time', with appeasement being the price. An expectation that very soon proved to be wrong, for Hitler's ambitions were insatiable and he interpreted appeasement as weakness.

But for the moment, with the threat of war seemingly put to rest forever, we lightheartedly completed our delayed flight. Flying over Israel to land at Amman in Jordan to refuel before flying on to our starting point at Habbaniyah. All aircraft and all crews landing safely to complete a really trouble free round trip, except for the slight hiccup of the diarrhoeal delay at Port Sudan. *En route* we had flown over two of the seven wonders of the world, one mystically invisible, the other just as mystically visible.

By November 1938 my two years in Iraq had been completed and now three years in India stretched before me. And so on the allotted day, with many of my troopship pals of two years ago, including Lofty Mee and, with oversized and made-to measure deep sea kit bags, the India bound draft assembled to make the return journey to Basra in those infamous and disgusting four horse or eight man trucks. The grandmother of all troopships, the Nevassa, was waiting at Basra to take us safely on the short journey to Karachi.

Once there and disembarked on to the quay, we each had to recognise and claim our own kit bag. So as the coolies started to unload we watched intently in order to make a quick getaway. The gang plank they were using was just that, a foot wide plank set at an angle of some thirty degrees, which bounced in contra rhythm as each heavily laden coolie sure-footedly made the trip from boat to quay.

Before leaving Habbaniyah I had tried to lift my own well stuffed kit bag, which was about three feet high and two feet in diameter, and with both arms linked around it and with an out-thrust stomach I couldn't even begin to lift it. So I looked with utter disbelief and amazement as I recognised my bag being speedily carried down that bouncing plank on the bent back of a tiny little Indian with legs going like clockwork matchsticks. It was a scene to be repeated many times later for these wiry little fellows could carry the most impossible loads without a stagger or any sign of distress whatever.

The Indian State railways were certainly an improvement on those of Iraq, imitative of the British system, but with all operatives noisily and argumentatively striving to carry out the bureaucratic and mechanical requirements of making the system work. Sometimes it did and sometimes it didn't.

Our destination in India (now Pakistan) was the North West Frontier, to the RAF station at Risalpur, near Peshawar, so a journey of about 650 miles confronted us. Eight to a compartment which consisted of bare slatted wooden seats plus two rope netted luggage racks. The latter proving to be vastly more comfortable than the seats. So as the journey was to take some twenty four hours or so, we took it in turns to enjoy this fortuitous luxury.

There was a kitchen attached to the train and the first meal it provided was surprisingly good, a sort of meat and vegetable stew. Then the evening meal arrived, it was meat and vegetable stew. Likewise breakfast and lunch the next day, with the ratio of meat and vegetables to liquid rapidly diminishing. Another hundred miles would have caused problems, both gastronomic and probably revolutionary.

For virtually the whole of our journey we would be tracking the river Indus, and I suddenly remembered sitting in the little upstairs bedroom of 28 Cobden Road swotting for a geography exam and memorising all the tributaries of the Indus; The Ravi, Jhelam, Chenab, and Sutlej, not realising that I would one day be so close to them.

As we trundled and rattled northwards we passed through and by many piteous and impoverished villages where it seemed that the people and the animals were as one, living together and virtually with each other. But the women in their colourful saris, carrying heavy pitchers of water perfectly balanced on their heads as they glided gracefully about their business, did seem to add a sort of mysterious dignity to the scene. But there was nothing mystic about their poverty, it was abject and absolute.

After some twenty four hours of clattering travel, starting, stopping and trying to enjoy the comfort of either seat or luggage rack, we arrived at the

RAF station of Risalpur, home to Number 2 India Wing and Number 39 Squadron, to which I was duly posted. The station itself was within sight of the foothills of the western Himalayas, a snow-capped and imposing horizon which never seemed to get nearer, even after half an hour's flying in their direction.

The North West Frontier of India enjoyed a particular reputation within the RAF and the army, being the locality in which the Fakir of Ipi and his followers, when not concerned with the planting and harvesting of staple foods, would insurrect and fight, causing service in that part of the world to be designated 'active'. Hence an award of the North West Frontier medal would confirm that the wearer had indeed seen some sort of military action, fighting the Fakir. A name that could be, and was, often mispronounced.

However, when I got there the Fakir had ceased to cause trouble, and the big fear at that time was a possible replay of the Quetta earthquake disaster of some three years earlier which had caused some twenty five thousand casualties. This explained why our bungalow windows had no glass, it was to allow a quick exit in case of a major tremor, which fortunately did not occur during my short stay at Risalpur.

Number 39 Squadron was equipped with single engined Hawker Hart light bombers powered by Rolls Royce Kestrel motors and they were a delight to work on. The Hart was a neat, compact and beautifully streamlined aeroplane and much faster than most aircraft in service at the time. Flying in them was exhilarating and enjoyable, notwithstanding the terrain to be flown over when visiting Fort Sandeman or Miramshah, when an engine failure would have caused more than a few worries to the crew, the aircraft and probably the Padre.

It was at Risalpur that I, in partnership with a wireless operator named Jones, bought for the equivalent of fifty shillings each, his and my first car, an old Model T Ford. It had been converted years before from an old 'Huck's' starter, the upper structure of which had been removed and replaced by some light alloy body work, making a reasonable looking open two seater. But proud ownership lasted but a few weeks for my co-owner, being a wireless operator, paid scant attention to topping up with oil. He went on a long trip, burnt out the white metal bearings, clanked back into camp and came to a smoking and permanent halt. I taught him a few new swear words, with which he quickly retaliated, telling me that I could just as easily have checked the oil. All very true – we got rid of our wreck and kept our friendship.

The particular aircraft that I had been assigned to, had prior to my arrival acquired a reputation for being awkward to start. So I systematically

A SHILLINGSWORTH OF PROMISES

ran through and checked all the known causes for such awkwardness and V for Victor responded splendidly, starting each time without hesitation.

But then a fly-past for some visiting dignitaries was scheduled, and the squadron was due to take off in formation, and of course V for Victor picked this particular moment to revert to its former antics. And as I wound my heart out on the starting handle and not realising I was within earshot of anybody I exploded, using all swearwords known to man plus a few manufactured on the spot. When it was all over I was more than puzzled to receive via our Chiefy a word of congratulation from the C.O. not only for the manful struggle but also for the innovative and interesting additions to his vocabulary.

1939 was now well on its way, with the expansion of the RAF at home beginning to accelerate. However, some investigative commission had decided that the forces in India should be reduced, meaning that some lucky lads would soon be on their way back to UK.

It was about this time that Portsmouth and Wolverhampton had reached the final of the F.A. cup, with Wolves very much the favourites and Pompey given no chance. I linked this with the possibility of being drafted back to the UK by making a bet with Jonesy that if Pompey won we would soon be on our way. Against the odds they did, and then within weeks we received the good news, it was to be via Bombay on the 25th May on the troopship Somersetshire.

The inconveniences and hardships of the return train and sea journey were more than compensated for by the general feeling of relief at not having to do a full five years abroad. And I was more than content to leave the so-called 'mystic East', with its many religions, involved caste system, overpopulation and its millions of flies. I certainly never came into contact with the sweet life so much enjoyed and written about by the favoured few of the British Raj. Passing through and by the not so unfamiliar landmarks of Aden, Suez, Malta and Gibraltar, we eventually arrived in Southampton on the 18th June. And there, as we lined up on the quayside, the Customs officers did a percentage check of our baggage. I must have been looking happily guilty for they checked my two and a half years of accumulated junk plus a few silk shirts and pyjamas, not once but twice. The happy look was because I had just received my travel warrant for the journey to RAF Hawkinge, near Folkestone, and I was feeling that at last there was some justice in the world.

On the journey to London and soon after leaving the outskirts of Southampton, one lad started to shout 'Look! Look!'. We all did and saw nothing and said so. Again he shouted 'Look, look, you moronic twits!' Politely curious, and curiously polite we asked 'What the bloody hell do you want us to look at?' All he answered was 'It's green, it's green, everything's green.' He was enraptured and then, as the miles of green English countryside flashed by, I too began to feel what he no doubt had felt earlier and stronger, – 'Home at last' – leaving far behind the heat, dust and arid harshness of those parts of the Middle East so favoured by the RAF

The journey home continued and, with a wallet bursting with six weeks' leave pay, I took a taxi from Waterloo to Charing Cross, and then tipped the driver a tanner for hoiking my heavy kit bag and cases on and off. I liked the feeling this gave and I dreamed 'I'm going to be rich one day'. Then modified it to 'might be' assuaged a few doubts by a 'why not?', finishing with a more realistic 'you'll be bloody lucky'.

As I re-travelled the familiar journey from Charing Cross to Folkestone Central I felt as if I'd never been away, all the well known landmarks came and went, until the Grammar School and then Cheriton Road Cemetery told me I was almost home. From the station I took a bus to Sandgate Road to await the next 'East Kent' to Hythe.

I had some forty minutes to wait so I lugged myself and my baggage the short distance to the Leas, there to sit and watch the sea and the passers by, while at the same time soaking up the fresh air, sunshine and beauty of what was then one of the most attractive spots on the whole south east coast. Then I started to feel sorry for myself, regretting my decision to join up. But I quickly blanked my mind and enjoyed the relaxation for a few more moments before staggering off to catch the bus to Hythe.

My bus stop in Hythe was opposite the Grove cinema which is now the site of a supermarket car park and I had slowly made my way to Stade Street when a husky voice from behind called out "Fred". So I looked back and there was Father, splay footed as ever, but smiling the happiest of welcoming smiles. And then, for the first time since I was a little lad he put his arms around me and almost kissed me, compromising in the end with a bewhiskered cheek to cheek nudge. Mother of course was at the front room window, watching and waiting, but allowed us to actually get into the house before giving me a mother's welcoming and tearful embrace. She was too shy to show her emotions in public, she said, but Dad didn't agree, saying something about courtship days, and the canal bank benches. Mother just gave him a glance and said "Don't be dirty."

Brother Bert, as usual, was away with the Navy and younger brother Tom was also away at sea, having joined the Merchant Navy as a kitchen

A SHILLINGSWORTH OF PROMISES

boy. That left just three of us to celebrate the homecoming, which we did in the pleasant surroundings of the garden at the Hope inn, which was only five minutes away and well within safe staggering distance of home.

The following day we had kippers for breakfast and a shoulder of lamb for lunch so things at number 28 were looking up. But Dad still had his allotment and Mum still from time to time let off the two front rooms to holiday makers. More now for the company than the money, she said.

July 1939 came and with it increased fears of what was happening in Europe, but my only fear was that I might run out of money before my leave was up. Meanwhile I was making the most of what Hythe and Folkestone had to offer. All the old pleasures of earlier days, the Central and Playhouse cinemas in Folkestone and naturally hours and hours on the beach close to home, sun-bathing, swimming and watching the talent.

Strangely the latter occupation made me realise that, after nearly three years of frustration I had become somewhat reticent and shy at making or receiving a pass. I surely recognised it when I got it, but I wouldn't or couldn't follow up with any chat, as I previously would have done. I was a worried man, but I still had the attractions of the town itself to sustain me.

Alone and in a mood of sad reflection I retraced a lot of my old favourite walks. Including the relaxing water's edge stroll along the beach between Hythe and the Grand Redoubt, my mind going back eight years to the happy abandonment of arrogant youth and I wondered what she was doing now. Most probably married, I thought, with no doubt a couple of demanding bread snatchers to love and look after.

But my leave duly came to an end and in late July I reported to the RAF station at Hawkinge, or more specifically to Number 25 Squadron, which was a night fighter unit equipped with Bristol Blenheims. I had seen a Blenheim some eighteen months earlier, it was the first one of its type to fly out to Habbaniyah but it had made a somewhat ignominious arrival by landing on its belly. I assisted in its recovery, but this was hardly enough to claim 'previous type' experience.

So it was a whole new concept for me, this all metal, twin engined monoplane looking at first sight a little cumbersome and tinny. But time proved that first impressions can be wrong, for the new configuration as presented by the Hawker Hurricane really convinced me that the progression from bi-planes to monoplanes was only natural. For the Hawker Hurricane looked remarkably like a Hawker Hart, only minus its top wing.

4 ■ The War (some lighter moments)

Being now so close to home, I applied for and was granted permission to 'live out'. This meant that after seven years of nothing but service life I was now able to enjoy at regular intervals a part time life in Civvy Street, where the current dominant worry was 'would there be another war or not?'

As I was already in the RAF I had little choice as to what I would do if war did come. I had by now a feeling of its inevitability but with absolutely no idea or foreboding of the evils it would bring. So what more could I and thousands of others do, except drift into whatever was coming and react according to conscience.

On buses, in shops and on the streets one could hear snatches of conversation giving voice to the anxieties and fears of the moment. Some, having read about the impossibility of breaching the Maginot Line a point of view widely propagated by the French – accepted the claim and were reassured. Others seemed resigned to whatever might come, with many assuming that it would be over by Christmas anyway, for Germany so far had only confronted minor nations. A few asserted or bragged that they would exercise their rights of conscientious objection, but the true British reaction was well voiced in a snippet of conversation from two muscular road workers to the effect that 'if the bugger did try anything he would get an effing good hiding'.

But the atmosphere of unreality and uncertainty quickly came to an end, and so did my short period of 'living out'. For on September 1st Hitler invaded Poland and a second world war became inevitable.

Number 25 Squadron and newly promoted corporal Hitchcock moved to their allotted battle stations at North Holt. The night defence of London being a main objective. But the sense of unreality still prevailed and even when at eleven o'clock on September 3rd Neville Chamberlain sombrely declared that we were at war with Germany it was still hard to believe, and everyone in the country, civilian and serviceman alike, wondered what the hell was going to happen next. Apart from a false alarm virtually within an hour of the declaration, nothing did. My promotion to the rank of corporal a few days earlier had meant that I had lost my mustering as a part time air gunner. I felt disappointed at the time, but in retrospect I suppose it was a case of the devil looking after his own. And as the war wore on, my respect for all air crew was that much greater for I was better able to appreciate the

A SHILLINGSWORTH OF PROMISES

high sense of duty that carried them through all the dangers and uncertainties of each and every operational sortie.

Night fighting in the early days of the war was a little like looking for a chimney sweep in an unlit coal hole. A matter of search, identify and destroy, and as the pilots only had radio ground control to assist them, it was a difficult if not impossible task.

So within weeks of the war starting the 'Boffins' came to the rescue together with several long-nosed Blenheim Mark IV's fitted with experimental radar, or A.I. (air interception) equipment. I had the good luck to be assigned to these aircraft, which were protectively kept in an out-of-bounds hangar. The A.I. gear accommodated in the nose of these planes looked very fragile. A mass or mess of plasticised cardboard, wires and little green screens, all very much 'out of this world' and strange.

These aircraft would take off in pairs, disappear over the North Sea and come back with the boffins and A.I. operators nattering about 'blips' or the lack of them. This special section of the squadron was eventually detached to Martlesham Heath in order to attempt actual night intercepting of enemy raiders coming in over the North Sea. A positive outcome to this venture was denied, not by any fault or shortcoming in the equipment, but by a dearth of enemy raiders at the time.

The phoney war continued but in November six aircraft from 25 Squadron together with 601 Squadron, took part in one of the earliest raids of the war, a strafing attack on the sea-plane base at Borkum. After that the Squadron relapsed into its more normal function of standing by as a night interceptor unit, with all its serviceable planes and crews at a state of instant readiness.

In January 1940 the Squadron was moved to North Weald and in the early months of the year, as well as being involved in protecting the North Sea convoys, trials continued with the airborne radar in the Blenheim IV's. A new aircraft, the Bristol Beaufighter, which was the first purpose built night fighter to be brought into service, no doubt reaped the benefit of these trials by having the most advanced form of air to air radar installed at birth, at last giving the crews a fair chance to make successful night interceptions. But the re-equipment of the Squadron with these up-to-date aircraft unfortunately did not take place until September.

Some months earlier than that, in May, the German forces had bombed and blitzed their way around the impregnable Maginot defences, via Holland and Belgium, meeting diminishing resistance as the British and French forces were forced to retreat. A quickly planned operation to evacuate as many troops as possible from France was organised as the retreating forces funnelled into Dunkirk.

Some of the squadron's ground staff were immediately detached to Hawkinge to be better able, with others, to service an aerial escort for the hundreds of little ships in their heroic attempt to extricate the beleaguered forces from the beaches of Dunkirk, and records show that from May 21st to June 4th this mixed flotilla of little and large ships was miraculously able to rescue some 340,000 troops. But amongst the many losses of men, ships and planes in this great operation were, sadly, one of my old pals from my days in Iraq, and the Hythe lifeboat, which to this day has never been replaced. All the heart-rending Pathe news film of the returning soldiers, together with my own slight involvement, brought the realisation that, in spite of the relative calm of the previous months, the horrors of a real war were now with us.

Shortly after, on June 19th, the Squadron moved northwards to Martlesham Heath, where the airfield bordered on to the A12, just north of Ipswich. As our flight dispersal point was sited close to the road some of us grabbed the opportunity each midday to nip up the road to enjoy the gastronomic delights of a roadside cafe, in the form of a man's size portion of eggs, bacon and baked beans. A contravention of standing orders but a welcome civilian interlude to an otherwise ordinary working day.

Further down the A12 towards Ipswich was the Deben club social centre where, from time to time, a dance would be organised, with always a good attendance from the local girls, all very much put 'in the mood' by Glen Miller and others. It was at one of these do's in the open air and in the blackout that one lively, tempting and co-operative partner sat on my lap and then wriggled delightfully to the rhythm of the music, setting my blood and thoughts racing. We immediately and inevitably fell in love. But it was a short affair, the total commitment lasting only long enough for each to savour what the other had to offer. The engagement was broken off and we finished the evening as just good friends or more accurately, just good intimate friends. Sex and love in these strange times had become something you did and not just something you talked about. I now also felt less worried, the arrogance of youth having temporarily returned, and after all I was still only twenty four.

Although the hazards of war-time life undergone by the RAF ground crews were minimal when compared with those of the air crews, living and working in locations which were the prime targets of the Luftwaffe at this time could set one's nerves tingling in moments of potential or incidental danger.

It was at Martlesham that, with the Blenheims parked out in the open at their dispersal points, that I, with another lad, was busily working on a stern frame change, with me on the inside putting nuts on the mushroom headed bolts as my pal systematically fed them in from the outside. The stern frame being the rear end of the fuselage meant that I was lying comfortably horizontal, so when the bolts stopped coming through the holes I imagined my mate had nipped off for a quick widdle, and I took the opportunity to dream a little.

After some fifteen minutes of fruitless fantasy I crawled out of the fuselage to find not a soul in sight. And hearing the distant pulsating throb of aircraft engines, I assumed that the Luftwaffe was busy paying an ill-intentioned visit to Felixstowe or Harwich. I had not heard any warning from the sirens or from my mate, who had no doubt scarpered off at high speed. Had the raiders switched their attention to Martlesham Heath, I would certainly have been very closely associated with some German pilot's claim to have destroyed one on the ground. And this would have certainly given me an unexpected opportunity to have an early, unwanted and difficult chat with Saint Peter.

I found my self-preserving mate sitting in the air raid shelter with his tin hat strategically placed over his wedding tackle. And as I wasn't feeling very charitable towards him at that moment I suggested that if his cock was in the same working order as his brain, he needn't bother.

The Squadron returned to North Weald at the beginning of September and resumed its night activities and whenever the German bombers mounted an attack we became busy. Likewise all the ack-ack batteries in and around London, and it was quite a while before we realised that the intermittent whistling sound one could hear when having a night time piddle in the open was the shrapnel fall-out dropping too close to be comfortable.

But no casualties were recorded, the only near thing was when one off-duty airman returning to his bed, cut his ear on a walnut sized piece of shrapnel which had penetrated the hut roof to make a mess of his pillow, just where his head would have been had a call of nature not deemed it to be otherwise.

A few days later we were the off-duty flight and as usual some lads kipped down early and others, including myself, were whiling away the late evening with a game of solo whist. Suddenly the hut door flew open and the duty sergeant, a Sergeant Milliner, who was a bit of a joker, screamed at us to get out of the hut and to run as fast and as far as we could over the camp boundary and away. Then adding as an after thought, "There's a bloody great unexploded parachute mine outside the door!"

We had heard nothing untoward so we knowingly grinned at each other and carried on playing. Some short while later one of the foursome, an LAC Knox, nicknamed Nervo of course, casually got up to wander out for a pee. In five seconds flat he came flying back yelling, "There IS a bloody mine out there!" as he disappeared out of the opposite door, having grabbed his tin hat *en route*.

To be convinced we all trooped out and there it was, no more than ten feet away, the parachute gracefully draped over it, and the pot-shaped detonator firmly rammed home.

Pandemonium followed for several minutes as the disbelievers and the bedridden hurriedly tried at one go, to dress, run, and grab their essentials before streaming out of the hut, over the boundary fence and away.

An inefficient German assembly worker or a friendly factory saboteur had undoubtedly saved us a lot of bother and a lot of lives. And never again did we take anything that Sergeant Milliner said other than very seriously. The following day a bomb disposal unit from the Royal Navy turned up to casually but efficiently, defuse the thing and take it away.

In mid June the Germans had overcome all French resistance and an armistice had been signed, allowing Hitler to concentrate and increase his activities against the UK. A main objective of which was the destruction of all RAF Fighter Command airfields, and North Weald was one of them. Although a lot of extensive but repairable damage was done to bases at Biggin Hill, Kenley and others, most enemy bombs aimed at North Weald seem to have landed on the other side of the fence.

It was about the middle of August that the Luftwaffe made the very wrong assumption that it had weakened the RAF to such an extent that it could now launch an all out attack. This resulted in the now well chronicled Battle of Britain, and all I can say about my part in it is that I was in the RAF at the time.

This great and prolonged air battle was a day time affair, and as I was in a night fighter Squadron, my feelings of pride, satisfaction and exaltation came the same way as for most others, that is when reading the score line in the morning papers. However, the tensions and excitement of the day-time scrambles from North Weald, with their resulting successes, certainly boosted our morale and our appreciation of the courage of those involved. And I would say that even Churchill's great summing up at the end of the country's 'finest hour', although clear and succinct, was still an understatement.

The Luftwaffe having failed to put out the RAF, switched tactics and concentrated on a vicious day time attack on London, but again lost so many aircraft that it then confined itself to high level night bombing of the capital. And that's where we came in.

But as yet our purpose-built Beaufighters were not one hundred per cent effective, for having come practically from the drawing board to immediate operational service, their teething troubles were somewhat of a handicap. But these were progressively overcome and the Squadron began to have its first successes by virtue of the new air interception radar fitted into these much faster and better armed aircraft. In an attempt to fool the Germans, this sudden improvement was attributed to the fact that our pilots' excellent night vision was due to a special diet, consisting mainly of large helpings of carrots. A belief that still gains some credence.

In spite of, or more likely because of, the demanding nature of war-time service, leave was still granted and thankfully received. And on one of these short breaks in October, my young brother Tom was at home, relaxing after having survived the sinking of his ship, the Auckland Star off the Irish coast of Connemara.

The U-boat had made a direct hit with its first torpedo and then the commander, suffering a slight attack of human decency, had given the crew a short time to abandon ship before finally sinking the vessel with two more torpedoes. The loaded lifeboats, spotting the beam of Borne point lighthouse, rowed for the shore and the crew eventually arrived knackered and hungry at Clifden. Tom continued with his career in the Merchant Navy incidentally, taking part in the evacuation of Singapore in the Orcades, and finally finishing up on the Queen Elizabeth, ferrying thousands of American troops across the Atlantic.

Hythe, like most coastal towns along the south coast, began to suffer the defacement of necessary and vital military installations and defences. It had also, in early October, received the attention of a returning German bomber, which emptied its racks before flying back across the Channel, disturbing the dead near St. Leonard's church and demolishing the Arcade in the High Street, where the old Picture Palace used to be.

The town also began to be deserted, large numbers of families evacuating to safer localities inland. Including old man Hilton. Apparently he had been standing outside his little cottage by the school chatting to my father, when a Hurricane came screaming in from the sea being chased by a German fighter. Old Hilton said "Bleeding hell, that thing had a bloody swastika on it." This was a bit too close to home for the old lad. The chat suddenly ended as he disappeared up the alley to his back door. And the next day Newman's removal van took him, his wife and his belongings to a 'safer haven'! near London, and I've never heard of him since.

The sea front and promenade of my childhood sadly began to change. The railings and seats disappeared, gun emplacements were built and mile after mile of steel pipe defences were erected on the beach itself.

It suddenly made me realise that 28 Cobden Road would really be in the front line if an invasion did come. I felt for the first time some foreboding and a lot of bitterness. But father said he would never move, and anyway Hitler would never attempt the crossing. Napoleon had baulked at it and so would Adolph. "Remember", he said, "that Channel's worth a guinea a drop."

This was a surprisingly accurate forecast, for the German bombing onslaughts on London and other cities, although doing immense damage, were ineffective, and they were losing so many aircraft and crews that their overall strategy was changed. And Hitler changed direction, launching an all-out attack on Russia in June 1941. Thereby lifting the threat of invasion and giving the British public and fighting services time to recover and rethink their own future strategy.

Also later in the year, when Japan attacked Pearl Harbour, bringing the USA into the war, the strain on the UK was eased somewhat and the future began to look relatively less threatening. In November 1940, 25 Squadron had moved again, this time to Wittering, near Peterborough, and returning there from a short leave early in 1941 I saw for the first time the extent of the damage in London, and wondered how Londoners still seemed to go about their business as usual. Especially as a vast number of them had probably spent the night sleeping on the platforms of the Underground.

I remember having to tread very carefully when taking the tube to Charing Cross, filtering my way through a mass of people sleeping in positions of unbelievable togetherness, with the atmosphere thick enough to chew. But there was no smell of fear. Just feet etc. All reminiscent of a troopship deck at midnight in the tropics.

At Wittering, the Squadron having now overcome the worst of the Beaufighter's teething troubles, started to have real successes, destroying thirteen aircraft in May and June, together with claims for some probably destroyed and others certainly damaged. Not in the glamour bracket of the day fighter squadrons, but a major success just the same.

I also had a first whilst at Wittering, in the form of my initial driving licence, issued by the 'Soke of Peterborough'. A learner's licence of course which allowed me to improve my skills and my confidence in a borrowed Ford 8. A bit of a rackety affair, but road worthy enough for war time operational binges in Stamford or Peterborough. A nostalgic highlight of one of these alcoholic sorties being when a well filled and happy companion stood on the parapet of the bridge in Stamford to have a fountainous widdle in the Welland, receiving looks of either disgust or admiration from the people passing by in the moonlit blackout.

The river Nene in Peterborough gave me a welcome surprise, for I found there a straight stretch of water with boating facilities providing exactly the type of sliding seat boat that was my big joy on the Hythe canal. So many of my days off in the summer months were spent feathering along a mile or so of the river, enjoying the relaxed exercising of every muscle in my body, except one maybe. But help was at hand for one morning a while later, whilst working in the hangar on a wing' change, the post arrived and an unexpected letter was flicked up to me. I thumbed it open and drew out a studio portrait of a girl's face, a face that I certainly could not recognise. It was perfect. Faultless in every feature and with every feature merging to form the prettiest of faces, made all the more attractive by a provocative and inviting half smile.

All this I appreciated in a matter of seconds, as I pulled out the accompanying letter. It was Kirsty's young sister Babs, and lightening mental arithmetic told me she was now sixteen. I was twenty five and the nine year difference blunted my instant enthusiasm. But curiosity and an inability to resist a beautiful smile, meant that I would inevitably and immediately accept the invitation to visit her in the family's new home at Stanmore, just up the hill on the western outskirts of Winchester.

This I did the following weekend, being received by Ma Price, as if 1936 was but yesterday. And by Babs as if tomorrow couldn't come quick enough. She was even more beautiful than the picture. How is it that boys just grow up, but girls progressively explode into gorgeous womanhood?

As we walked down to Winchester on our first evening out, we stopped under the railway bridge for a first consuming kiss. Not the most romantic of spots but it was unforgettable, for this gorgeous girl gave me the kiss of my life. It was the wantonness of inexperience and I was the willing and happy recipient.

The rest of the evening passed in a haze, and not being willing to trust myself, we caught an early bus home. Then, after a long natter with Ma over several cups of tea, my mind returned to normality and Babs and I went to bed, in different rooms. Ma was a bad sleeper and came up later. I was still awake when she popped into my room to whisper,

"Come, come and have a look."

We tiptoed to the open door of the other room and Ma pointed towards the window. It was a bright moonlit night and the diffused rays angling through the window, revealingly silhouetted the curves and two main assets of a naked Babs, fast asleep on top of the bed.

There was nothing lascivious in this little episode. Ma was proud of her beautiful daughter and she wanted me to feel the same. But pride was already the wrong word and I was having great difficulty in convincing myself that I should wait at least a couple of years before consummating any of the dreams or evil intentions that were running through my mind. It was the moral decision to do just that, that proved to be my undoing.

At the beginning of January 1942 there were strong rumours that the Squadron was to be moved to Northern Ireland to Ballyhalbert, situated in that droopy tongue of land that hangs down just south of Newtownards, and this would mean an end to any short or long weekends in England.

I remember sitting in the loo at the time, when a couple of 'erks' came in to have a conversational piddle. They weren't at all enchanted at the idea of a visit to the Emerald Isle, but they optimistically suggested that maybe on the trip over, they could push overboard a couple of bloody corporals as well as that cynical sod Sergeant Hitchcock. One of them remarking that he would rather do jankers than get a bollocking from him. I silently accepted this as a back handed compliment and at the first opportunity I got them together to tell them "The next time you want to commit accidental murder, do it with your hands on your hearts and not on your cocks," and left them to work it out. The rumour became fact and at the end of January the aircraft were flown over. The ground crews, spares and equipment made the journey via Stranraer to Larne to arrive at Ballyhalbert late at night in pouring rain after an uneventful trip, free from the threat of U-boats, rough seas, enemy aircraft or fed-up 'erks'.

We stayed four months in Northern Ireland and I'm sure it rained at least every other day, making the new concrete runways the only solid thing in a sea of mud. And the first Beaufighter to veer off on landing was soon feet deep in sludge, also the Cole's crane brought in to lift it. This happened several times and the CO threatened virtual life imprisonment to the next one that ran off. And who should that turn out to be? – Oh yes it was.

Weekend leaves, weather permitting, were usually spent in Bangor, which being a seaside holiday resort had a selection of lovely Irish mums providing bed and breakfast. The bed usually being large and comfortable with beautiful white sheets and the breakfast a mammoth feast of crisply cooked potato cake, egg and bacon.

Any afternoon or evening off could be spent taking a quick cycle tour along the Strangford Loch or in a pub at Donaghadee, where the art of drawing off a pint of 'God's gift to the unwary' was repeatedly demonstrated in the form of glass after glass of expertly defrothed Guinness.

Whatever element of the overall strategy of the war that had deemed it necessary for 25 Squadron to be stationed in Ireland soon changed, for in May we were packing up once more, to be transferred to Church Fenton in Yorkshire. And I had been assigned to the advance party which was to fly over in an old Handley Page Harrow transport plane. When it turned up, who should the pilot be? None other than Tubby Hilton from Harvey Grammar and Iraq days, and he promised faithfully not to land nose down halfway across the Irish sea. He didn't, and we all arrived safely. We had a final chat, wished each other good-bye and good luck, and I've never seen him since, either in or around or away from Hythe.

The Squadron's activities during the early months at Church Fenton became somewhat routine due to the inactivity of the Luftwaffe at this time. Although totally engrossed in our own contribution towards winning the war, Church Fenton seemed somehow remote from the activities of the real conflict going on in Russia, North Africa and the Far East. And so we avidly read the newspapers, having the same concerns, doubts and hopes that the whole nation felt at the time. The Squadron of course had its occasional successes during this period and hoped for more when in October it received the first of its new Mosquito night fighter Mark II's. Flight Lieutenant Joe Singleton had an early success, damaging a raiding Dornier.

My own efforts came to an abrupt end at the end of November, for an attack of mumps necessitated twenty eight days of isolation in hospital at Pontefract. I was accommodated in one large room, which had an open coal fire, making it warm, cosy and comfortable.

The day nurse was a little girl, quick and efficient, who only stayed long enough to do what was necessary, but the night nurse was a little larger, somewhat slower and inclined to chat in a horizontal position. I nearly fell in love, but escaped to normal life just in time, cured of mumps, bumps and sundry dangling aches, to be granted a few days sick leave augmented by a Christmas break.

In spite of rationing and restrictions Christmas 1942 was a happy one, Mother and Father and myself gorging ourselves on a thin-thighed guinea fowl that I had bought from a little shop at the top end of the old High Street in Folkestone. There wasn't much choice really, for it was the only thing left, languishing alone on the marble slab, pleading for a buyer.

Cobden Road itself appeared to be largely deserted, there being only a handful of families left, the Griggs, the Newmans, the Blackmans, the Pilchers and maybe others. Father, along with many other local men, was enjoying sustained employment, working on new installations somewhere between Dymchurch and Dungeness, camouflaging buildings to look like fishermen's huts or houses. Mother was doing her bit with the Women's Institute, serving tea and wads to the 'boys' at the Institute in Prospect Road. The military establishments at Hythe and Shorncliffe ensuring an appreciative clientele.

The return to Church Fenton after the Christmas break had an added interest for the new Mosquito was a beautiful aircraft of all wooden monocoque construction powered by Rolls Royce Merlin engines, and it was a rewarding and pleasurable plane to work on. It had its teething troubles naturally and the mention of exhaust shrouds was usually prefixed with a volley of swear words, for they burnt out with quick and monotonous regularity. A minor fault which was quickly solved by the experts at De Havillands.

My occasional visits to Stanmore increased in tempo for it was almost two years now since I made my vow 'not to'. So on this visit early in 1943 I proposed and was accepted, taking Babs on a romantic weekend to Hythe. Mother was noncommittal, but Father was entranced of course. Mother said "She's a bit young, isn't she?" and Father warned "You'll have a bit of a job hanging on to this one, lad, she's far too attractive."

The weekend was in one way non-productive. Babs had been given the front bedroom, Ma and Pa took the middle room, that left the little back bedroom for me, with a squeaky passage in between, with Ma's Victorian ear hole on the qui-vive for any midnight meanderings. I didn't even try.

On the return journey we parted company in London. After a clinging good-bye at Waterloo, Babs caught her train to Winchester and I continued on to Leeds and Church Fenton.

As the Mosquito could almost be considered revolutionary in construction and design, courses at the manufacturers were made available. And the lucky ones, including myself, enjoyed courses at Hatfield and Derby, enabling us to more quickly grasp the advanced technologies involved and to appreciate how quick and massive these had been from just a few years ago. Variable pitch, contra-rotation propellers and two stage two speed superchargers,

A SHILLINGSWORTH OF PROMISES

rated altitudes and R.A.E. injectors all made it seem as if fifty years of development had been compressed into something less than five.

The Squadron's night time role now included the carrying out of night sweeps over the continent, bringing successes which put railway engines and trains on the score sheet alongside the Dorniers and Heinkels. In the summer of 1943 three aircraft from the Squadron joined up with three from a Polish Squadron and three from an Australian Squadron to form a composite Flight at Predannack in Cornwall. I was happy to be detailed for this assignment, selecting the accompanying ground crew myself, with the approval and blessing of the Squadron Engineering Officer, Flight Lieutenant A.E. Gunn.

This unit had been formed to carry out long range patrols over the Bay of Biscay, to discourage German aircraft from attacking the routine patrols of Coastal Command. It was a hectic few weeks, the biggest hazards being the instant blanketing of the airfield when the sea mists rolled in, and the insistence of the Polish pilots that temporary unserviceabilities just could not happen. One had the feeling that their dislike of the Germans was such that they would fly anything as long as it would get off the ground. Sadly though on one operation one aircraft failed to return. Now, closing my eyes some fifty years later, I can still see the cheery smiling wave of the dark haired, newly married young pilot as he climbed into the cockpit before taking off. By the nature of our job and the bloody war, these moments did arise, but this particular one somehow focuses more clearly and more often in my mind than the others.

Now back at Church Fenton I rejoined 'B' Flight to carry on as before, with the two other senior N.C.O.'s, a Freddy Hindel and a Freddy Gilbert. We were collectively known as The Three Freddies.

Freddy Gilbert was married and had been granted permission to live out, occupying the two top rooms of a small cottage with shared use of the outside loo, but with the added convenience of a broken handled piss pot under the bed. Freddy G. was late returning home one evening and, not wishing to disturb the household, he barefootedly started to feel his way up the stairs in the pitch darkness. But his wife, anticipating Freddy's needs, had also picked the same moment to creep silently downstairs, precariously holding the broken handle of a full gozunder. Suddenly there was a tumbling mess of bodies, arms and legs, all receiving a full urinary baptism. Initial surprise and anger turned to raucous laughter on realisation of what had happened. Gravity had ensured that Freddy, being the underdog, had received the maximum benefit from the encounter. He came in the next morning wearing his 'best blue' to give his own version in somewhat more expressive and explicit language. Towards the end of 1943 Freddy Hindel gained his engineering commission, Freddy Gilbert was posted, and I was promoted to Flight Sergeant, taking over 'B' Flight for a short while, before becoming Flight Sergeant in charge of the Repair and Inspection section.

On December 19th the Squadron began to receive the first of its new Mosquito N.F.XVII's. It also underwent a short two month stay at Acklington on the North Sea coast, a few miles north of Hull. And I remember every one of them, due to a missed bus on a wet and windy winter's night after a longish session in one of Hull's centres of delight, the Paragon.

February 1944 brought a move south to Coltishall in Norfolk, where the new N.F.XVII's soon proved their worth, the Squadron having twelve successes during February and March.

The Three Freddies: Hitchcock, Hindel and Gilbert.

A SHILLINGSWORTH OF PROMISES

Norfolk, with a multitude of newly constructed airfields, was now virtually one big American Air Force base, and we were in the middle of it and could appreciate the origination of the jealously triggered and well worn complaint that they were overpaid, oversexed and over here. All true. But could we have done without them?

By this time the pattern of the war had changed. The Eighth Army had cleaned up North Africa and, together with the Americans, were sorting out the Italians in Southern Italy. And Russia, having turned the tide at Stalingrad and lifted the siege of Leningrad, was beginning to menace the Fatherland from the east.

Bomber Command by night and the USAF by day were bombing hell out of Germany in an attempt to destroy their factories and military installations. And, just as importantly, their morale. Quite heavy losses were sustained during these operations, making one marvel at the dedication and courage of the crews. A different sort of courage to that required of a fighter pilot, for the bomber crews, on each operation, had to undergo hours of nerve wracking flying, heading for and returning from well defended targets, realising all the time that disaster could well be only a moment away.

The differing reactions of the Americans and the British to the stresses of the times, I think was very well illustrated one evening at the bar in the sergeants' mess. Two damaged Fortresses returning from a raid had been forced to make emergency landings at Coltishall, and the crews were naturally and ebulliently celebrating their success and safe return. Then one of our night fighter pilots came through the bar before going in to have his supper. A gentle enquiry as to how he'd got on, received a nod and a "Yes, we managed to get one." One of the Americans then asked, "What did he mean, he got one?" On hearing the answer his reaction was one of disbelief. Not of the claim, but at the matter of fact way it had been made.

On a long weekend leave in May I was surprised to find brother Bert at home enjoying a few days in Hythe. Like me he also loved to take long walks around the town, and this day we decided to enjoy the Channel views from Cliff Road and the gentle descent into Seabrook, returning along the tree lined north bank of the canal to Twiss Road, the seafront and home.

But we got no further than a few yards past the old railway station for we were unexpectedly challenged by two well armed army guards. Cliff Road had become a protected area and out of bounds to everyone. We could see further along the road a mass of army transports sheltering under the trees. We presumed rightly or wrongly that it was a tiny part of the massive army of vehicles, tanks, guns etc., being assembled for the second front, which was but a few weeks away.

Then, in early June, every member of the Allied forces received a printed letter from the Supreme Headquarters, Allied Expeditionary Force carrying the signature of General Eisenhower. It said, more or less, 'The big day was almost here and the Allies were about to give the German war machine its come-uppance. We had already, since 1941, given it a right old rollicking and had seriously reduced its air strength and capacity to fight on the ground. We now had a vast superiority of weapons with a large reserve of trained men to turn the rollicking into a rout. It won't be easy, and the eyes of the world will be on you. Good luck and God bless!'

It started on the evening of the 5th June, making the 6th the first full day of the landings. My absolute and full appreciation of the dangers undertaken by those directly involved did not really come until some forty seven years later, when I visited the Normandy beaches.

I had of course read many accounts of what took place on the landing beaches of Utah, Omaha, Gold, Juno and Sword. But standing on the low cliffs looking out at the remains of Mulberry harbour and surveying the shoreline, I was struck by a realisation of the kind of hell those lads must have gone through. Their ultimate success was nothing less than a man-made miracle. A visit to the British, American and Canadian cemeteries in the locality gave a sombre reminder of the price that had been paid. The whole area should be made a place of pilgrimage for the thousands of British and French people who, in spite of the hardships of wartime, were only marginally inconvenienced. And that would include myself.

While the miracle centred around Arromanches was taking place I was still at Coltishall. Then when the V1 flying bombs, or 'doodlebugs' as they were called, started to come over in large numbers around the end of June, the Squadron immediately became involved in night operations against this growing and glowing menace.

As they had a speed of up to four hundred miles per hour, some of our Mosquitoes were re-engined with more powerful Merlins to give a better chance of a dived interception. Wing Commander Wight-Boycott D.S.O. was our C.O. and his aircraft was the first to be modified and he gave me the privilege if not the pleasure of accompanying him on the test flight.

He climbed high in the sky and then put the nose down at full throttle, finally having a trial of strength with the joy stick in order to level out. I didn't feel comfortable and I don't think he did either. The De Havilland specialists were consulted and a slight change in the tail plane angle of incidence corrected the tendency to stay in a steep dive, thus making it possible to perform a safe diving attack on the VI's.

With bombing attacks on the launching sites, radar directed air interceptions and anti aircraft fire, the menace was considerably reduced. And records show that of the 7840 launched, 4260 were destroyed by 29th March 1945 and in the final stages ninety per cent of the launches were being destroyed.

At the end of October 1944 the Squadron moved once more, this time to Castle Camps, and at the end of December I moved even further to Milfield near Coldstream and Berwick on the Scottish border, to join a new Operation Training Unit. This unit trained Typhoon and Tempest pilots, as there was an urgent need for them on the second front.

I remember the new Hawker Tempests being delivered straight from the factory, piloted by women of the Air Transport Auxiliary, all making beautiful landings. Puncturing the ego of a few of the more macho lads under training.

Also at Milfield I had my first contact with W.A.A.F. mechanics, and made the tactical error of allocating one to each maintenance crew. One girl to six boys, it was fatal. So I formed a complete crew of all girls and their attempts to prove that they were as good as, if not better than the men, created healthy competition. There were mishaps of course, both technical and emotional, and being by now an old hand at both, these were soon smoothed over. And I was likely to be an even older hand, for I had applied for and been granted a second twelve years of service.

Milfield was a long way from Stanmore, but Babs was now working as a telephone operator in the exchange at Winchester, so communication was no real problem. I hadn't been able to get down to see her for some fourteen weeks or so, last year in fact, for it was now March 1945. Her new job had made it easy to have a natter now and then. But nattering turned out to be not enough, for late one evening on being called to the phone, Babs' trembling and tearful voice told me that she had broken our engagement and was going to marry a twenty one year old air gunner!

Somehow I wasn't all that surprised, other blokes weren't blind, and this one certainly wouldn't have been inhibited by any age difference. Maybe there's a moral here, but at least I had a clear conscience. I went to bed humming 'On top of old smokey', the words seemed to be remarkably apt.

'On top of old smokey, all covered with snow, I lost my sweet lover by going too slow.'

The real war was still going on and the Allies were now unbeatable favourites to win. The Americans had liberated Paris, with De Gaulle in attendance, all resistance in Italy had been overcome and Southern France was again free.

Now Germany itself, having received a massive pounding during the last year was in no condition to withstand the final onslaught of some nine thousand aircraft and the Allies broke through to meet up with the Russians on the river Elbe.

Hitler killed himself on the 2nd May and Donitz surrendered unconditionally on the 7th and the war in Europe was over.

In June the O.T.U. at Milfield closed down and I returned to 25 Squadron at Castle Camps, to experience horrors almost as bad as the war. Serviceability of the aircraft was no longer a priority, and re-installation of strict service discipline now became paramount. One could almost feel our war time heroes going through their list of instructions on how to become good peace time Station Commanders. The sound of stamping feet again echoed across the parade grounds, and those old first world war rifles were once again being sloped, presented and ordered. I felt discouraged.

The final freeing of the world from tyranny (I'm talking here of the Japanese) came when the massive destruction caused by the two atomic bombs on Hiroshima and Nagasaki compelled the Japanese to surrender quickly and unconditionally on the 14th August.

5   *Peace, sadness & a Cairo wedding*

The monotony and inactivity of the first few months of peace-time was enlivened a little, when a detachment from the Squadron was sent to Lubeck in north east Germany. I flew over in the Squadron Anson and was amazed at seeing the extent of the damage suffered by the German towns and cities. It was absolute devastation, acre after acre of roofless and broken buildings surrounded by rubble with just the cleared streets to separate them.

The thought occurs to me at this moment in 1992, with Germany and Japan rebuilt and dominating the world economically, with their citizens enjoying the best standard of living they've ever had, that perhaps the best way to win a war would be to lose it.

My short stay in Lubeck is remembered for just two things. One is that the locals there would do almost anything for a single cigarette, and two, that food seemed not to be a worry. A point reinforced by the meals that were enjoyed in the mess, heaped plates of quality nosh coming legitimately, or maybe not, from nearby Denmark.

We flew back to Castle Camps, again in the Anson, and had to land twice *en route* to check our bearings. And the trip over the North Sea was not uneventful. We had two navigators on board and they decided to change over about half way, and during the squeeze of this manoeuvre the engines suddenly became silent. It was some twenty seconds before the pilot realised that the caged switches had accidentally been switched to the 'OFF' position. A quick flick upwards brought the engines spluttering back to life and saved us from ugly thoughts of a cold North Sea ditching.

With the war over the RAF began to shrink, making continuity within a unit somewhat difficult, aggravated by the fact that it almost needed an earthquake to motivate masses of de-mob happy 'ack-emma's'. The pattern and future of one's chosen profession at this moment was a bit obscure, and this feeling of uncertainty was practically universal.

It was little better at home, and Hythe certainly was a changed town, and would need years to recover. Continued food rationing, utility goods and the black market would become ever more irksome as the memories of war receded. And of course many thought that the new Labour government was nothing more than an untimely self inflicted wound. Bleeding the country by getting its priorities wrong. Concentrating on social change and nationalising everything in sight when it should have been rebuilding and modernising factories worn out by years of unavoidable war time neglect.

We didn't rebuild, but Germany and Japan did, and reaped the rewards, introducing social change when they were really able to afford them, though I suppose it must be said that we helped Germany quite considerably, for it didn't have the expense of demolishing its old factories, we'd already done it for them.

Even in peace time the Squadron continued its nomadic existence, moving once more in January 1946 to Boxsted near Ipswich, where the Station Engineer happened to be Squadron Leader A.E. Gunn. We had a long chat about bygone glories. I simply said "Well, you were posted and I went away for a while," and like the blond instructor at Halton I left it at that.

Soon after that my seven and a half year association with 25 Squadron came to an end, for in July I was transferred to number 24 Reserve Centre at Reading. A newly formed unit with a staff of eight, working from a large private house 'Sylvesters' in Berkeley Avenue, giving technical lectures to weekend airmen of the Volunteer Reserve in classes of usually some six or seven in number. A pleasant, interesting and satisfying job, totally different in nature to any previously held. And giving ample opportunity in the slackish week days for various private activities.

The oddest of these being when we tried to grow mushrooms in the unused cellar, buying the basic elements of the enterprise in kit form, following each and every instruction religiously, and promising all and sundry a share in the harvest.

After six weeks of concentrated endeavour we gathered just two mushrooms, and then waited two more weeks for late arrivals that didn't. It took an invective infested half day to clear out the mess. Twenty Four Reserve Centre came under the control of Reserve Command at Middle Wallop which sometimes called on us to help out with other units and that's how I found myself in digs at Eastleigh when standing in for an absent member of Southampton University Air Squadron.

Whilst there I had a slight *contretemps* with the C.O. for his pilots tended to treat the Tiger Moths as being totally infallible and became upset when I insisted on an accumulated series of small repairs being done. So my stay was curtailed, but not before I'd had a surprise visitor one evening on returning to my digs.

I had called in at Stanmore on the way from Reading for a chat with Babs' mother. And Babs had been able, by the nature of her job and the telephone, to find my address, and had taken an early opportunity to come down to see me. I was pleased and then sorry to see her, for she was unhappy and troubled. Her marriage was apparently going through a sticky patch but, as I was still not out of love with her, I was not the person to give advice, and that made my next move a little awkward.

The choice was between being a slightly over aged lover or a slightly under aged father figure. The former leading undoubtedly to unpredictable complications and maybe again final disappointment. So I chose the latter, offering sympathy, understanding and a quick trip back to Winchester on the next bus.

Although my love life was somewhat erratic, stopping and starting but never climaxing, brother Tom's was progressing smoothly. He had left the Merchant Navy and found a job as a painter, removing the stains of war from the Hotel Imperial. Early in 1947, after a short courtship, he married a local girl, got the sack, and moved to Hayes in Middlesex. He found a permanent job on the maintenance staff at Nestlé's where Brenda, his wife, spent her days packing chocolates. And they lived happily ever after, having two children, a boy and a girl who eventually blessed them with three good-looking grandchildren. Thereby ending a long nosed family tradition.

Later in the year, after spending a month at Chivenor in Devonshire, looking after two old Avro Ansons, which were being used to give young Air Training Corps lads their first experiences of looking down on the world, I returned to Reading. I was met by a Warrant Officer Fox, a tall dry old stick, who I remember miffed and puzzled an over critical young stores officer, who had been telling the men to repair their socks instead of changing them, by presenting for exchange a tie in perfect condition. On being told there was nothing wrong with it he said "Oh yes there is, it's much too tight." The message was received and understood.

W/O Fox told me that the orderly room had phoned through to let me know that I was due to attend a fifty five week advanced training course at Locking near Weston-Super-Mare, starting in December. This was excellent news for it meant that I would be brought right up to date with all the recent technical advances, including the now operational jet-engined aircraft.

The winter of 1947 was a rough one, so we anticipated that the central heating would be turned on – it was. But due to the fuel shortage only just high enough to prevent the pipes and not us from freezing up. It wasn't pleasant sitting in the lecture rooms in overcoats, trying to take notes with mittened fingers dampened by surreptitious attempts to wipe away the winter dewdrops. However, temporary reprieve from this Arctic hell was near, for the school closed down and we all went home for the Christmas break.

Brother Bert was now based at Chatham, so it was no surprise when he decided to spend Christmas at Hythe. His wife Mary being quite happy to celebrate the seasonal festivities with her guests at her newly opened boarding house in Southsea.

The atmosphere at home this year was a little depressed, for Father had recently had a prostate operation, and his convalescence was not going well. But this did not affect his inherent sense of humour, and with the family around him his morale, and Mother's too, rose considerably.

Now with the break over I returned to Locking to survive the remaining winter months and the rigours of continuing school life. Undergoing the same delightful torture was Lofty Mee and the only thing that had happened since we last met was a bit of a war, which we both seemed to have weathered fairly well. He was still as ruggedly or, more accurately, raggedly good looking. Tallish, square jawed and passionately sincere in his relations with those he chose to call his friends. A good lad to have around if ever you needed any sort of moral support.

As we progressed through the course we were constantly being made aware of the speed and depth of the technical advances that had taken place since our original training some twelve years ago. But the present seat of learning made it easier, being less irksome and closer to civilisation.

Weston-Super Mare itself, being a seaside resort of some repute, satisfied most of our off duty wants. Its beautiful sands, superb fish and chips, organed cinema and welcoming pubs providing everything except 'the other'. It was there, but it wasn't exactly provided. I had no heart to go searching, but at lunch times I took consolation watching a lovely red-headed W.A.A.F. cook. It must have been the sensual flick of her wrist as she sploshed dollops of nosh on my plate that captivated me. But I had no chance, for there were younger and better looking lads in the queue, hoping for something more than a dollop of mash or the smile that came with it. All I could do was to wish them luck.

Sometime about the end of July 1948, on the final stage of the journey to Hythe for the end of term leave, I fell to pondering on my life to date. I'd done a lot of travelling, but had I really got anywhere? A positive past maybe, but a future with no definite destination, except perhaps to a crematorium somewhere. Morbid thoughts, neutralised a little by a touch of nostalgia as the old Grammar school came into view. I was suddenly a little boy again, capped and satchelled, and fighting the queue for a bag of hot chestnuts from the old fellow at the gate, hoping that the rattling school bus wouldn't leave without me.

When I arrived home, Mother greeted me with a soft smile, but there was sadness and a barely suppressed tremor in her voice when she took me aside to tell me that Father had been diagnosed as having cancer, and as yet he hadn't been told.

Father himself was sitting in a well cushioned arm chair in front of the living room window, with his good ear glued to the loud speaker of the wireless. He had his eyes shut and was chuckling to himself, so I waited a while before interrupting to say my hallo's.

I was still trying to absorb the shock of Mother's news, so looking into Father's eyes and seeing the twinkle of welcome there pulled at the heartstrings and it was difficult to control the black emotion that welled up.

The following day Father asked me to take him for a walk. He wanted to walk along the sea front towards Seabrook as far as the slipway, and then across the raised path over the golf links to the canal bank, and on to Seabrook Road. I tried to discourage him from taking such a long walk but he insisted, saying it would give him time to talk.

I learnt more about my old Dad in the next hour or so than in the previous thirty two years. He told me about his early struggles as a boy in London, how he'd met and courted Mother, how they suffered the miseries of the 14–18 war and how they'd worked together to bring up the family. This and much more. It seemed as if he somehow wanted to let me know that, despite the circumstances and ordinariness of his life, he hadn't really failed. When eventually the stories petered out he fell silent for a while, and then a fleeting smile crossed his face as he looked at me and said, "I do know, Son."

Then he jokingly prophesied that he wouldn't be drawing his old age pension, or if he did it wouldn't be for long. And he didn't want any long faces, tears or wreaths, but a few chrysanthemums wouldn't be refused.

Father died on the 24th November, just thirteen days after he'd qualified for his pension, and I could almost hear him saying "I told you so". He is buried in the beautiful and quiet little churchyard at Saltwood. Not all that far from the Lych gate which he and Mother used to find so protectively useful in their courting days.

It now fell to us to find a way of helping Mother, but she was doggedly insistent that she could get by on her widow's pension, and did not want any help. This was not easy to accept, especially as I, the only unmarried son, could easily afford to make things a little easier for her.

Of the terrace of three houses, 26, 28 and 30 Cobden Road, ours was the only one that still had its original occupants. I knew that dear old Mr

Simmonds and his wife had both passed on years ago, and now a Mr and Mrs Allen were renting the place. I also knew that the clothes line of number 30 ceased some years back to display the split-legged Victorian drawers of old Mother Crump, but I hadn't as yet made contact with the occupant of the somewhat more modern but less convenient replacements that now fluttered in their place.

Fortunately at this particular moment the Hamer family who owned all three houses decided to sell, with the sitting tenants having first choice, as long as a total price of fifteen hundred pounds was obtained for all three.

Obviously if I bought number 28 then Mother would have no alternative but to live rent free. So I called in at number 30 and introduced myself to John and Meg to find out how they felt about things. They had already decided that they would like to buy. But the tenants of number 26 had no such wish, so the only way John and I could settle the deal would be to find a buyer for Allen's house. But with a sitting tenant that would be difficult so we decided to offer six hundred pounds each for our own, leaving an asking price of three hundred pounds for number 26. This offer was turned down. Then I approached brother Bert and told him he could buy the house next door as an investment for just three hundred pounds. He, with eventual retirement in mind, accepted. The whole thing was soon settled, and Mother lived rent free, I lived with an easier conscience. John and Meg were happy and Bert finally retired, to modernise and live at number 26 for a few years before selling it for thirty thousand pounds and emigrating to Tasmania in 1982.

The course at Locking came to an end in January 1949, and then after successfully passing the final examinations I, together with others, including Lofty Mee, were detailed to attend another four or five week course at St Athan in South Wales in order to qualify as inspectors of the Aeronautical Inspection Services. (A.I.S.)

To date the only time Lofty Mee's path and mine ever crossed was either on courses or troopships. So it came as no surprise that soon after the St Athan course was over we found ourselves leaning on the rails of the 'Empire Trooper', just watching water again, *en route* for the Canal Zone in Egypt, having left Southampton on the 14th April.

The journey to Port Said, in spite of the passage of eleven years since the last one, was virtually the same. Troopships don't change, neither do seascapes, but the Bay of Biscay was a little more friendly this time.

Since the British military presence in Egypt was now confined to the Suez canal area, it was but a short journey after our arrival at Port Said in

A SHILLINGSWORTH OF PROMISES

April to our final destination at El Hambra, far removed from any of Egypt's world famous tourist attractions.

Our stay at El Hambra was transitory and we were initially accommodated under canvas. And Lofty Mee, Dick Temperton and I having been together since January, shared the same tent. Within days we were finally separated, Dick and I were posted to the A.I.S. Test Centre at adjoining Kasfareet and Lofty went to El Firdan.

Some of the tests at the centre meant checking to up to six places of decimals, so the building was temperature controlled, which was not only essential for the work, but a cool bonus to we lucky few that worked there.

Christmas 1949 came and went and I can remember nothing of it, maybe an alcoholic lapse of memory, but more likely because it was totally uneventful. But soon after, early in February, as I was quietly working at my bench, I became aware that someone was standing behind me. It was the station Engineering Officer who surprised me by asking if I had ever been to Cairo. A positive answer triggered the next question. "Would I like to go there again?"

Before showing any great enthusiasm, I asked, "to do what exactly?"

I learnt that it would mean a stay of three months in civilian clothes at a small Hotel Pension, which would be used as a base from which I would have to travel daily to a factory in Shroubra. And the job was to check and supervise the manufacture of steel furniture being made by the Delta Trading Company for the RAF Checking would mean seeing that the company kept strictly to the agreed specifications and supervising would mean a quality control check at all stages of manufacture.

It was a bit of a challenge but as I was due to do my third all night guard duty in less than a fortnight, I naturally, willingly and happily said "Yes".

So within a week, dressed in my only sports jacket and flannels, carrying a small case containing toilet necessities and a change of underwear, I turned up at Cairo railway station to be met by a Bill Irvin, who took me in a neutralised RAF 15 hundredweight van to the 'Hermitage Hotel Pension' in Sharia Kasr-el-Nil, where the proprietor was known only as Nick, or Nick the Greek.

Bill was the resident 'Local Purchase' supervisor and had been in Cairo a number of years. Very experienced and if necessary, could be as devious as those he had to deal with. He operated from an office in Sharia Soloman Pasha and was the link man to RAF H.Q. in the Canal Zone.

Also staying at the Pension was an RAF clerk working at the British Embassy with a Flight Lieutenant Chapman who dealt with all the administrative details. In Cairo also at this time was a member of the Special Branch of the RAF police, a Flight Sergeant Bob Comber, and what his function was I never found out, even though we became close friends. Both Bill and Bob were accompanied by their wives, and had flats away from the Pension. The factory at Shroubra on the outskirts of Cairo and sited next to the Sweet Water canal, was quite a surprise. It being well built and well equipped with all the equipment necessary to produce the metal furniture that the RAF had contracted for.

One morning on my second or third visit to the factory and when passing along a veranda fronting the offices, a rich English voice called out "Good morning – you are English aren't you?" It was easy to make the admission and he invited me in to share the first Turkish coffee of the day. A sweet dark drink, taking only half a dozen sips before reaching the bitter sludge at the bottom, and always followed by a glass of water, but a guaranteed quick lift to start any day.

The voice belonged to a retired Royal Engineer, Major Hemming. He had recently become the engineering and production manager at the factory and therefore we had a mutual interest and it made life that much easier.

And life itself began to feel freer and likewise my spirits. The more so because my anticipated three months in Cairo had been extended indefinitely. But this sense of unfettered well-being suffered a temporary setback when we learnt that Nick had mysteriously disappeared, leaving us high and dry. A search for a new Cairo home quickly followed and by the evening I was on my way to 26 Sharia Antikhana to the 'Pension Suisse', owned and run by two Swiss sisters, Erica and Hedy Frey. They also had another smaller pension situated in the Cairo suburb of Maadi, where their mother resided and presided. Maadi, in stark contrast to the frenetic city life of Cairo, was a peaceful and restful place. And the beautiful garden around the eight room pension was a marvellous mélange of Jacaranda, Palm, Mango, Lime and Guava trees, intermingled with colourful beds of Poinsettia and Jasmine.

I knew how and why my life had brought me to 26 Sharia Antikhana but how did Erica, Hedy and their mother Maria come to be so settled and established there?

This story starts in 1899 when the unmarried Maria became friends with a Julie Bosshard when working at a milliner's shop in Basle, Switzerland. Julie had a boyfriend who was a Maitre d'Hotel in Arosa, but he had emigrated to Egypt to take up a more remunerative post. So Julie decided to follow him. But when she arrived in Cairo her boyfriend was courting a new and newly pregnant girlfriend and he had little alternative but to marry her.

A SHILLINGSWORTH OF PROMISES

Julie then found a job as a nurse with an Egyptian family headed by Zaki Bey. Although his wife was of the Turkish aristocracy he still fell in love with Julie and then made a special trip to Istanbul where he took her as his second wife. They then returned to Cairo.

Years later and some few months before the outbreak of the 1914–18 war, Maria was invited by Zaki Bey and Julie to spend three months in Cairo to help alleviate a sinus problem. By this time Maria had married and had three children, Rene aged ten, Erica aged eight and Hedy aged seven. All destined to go to Egypt, for Maria now had the country in her blood and was determined to live there.

So in 1924 the family duly arrived in Cairo and rented a flat in Sharia Antikhana. Erica was a qualified coiffeuse and was soon working in a salon in Sharia Kasr-el-Nil and Hedy found a job as a chambermaid at the Hotel Continental. But Rene was not impressed and returned after a few months to Zurich. Erica too returned to Basle in 1930, with her husband Freddy. And Sylvia was born in 1932, all returning to Cairo in 1934. The same year that number 26 Antikhana was built and the family, without Maria's husband who had sadly died of typhoid in 1933, took the two top floors to create the twenty three room 'Hotel Pension Suisse'. Freddy became disenchanted with Cairo and returned to Zurich in 1939, making a divorce inevitable.

By 1937 Sylvia was back in Switzerland and at school in Lausanne, but came back to Cairo when war in Europe threatened, catching the last peacetime sailing from Genoa. She spent the war years at convents in Heliopolis and Zamalek, and in 1946 returned to Lausanne to complete her education.

The Pension Suisse prospered, becoming approved during the war for use by Allied officers, and after the war by lesser mortals, hence my recent arrival there, to enjoy the company and hospitality of Erica, Hedy and their mother Maria. And to meet Julie who, after Zaki Bey had died, lived for a while at the Maadi pension, before finally moving into a small flat close by.

My attitude of accepting life as it came began to change, and the light at the end of the tunnel vision of service life seemed to be brightening. Being in civilian clothes and with no 'Daily Routine Orders' to be concerned about, and getting away from the conversational limitations of an unmarried serviceman's life, together with wider social horizons all helped to bring about this change of mood.

In August Erica took a month's holiday to be with Sylvia, staying with a Madame Channon at Pully, near Lausanne. Before leaving she told Hedy to make sure that I was well looked after, as she thought I was looking hollow cheeked and pale and not eating at all well.

Of the two sisters Erica was seemingly the dominant one. They were both very good looking, a mature consequence no doubt of being quite beautiful in their younger days. Erica was blonde, chic and the quiet one, always busily concerned with the efficient running of the hotel. And her fluency in German, French, English and Arabic made it easy for her to relax when necessary with any or all of the guests.

Hedy was the plumper, more lively one, multi-lingual like her sister, with an easy and uninhibited approach to everyone, refusing to be intimidated in any way, and judging people purely by her own reactions. She was a total Anglophile having spent a year in England at the age of seventeen as masseuse to Lady Portman at Uckfield, at the same time teaching her French and exercising the dogs. And a two month holiday in Torquay in 1931 with her then boyfriend, and the good years spent with the officer guests during the war, all increased her sympathy for anyone and anything British.

Now her delegated concern for my well-being soon became apparent and I, not knowing the real reason for it, felt uncomfortable but none the less flattered. She seemed to enjoy listening to me, and I to her, and it was then that I became *au fait* with the circumstances of the arrival of the family Frey in Cairo. But at this moment it was my lack of appetite that was the problem, so Hedy thought it would be a good idea to have a word with Hassan, the chef. He was a large, likeable Egyptian and had learnt his skills under the direction and supervision of an Austrian chef at Mena House. So it was no surprise to find that *apfelstrudel* was frequently on the menu, and to watch him making and conjuring with the very thin pastry was impressive, not a hole or tear in sight. And his *aubergines au gratin*, his *poivrons* or *courgettes farcis*, his *macaronis au four* together with other equally delicious dishes quickly cured my loss of appetite.

Towards the end of August, in the cause of fattening me up, Hedy suggested that we might spend an evening gorging ourselves at the 'Restaurant des Pigeons' on the other side of the river in Zamalek.

So in the shaded and dimly lit garden of this high class noshery we chose a table overlooking the Nile, and spent the evening drinking, nattering, eating and getting to know each other. We found just one tenuous link between us from out of the past, for a Guy Hayes had been one of her war time guests. He had also been the C.O. of 55 Squadron in Iraq when I arrived there in 1936.

We began to spend more and more time together, not exactly the *coup de foudre* of romantic novels, how could it be? For we had both been taken off the shelf a few times to be looked over, tried out and put back again.

A SHILLINGSWORTH OF PROMISES

But romance did finally blossom and it was Hedy who suddenly posed the question, "Why don't we get married?" Without hesitation I agreed "Why not?" And that was the beginning of thirty five long years of sustained respect, affection and love, in that order. In later years I often asked her why, of all the men that had passed through the hotel, she had picked on me. The only answer I ever got was, that the spirit of her father had told her "This is the one." Hedy was a believer, even unto spiritualism, and this ran contra to my agnosticism. But if she believed her father had been speaking the truth, then who was I to disagree?

My letter home was a surprising shock, or a shocking surprise to Mother at the speed of things, but she had every faith in me, and sent her blessings. Erica had returned from Switzerland and was clearly astounded at the outcome of her advice to her sister to look after me.

Fortunately the slight delay in completing the complicated paper work only postponed the wedding for a few days, and so on November the 11th 1950, my thirty five years of independence and self-indulgence came to an end. On the morning of the 11th and waking early, Hedy, myself and Bob Comber, the best man, took off in Major Hemming's car along the desert road to Abu-Sueir and 205 Group H.Q. There to be married on British soil by the Directorate of Legal Services. The ceremony seemed a little incongruous and somewhat unreal, and I felt extremely sorry that all involved had to be so 'ceremoniously' inconvenienced, but very thankful none the less. After handshakes and good wishes we all piled back into the car for the rush back to Cairo to be in time for the special lunch. Hoping to take a nap afterwards, before the real ceremony in the chapel of Cairo cathedral at six o'clock.

Hassan had excelled himself preparing the lunch and I had excelled myself washing it down so a pre-marital nap became imperative. But there was a constant stream of happy, congratulating guests who turned the nap into a nightmare. So even after a shower and a change into my wedding suit, I still felt a little windy and woozy. However, Bob and I scrambled into the hired car to arrive in time at the cathedral to wait, seemingly straight and sober, for the sound of 'Here comes the bride'. She did, and then the seriousness of the occasion took over and I responded loud and clear, remembering every detail as rehearsed the week before. With the ceremony over Hedy and I walked arm in arm back down the long aisle of the echoing cathedral to be endlessly photographed at the door before hurrying down the steps to the car waiting to take us the short distance back to the hotel. Then a long rest, a cool shower and a quick change saw us fit for the all night reception. I'd never before in my life been so friendly with so many people I didn't know, and the happy multilingual buzz left me in somewhat of a conversational vacuum. I grimaced and nodded and shook my head hoping for the best. A Germanic nod to Frau Berli, a Grecian shake to the Greek grocer, kitchen Arabic to the Caireans, and school French to the rest. Except to Tommy Dando the Odeon organist and the locally based RAF lads, when a slightly alcoholically enhanced English was thankfully received and understood.

Hedy and I left just before midnight to spend a two day honeymoon at Maadi. That sufficed for the moment, a longer one had been planned for some time in the future.

The work at the factory was running smoothly and as there was now an extended contract, my stay in Cairo seemed safe and assured. So Hedy and I were soon comfortably installed in a self contained flat on the fifth floor of the hotel, and we were now able to entertain our friends in privacy.

Bridge sessions soon became a regular feature and a source of many new friends, apart from maybe a few quarrelsome and over dedicated enthusiasts. My bridge at first was a bit tentative but, aided by the hours I had spent over the years playing solo whist, I soon managed to hold my own. Instinctive rather than classic bidding and some unconventional play sometimes puzzling the local experts. I thought it was skill, they mainly called it luck. They were probably right – or wrong!

Amongst these experts was a Baron von Schulmann and his wife. He was a tall, always impeccably dressed man. Handsome, with wavy silver grey hair and bushy dark eyebrows, and had a somewhat imposing presence. His wife on the other hand was a wrinkled nosed little charmer, with something I appreciated, a slightly coarse cryptic humour. And on one occasion with her husband as partner, she had made an opening bid of one spade and after waiting some consider-able time for a response, she grinned and said "Kom schon, mein alter furz

Cairo, December 1950:
Newly married – obviously.

A SHILLINGSWORTH OF PROMISES

Kasten, sag etwas." The old 'fart box' looked up, wriggled a bit and then passed. I assumed it to be a term of endearment, but later I did find it would sometimes be prudent to avoid crossing his slipstream.

The pyramids of Giza could be plainly seen from the roof of 26 Sharia Antikhana, and although each year thousands of people came from all corners of the world to wonder at them, by some perversity of nature I couldn't even be bothered to take a taxi ride to do the same. The relative attractions of ancient and modern for the moment being biased towards what is and not what was.

It was the live twentieth century Cairo into which I had luckily been pitch forked. A city half oriental, half westernised, half attractive, half repugnant. Moslems, Christians, Jews, Egyptians, French, British, Germans, Greeks, Italians and others all living in noisy and suspect harmony, aggravated at this particular time by the struggle between Communism and the Moslem Brotherhood going on in the cafés and meeting places for the hearts and minds of the people.

We would spend many hours in the evenings just watching the Cairo street life from our fifth floor veranda. Just the ordinary comings and goings of Cairo's ordinary citizens, but how different from the sedate activity of street life in our European capitals. A couple of taxi drivers shouting and gesticulating, threatening to knock hell out of each other over a ten piastre lost fare. The cosily idle, sipping coffee on Groppi's roof garden opposite. A draped coffin being rushed to the cemetery before the sun went down. The makwagi delivering the day's ironed laundry, and the ever happy and legless Ibrahim scooting along on his little home-made four wheeled 'skate board', never very far from the Pension Suisse where he had been befriended by Hedy's mother Maria some twenty two years earlier.

These scenes were the fascination of the place, mixing easily and strangely with the trappings of European cultural life, the opera, the theatre, classical concerts, cinemas, sporting clubs, restaurants and night clubs.

So it was not surprising that my appreciation of things cultural was hoiked up a couple of notches. And it was at one of the piano concerts given by the old and famous Artur Rubinstein, where I was introduced to Frederic Chopin, and we've been very good friends ever since, often spending a consoling hour or two together. But as a change from high culture, Bill Irvin, our street wise Cairean friend, would take us on a tour of the earthier fleshpots to see and be captivated by classical belly dancing, performed to perfection and at very close range. Who really wants to look at pyramids? They haven't moved for centuries.

Nobody living in Cairo could avoid, or want to avoid, visiting the Mouski. This world renowned market place being a never ending source of surprise. The atmosphere is intimidatingly friendly and sharing many cups of sweet Turkish coffee is part and parcel of any bargaining.

The near claustrophobic, crowded, narrow streets smelling of herbs, spices, carpets, heated metal, candles and coffee, mixing with the individual smells from a myriad of tiny open fronted workshops, would make even a single visit unforgettable.

The skill of the artisans making the silver inlaid copper and brass work, the ivory inlaid boxes etc. was hereditary and unique. And when I watched them at work I was always intrigued and impressed at the quality of work they turned out, squatting at their tiny foot driven lathes in hunched concentration, impervious to the noise and bustle going on around them. As was the little white whiskered benign looking Abdel, curiously and endlessly knitting pullovers as he sat in his kiosk flogging lottery tickets.

In the absorbing atmosphere of a settled life in Cairo, the months flew by, but there were increasing signs that the resentment to the presence of Europeans was growing and hardening.

It was not unusual that, when walking side by side along a crowded pavement, one would be deliberately forced to step aside. Something to do with territorial rights I suppose. And on several occasions, when passing through the fruit and vegetable market in the evening on our way to the cinema, we would be the target for some poorly aimed rotten fruit. Disconcerting more than frightening, but it certainly made us wonder how and when this undercurrent of unrest would crystallise into some form of action. One servant in particular, having spent the previous evening listening to his revolutionary friends, would become sulkily resentful and very hard to handle the following day. But as the day wore on the charm and concern of Hedy and Erica would eventually bring a smile and take the edge off his indoctrinated discontent.

Listening to the two sisters exercising their multi-lingual talents always filled me with envy, as they, in the course of a few minutes, would switch from German on the phone, to Arabic to the servants, to French to a guest, and then to English if I came on the scene. And of course they were the conversational lubricant to the chatter of any bridge or social evenings.

However, on a couple of occasions no lubricant was called for. For a 'Yuggie Pascoe', a New Zealand travelling mate from thirteen years ago, on 55 Squadron's round trip, turned up, in transit through Cairo with his wife and daughter, and we spent a lively evening together in our flat. I was maybe

A SHILLINGSWORTH OF PROMISES

surprised but certainly pleased to learn that he had progressed from aircraftsman 1st Class to Flight Lieutenant in the intervening years. However, the following morning he passed out of Cairo and my life, but not so our second visitor.

It was none other than Lofty Mee, the date being July 1951 and he had come up to Cairo to meet his daughter who was due at the airport the following day. We spent a nostalgic evening together, not so alcoholic as on previous occasions, for I had by now forsaken the bottle, apart from a glass of plonk now and then, young or vintage. My proletarian palate being unable to appreciate any subtle difference between one or the other. But I did abide by the restaurant ritual of approving any offering with a cursory nod, unless there happened to be some visual evidence of a deteriorated or broken 'bouchon'.

Lofty's visit of course foreshadowed a coming move, and so it was no surprise when a few weeks later I learnt that my tour of duty in Egypt was due to come to an end in September. So Hedy and I quickly began to plan the where and when of our delayed honeymoon. We had been granted permission to make our own arrangements for the return to U.K., being warned that there would be no financial re-imbursement, except for the cost of the rations that we would have taken had we gone by troopship. It was all of £12 I think.

We now spent rather more time than usual with Hedy's mother at Maadi, the journey from Babalouk station taking only twenty minutes or so. The coming departure of Hedy from her family was going to be sad, with Marie feeling the end of an era had come. Erica's daughter Sylvia would be returning to Cairo to replace Hedy as second in command, and that solved what would otherwise have been a crisis of conscience.

The actual day of departure in mid September soon arrived, and then after struggling through an emotional half hour of handshakes, heartaches, kisses and tears, we eventually climbed into the waiting taxi to just hold hands and say little as we hooted our way through the overcrowded and familiar streets to the station.

After a short wait Hedy and I, together with six pieces of luggage plus a hat box (which I soon learnt to recognise from a hundred yards) were safely loaded onto the train. The three hour journey to Alexandria was a hot, dusty and uncomfortable start to our holiday. And the discomfort continued, with an argumentative and abusive taxi driver, followed by a slow and awkward passport check. This was more than enough to convince us that we were leaving Egypt at just the right time.

This feeling seemed all the more justified after we had boarded the 'Esperia', to enjoy a shower, a change of clothes and an evening meal, followed by a stroll on deck in the cool of the evening before retiring to our two bunk cabin. One up and one down, not quite the ideal arrangement for the first night of a delayed honeymoon, but it turned out to be not a problem.

For one and a half days we relaxed and enjoyed the on-board comforts, and renewed our acquaintance with the Mediterranean dolphins. The first port of call at Syracuse allowed us to stretch our legs ashore for a couple of hours; long enough for me to sample my first 'Expresso' from a strange and hissing chrome contraption mounted on the bar of a quayside cafe.

Ten hours later and we were at anchor in Naples bay and, after taking a snap of Hedy loafing on the ship's rail, with Vesuvius in the background, we went ashore for several hours. Then, after having visited the cathedral and been impressed by the gilded grandeur of the place, and by the comings and goings of a multitude of Italians going about their devotional duties we made our way by foot and taxi to a balustraded viewing spot high on the hills overlooking the town and the bay. This bird's eye view of Naples, with its shimmering blue bay alive with boats, although remarkably picturesque, in no way convinced me that the advice 'To see Naples and die' had any real validity. I could think of better places in which to run out of heart beats.

Another sixteen hours or so aboard the Esperia took us to our seaborne destination of Genoa. Then, having gathered our six pieces of luggage and the hat box, we taxied to our hotel in time for an evening meal, and for Hedy to sweetheart the manager into stowing our luggage for a few days, allowing us to swan off unencumbered the following day. After a breakfast of eggs and bacon, desecrated by being cooked in olive oil, we caught a bus to Rapallo. A journey of some 35 kilometres along what, for the most part, was a tree-lined coastal road, running at varying heights above sea level, crossing an inlet or two before reaching the well known resort itself.

There we searched for and found a likely looking small restaurant. It was called 'The Pergola' and, after a quick glance at the menu, we ordered two portions of 'La Friture'. These handsome helpings of tiny, crisply fried fish immediately brought back childhood memories of Mother's efforts with the small whitebait, when we managed to catch them using a small shrimp net as they shoaled close to the shore on a calm day.

Hedy, although not exactly fluent in Italian, was able to enquire of the owner as to where we might find a reasonably priced hotel for a few days. At this, his speech and arm waving became even more friendly and animated as he invited us to look at a studio flat on the first floor.

A SHILLINGSWORTH OF PROMISES

It was brand new, and we were to be its first occupants, for it had only been completed a few days earlier. He offered us two days rent free as a thank you to the powers above for having so quickly blessed him with guests. As we had only intended to stay for two days we accepted, but split the difference and paid for one.

We enjoyed the stay and the virgin porcelain bath, eighty centimetres square and waist high, with a built-in seat for comfort. It was a tight fit sitting side by side, but adequate enough for a soapy and carefree tubbing.

After a trip to Santa Margherita, accessible by boat only, and then to the sheltered little inlet harbour of Portofino, bottle necked and shrouded by well wooded steep slopes, we left this fascinating part of the Ligurian coast and returned to Genoa. There to stay overnight and to resurrect our six bags and a hat box and catch a train to Verona via Milan. 'Bill Shakes' came to mind, but we neither met the Two Gentlemen nor found the balcony from which Juliet enquired of the whereabouts of her Romeo.

The hotel we chose backed onto the river Adige, and was very comfortable and very expensive, so we decided to eat out. After wandering around for a while we skirted the old Roman amphitheatre and then turned off into a side street, to be suddenly assailed by a mouth watering whiff of something good. Then, with only food on our minds we sniffed our way to a tiny and somewhat unprepossessing looking restaurant. But undeterred we went in and were more than satisfied by being served with a meal that easily matched the whiff. And even more satisfied after it had been washed down with more than several glasses of full bodied red wine. We went back to the hotel, mellow and replete to sleep soundly until the morning.

Then, having showered and breakfasted, we accompanied our six-plus-one travelling companions to the railway station, to continue our scenic journey over the Alps to Austria, following the valley of the Adige, where road and rail climb and intertwine their way through and over the Brenner pass to Innsbruck.

Arriving late in the evening we were met by Herr and Frau Ffanselter, friends of Erica, and soon to become friends of ours. Their home close to the river Inn was warm and homely. He was a tall thin lad and was delightfully Anglophile, as was his wife, a comfortable, well rounded little lady, whose cooking threatened to do the same for us. And the early morning aroma of her freshly ground coffee was, and is, unforgettable.

Our first day in town naturally took us to the famous Marientheresa Strasse, to be underwhelmed by the 'Goldener Dachl' and overwhelmed by the comfort and service of Schindler's coffee house. The cosy, leather seated alcoves and the delicious, cruelly irresistible pastries, the coffee, snow capped with whipped cream, together with the tranquillity of the place, kept us anchored far longer than was politely necessary.

Then a window shopping stroll along the arcaded shop fronts proved too much; for an uncontrollable urge to spend suddenly overtook us. Fortunately, good sense prevailed and, as England was our final destination, we spent the next half hour trying on a variety of raincoats.

I chose a longish, high collared and belted affair which would have been approved by any Hollywood private eye. And Hedy's choice was little better, 'Al Capone and his moll' as someone observed years later.

The kitchen window of the Ffanselter's home looked out northwards onto the Hafelekar and the bedroom window southwards to the Patscherkofel, both being snow capped mountains of some seven thousand feet, and both accessible by cable car. So we cabled up both of them, being intrigued by the rides, entranced by the snow and seduced by the views. Experiences that our hosts, strangely enough, had not, over a period of some fifty years, found to be at all necessary.

Five days later, and with hand luggage only, we took a train and bus ride to Langenfeld, in the southern Tyrol. A small village nestling in a valley and ideally situated for long walks through the pine woods and leisurely strolls beside its rock-strewn streams.

Our small Gasthaus reflected the tranquil nature of the place, except of course when the *bierstube* suffered one of its many convivial eruptions. Then the smoke, beer and noise, musical and otherwise, would combine to form an exciting and potent mix.

It was on one of these evenings that two new guests, young and in love, came to stay in an adjoining room. And with their bed set too close to the wall the inevitable rhythmic rattlings, squeaks and moans tended to keep us awake. We thought of shifting our own bed to make some sort of competitive retaliation, but then thought better of it. It was a wise and face saving decision for, by the time we eventually dropped off to sleep, the score was already three to one in their favour.

The following day our two young friends, bright eyed and eager, came with us on the same little eight seat bus, as we yawned our way over narrow unmade roads and precarious bridges to the ski resort of Obergurgl. It was between seasons, so it had little to offer but magnificent views and hot coffee. We partook of both and then returned to Langenfeld.

This time wide enough awake to better appreciate the courage and optimism or faith of our driver.

A SHILLINGSWORTH OF PROMISES

Our stay in Langenfeld came to an end and we returned to Innsbruck to receive the sad news that Hedy's mother had quite suddenly been taken ill and, after a few days in hospital, had returned to 26 Sharia Antikhana where she suffered an unexpected and fatal heart attack.

Hedy was heartbroken, but the tears were slow to come. It was useless to just sit at home with a thousand thoughts going through our minds, so we wandered, close held and silent, into the town. And not knowing exactly where to go or what to do, we caught a tram to Igls. On leaving the town the track passed through a thick wood, climbing slowly as it meandered through the overhanging trees, with only a few intermittent rays of light penetrating the autumn foliage.

It was consolingly beautiful, as was our return to town, by foot, along the river bank, where Hedy at last started to cry. Great strangling sobs that slowly subsided into short choking bursts, and then finally into easy flowing tears as she slowly and finally regained her self control, to make unwanted and unnecessary apologies.

The Ffanselters welcomed us with heart-warming and sympathetic concern, insisting that we eat, drink and talk a little before going to bed. This we did, but we retired early. Hedy, emotionally exhausted, thankfully and quite quickly dropped off to sleep. It was some time before I slowly withdrew a numb and aching arm, and a few more long minutes before I too finally managed to find some sleep.

We spent the next two days very quietly at home with our new Austrian friends, and succeeded in teaching them the rudiments of bridge, the hazards of filleting plaice, and the frustrations of trying to produce consistently good Yorkshire puddings.

I had also managed to correctly forecast for Franz the result of three English football matches which helped him to win the equivalent of twenty odd pounds on an Austrian football pool or lottery. And this added to his sorrow at our departure, regretting the loss of a source of infallible information. Both they and us were genuinely affected when the time came for good-byes, and both Hedy and Trudi had wet eyes when the taxi came to take us and the hat box *etcetera* to the station to catch our train to Zurich.

This journey of some five hours took us through the most beautiful of Tyrolean countryside where hundreds of geranium bedecked chalets nestled haphazardly and at all levels on the pinewood and grass slopes that bordered each and every lush valley. With four to five thousand foot newly snow-capped mountains blessing and dominating the whole scene. In spite of the beauty all around us, the train noise and the hypnotic effect of all the posts and trees rhythmically flashing by caused us both to doze, only to wake abruptly whenever the train tunnelled its way through an intervening mountain.

After a couple of hours or so we crossed the Rhine and the Swiss border at Buchs, and very soon we were skirting the southern bank of the Walensee, where the mountains on the opposite bank drop sheer into the water. And within half an hour the lake of Zurich came into view and, following its southern bank we slowly dropped down into the comparative flatlands of northern Switzerland to arrive in Zurich itself, where we were met by Hedy's brother, Rene.

A short trip in his car took us to Zollikerberg, and a lovely welcome from the family; Elizabeth and the three children, Maja, age nineteen, Jurg thirteen and Armin ten. Rene, if not a master chef, was very adept around the kitchen and apparently did all the cooking if guests arrived. But I came to suspect that he preferred the kitchen and an unchallenged slurp or two, than to have to listen to his wife. A compulsive talker with an uncontrollable tendency to use friends and family as legitimate and silent conversational targets. And it would be fatal to be trapped as the last one of any surreptitiously shrinking audience.

However, we spent a long and happy evening together, which was a soothing tonic for Hedy, as she enjoyed the happy family chat, and the showing of Rene's films of their holidays on the Spanish Costas when they were still nothing but miles of empty sandy beaches, small bays and fishing villages.

After the atmosphere and the poverty of Cairo, one could almost smell the wealth of Zurich. Neat, spotless, orderly, everything and everybody seeming to tacitly accept there was some sort of divine right to such affluence.

We didn't stay long enough to see if any of this surfeit of lolly should wear off on us, for within a couple of days we were saying our good-byes to get an afternoon train to Basle, to be in time to catch the three minutes past midnight connection to Boulogne.

Taking a couchette we slept our way across France to wake up north of Paris. Easily in time to have a leisurely freshen up and a breakfast of coffee drenched croissants before finally arriving at the quay to transfer ourselves, our luggage and Hedy's flaming hat box onto the ferry. It was a smooth and sunny crossing to Folkestone. And the date was 30th October 1951.

6   *Goodbye RAF, hello LAF*

Our arrival at 28 Cobden Road was happy but tentative, for there were innumerable questions to be asked and answered. But Mother had foreseen that we would be hungry and, after the initial emotional greetings and mutual weighings up, we started to unpack and settle in, and Mother disappeared into the kitchen.

Hedy was intrigued and amused by the old marble topped wash stand in our bedroom, but the amusement turned to petrified fear when I introduced her to our zinc bath hanging up in the outside loo. So within a week Sprinks and Son were turning the little back room into a bathroom, complete with a bidet which had a central spray. This apparently caused a lot of ribald cockney comment from at least three of my well tickled aunts.

The evening meal of roast pork, roast potatoes, Yorkshire pudding and sprouts, with apple pie and cream, followed by coffee to finish, was the beginning of a close relationship between wife and mother-in-law. For Hedy now grudgingly admitted that it certainly wasn't only the continentals that knew how to cook. I had already laid to rest their other most arrogant and monstrous misconception.

As Hedy had been dogless for some five weeks, the second day of our return saw us making our way to Headcorn in search of a white bull terrier. We returned with ten month old Rolfe, a robust and playful dog, and from there on in we were three.

Then, as two of us waited outside Boot's shop in Folkestone, a smallish, smart and elderly lad approached and gingerly asserted "Hitchcock, isn't it?"

It was Mr Emerson, my old French master and during our conversation he sympathetically observed, "It was a pity about matric, wasn't it?"

At this point Hedy came out of the shop and was introduced and, with her slight accent and his assumption, they were soon gabbling away in French. Then, after a short three-way chat in English, his parting handshake brought a friendly, "We should've tried harder, shouldn't we?"

I puzzled for a while as to whether he meant a 'we' we, or a 'me' we, or a 'you' we. I shared the blame and settled for a 'we' we. On Armistice day, Father's birthday and our wedding anniversary, I had to rejoin the RAF So leaving Hedy and Mother to share the kitchen, I followed my draft instructions and reported to the Central Trade Test Board at Henlow. There to find that I was now to be an examiner and, remembering my own ordeal sixteen years before when passing out from Halton, I immediately made up my mind to be kind and cajoling in extracting hidden knowledge from nervous candidates (as I had been). I found it to be harder than expected.

Very early in the new year of 1952 Hedy joined me in Baldock where I had found a flat. It was part of a very old house which had a walled-in garden, a boarded-up well in the kitchen, and a headless ghost of a highwayman's victim in the loft. Rolfe enjoyed the garden, Hedy was careful in the kitchen, and I avoided any possible contact with our non-talking ethereal friend.

On the 26th January in this same year the strong undercurrent of anti-British feeling that we had sensed in our last days in Cairo, erupted into riots, culminating in Black Saturday when anything British was attacked and burnt. We of course eventually received the horrible details from Erica and Sylvia, who fortunately had suffered no direct hurt. And they, in spite of all the difficulties, decided to stay on in Cairo and carry on with the business. Late in the year King Farouk was forced to leave Egypt when Neguib took power, only to be ousted himself by Colonel Nasser some eighteen months later, bringing some sort of precarious stability to the country.

And my own stability did not last very long, for in August I was transferred to Kirkham, near Blackpool, to the new and interesting job of testing the trade worthiness of the young mechanics at the end of their courses.

So once again I went flat hunting, whilst Hedy returned to Hythe to enjoy a relaxing couple of months, swimming, walking and enjoying Mother's English-cum-cockney cuisine. She also made new friends starting with Muriel, who turned out to be the wife of the Folkestone Customs Officer who had picked his way right through our luggage, including the hat box.

I eventually found a lovely little top floor flat at number 10 Lytham Road, Lytham-St-Annes, which was owned by a stockbroker and his Irish wife. It overlooked the Ribble estuary and the sand dunes running along to St Annes itself. Ideal territory for exercising the dog and us. As we were only five miles or so from Blackpool, we sampled a lot and missed a lot of what it had to offer. Hedy being a little surprised at the Continental flavour of some of the entertainment, appreciating Jean Sablon and Les Compagnons de la Chanson, of Jimmy Brown fame.

What I did not enjoy one particular evening was the 'after you, Dad' advice given to me by a young girl as I stepped back to let her onto a bus. I was only thirty eight. It took Hedy hours to massage my ego back to even questionable good health.

Our simple but satisfying pattern of life continued and we contentedly drifted into 1953. I was happy with life at Kirkham, each and every candidate providing a different and sometimes difficult challenge to winkle out the best he had to offer. To decide a level at which to pitch the first questions, each lad's performance in a previously taken multiple choice paper would be taken as a guide.

On one particular occasion it became very clear very quickly that a previous mark of eighty five per cent on the written paper must have been a fluke. The lad was told his attained mark would stand, but would he co-operate in an experiment by sitting another paper. He did, and again scored a high eighty per cent, but admitted he had guessed all but four of the questions.

I unfortunately had to tell him that he had failed the oral part of his test, and had been recommended for further training. At the same time it was suggested that he might apply his uncanny talents to the football pools. He said he hadn't done so, so far, but he might try.

Some weeks later I had a letter from him, thanking me and enclosing a couple of quid for a drink, as a thanksgiving for a two hundred and fourteen pounds win. I replied and thanked him, suggesting he should increase his stake and not to lose my address.

Reading Station Routine Orders one Monday morning in July, I was interested to read that volunteers were being asked for to present themselves for vetting, with a view to joining a training mission attached to the Lebanese Air Force. That evening Hedy and I discussed the possibilities and the following morning I applied, and by Thursday I was travelling to London to be interviewed by a female member of the A.F.L.I. section at the Air Ministry. She was totally unconcerned as to my qualifications, simply asking did I think my wife would be able to cope with life in the Middle East. I gave her a brief but comprehensive precis of her twenty seven years in Egypt, which elicited a smile and a nod as she wished me good luck and a safe journey home.

Within a week we were leaving Lytham for Hythe for four days leave during which we should report to Hawkinge for inoculations before reporting to Stansted Airport to fly to the Lebanon.

We had decided that Rolfe would eventually join us, and Mother a little reluctantly agreed to look after him meanwhile. So in August, on a fine cloudless day, we took off in an RAF York, together with Bill Sinclair, Jock Findlay, Paddy Pulford and their wives and sundry other passengers, to throb our way south across France to land at Nice, refuel and fly on to Malta. The next day brought a monotonous wave watching trip to Cyprus, where we landed at Nicosia.

Sitting opposite us on the plane had been two young wives flying out to join their husbands in Cyprus, and as we taxied in one of them recognised her husband waiting on the tarmac and jumped up in excitement. As she did so her knickers dropped to the floor and joy turned to red faced embarrassment, which in turn turned to laughter when, as she bent down to lift them up, her friend smilingly asked, "Hardly worth the bother, is it?" She lightly stepped out of them, putting them in her bag as she giggled her way off the plane into the arms of a delighted and lucky army corporal.

To our surprise the four men in our party were transferred to a Lebanese Air Force De Havilland Dove for the final stage of the journey to Rayak in the Bekaa Valley. But the wives, for some reason of security or procedure, were taken by Middle East Airlines to land at Beirut airport to pass through all normal civilian controls. Eventually arriving by car at Rayak some five hours after the men.

As we were a replacement mission there were no complications on our arrival and our allotted accommodation had been adequately prepared. Four flats in one building, with the clubroom and one other flat close by in another. All situated close to the perimeter track on the far side of the airfield, away from the hangars.

The Bekaa valley lies some fifty kilometres inland from Beirut, with the Lebanese mountains between it and the sea, and the anti-Lebanese mountains to the east, forming the border with Syria.

During the summer months the valley is somewhat arid with the parched greeny brown flora waiting for the winter rains, and then the spring, to change everything dramatically into a burgeoning expanse of colour. And the wooded lands rising to the sometimes snow-capped mountains behind Beirut were a welcome source of relief from the heat of any Mediterranean summer.

Beirut itself was an attractive town, reflecting a strong French influence both in architecture and language, and in the nature of its clubs, shops and outdoor restaurants and casinos. A veritable little Paris by the sea. And to make life even more serene, at this particular time, the country was politically pro-western, especially with the British.

So we had no great problems in settling down and quickly decided that Rolfe should join us. To prevent any hassle for Mother, we contacted the R.S.P.C.A. at home. They co-operated one hundred per cent and offered to supervise his inoculations and his dispatch by air, for a very modest fee of

A SHILLINGSWORTH OF PROMISES

thirty seven pounds. We sent them a cheque for fifty pounds and Rolfe was soon on his way, earning notoriety for a day, as there was a full frontal photograph of him at Heathrow on the front page of the London evening papers under the headline, 'Rolfe flies to the Lebanon'.

His plane arrived late at Beirut and Hedy had to turn on all her charm to sweetheart the airport staff into releasing him straight away. They did, and then, having signed the paperwork we were able to free him from his crate. He immediately baptised a handy bush with a powerful, pungent and well directed and time consuming piddle, before he jumped nonchalantly into the car, to spend the whole journey back to Rayak in a mood of resentful affection.

The arrival at the end of September of Flight Lieutenant Geoffrey Weeks and Flight Lieutenant Ken Hirst, together with their wives, brought the mission up to full strength, including Flight Sergeant Tonks, a 'left over' from the previous mission.

The Lebanese Air Force at this time was quite small and the object of the mission was simply one of training, both on the ground and in the air. The Lebanese ground staff were a mixture of servicemen and civilians, working well together and with us.

But language did cause a few hiccups for communication was restricted in the main to either Arabic or French. There were a few, however, that did speak English, one being Fouad Khairella, a fine mechanic with a flair for correctly diagnosing the most complicated of faults. He also constantly tried to improve his English, one day posing the question, "What's the difference between 'slowing down' and 'slowing up'"? I wasn't able to satisfy him, or myself for that matter.

Our 'living out' status meant that we had to organise regular shopping trips to Zahle. A compact, busy town about ten kilometres away, tree lined and beautiful. It provided most of our wants, including a small hospital. Shopping for pleasure or for amusement meant a visit to Beirut, to enjoy the cinema, the beaches and the larger shops, where all European brands were readily available. And the cinema had most of the later releases, 'Seven Brides for Seven Brothers' springing to mind.

A monthly trip to Nicosia in the Dove completed our shopping requirements, when both the club bar and the families could restock with spirits and fags at N.A.A.F.I. prices.

The winter of 1953/54 turned out to be quite severe, the mountains quickly becoming snow covered, and Rayak itself had a foot of snow, enjoyed by Rolfe if not by anyone else. But his main worry was a lack of local trees.

So with an early spring and the help of Monsieur Fournier, the French caretaker, gardener and general factotum, we managed to provide him with a choice of four, all planted within sniffing distance of our front door.

It was then only a matter of time before ambition tempted us to dig over the adjoining patch and plant beds of Zinnias, Love-Lies-Bleeding and Hollyhocks. And the fertility of the soil was such that they grew quickly and healthily to full bloom, the Hollyhocks reaching a height of ten feet or so. Later, in late spring, Monsieur Fournier and Hedy were busy planting beans and peas, these too quickly reached fruition and our dinner plates. And the seeds of Hedy's enthusiasm for gardening in later life had also been well and truly planted.

By now we were all settled in, with each family organising its own off duty pleasures and leaves. But most evenings the bar would be the main attraction, with an occasional 'do' being expertly planned by Geoffrey Weeks and his wife Gay, when there would be an influx of invitees from Beirut.

One of whom, after one particular party, accused Hedy of nearly killing him. For on his way back, and as he was enjoying a tyre squealing descent around the hairpin bends into Beirut, he suddenly remembered the punch line of one of her not-so-clean jokes, burst out laughing and came within inches of becoming airborne. The routine of training and servicing was running smoothly, except for the eternal delay in getting spares. But the routine was enlivened now and then with a trip or test flight with Ken Hirst. With a little too much enlivenment when, on one occasion when, landing a Harvard trainer, he dug the nose in after making a perfect touch down, and I had to struggle for ages before I could open a slammed shut hood and jump out.

He was a bit shaken and disgusted with himself and, looking at me he asked, "Are you alright? You should be, you're looking calm enough." I didn't bother to tell him it was probably because my normal pulse rate was only fifty two and, remembering Tubby Hilton and Iraq, I consolingly remarked, "Don't worry, It's not the first time. I'm getting used to it." His answer was quite short. "Balls!"

After lunch some few weeks later I worried Hedy by complaining of acute stomach pains. Doctor Daoud was called and he quickly diagnosed appendicitis, and within the hour I was in the little hospital at Zahle having my pubics shaved off by a young Palestinian.

The hospital was not exactly primitive, but maybe just a little unorthodox. For when the time came for the operation, I was invited, clad only in a cotton smock, to follow my Palestinian shaver to the operating room, where

A SHILLINGSWORTH OF PROMISES

I was taken over by a friendly Italian nun, who told me to lie down on the operating table. She then needled me in the shoulder and the next thing I knew was waking up in bed minus my appendix and hearing Hedy enquiring as to my health.

All went well except the semi-liquid diet caused flatulence and pain, which was relieved by my Palestinian pal pushing a well greased rubber tube up my arse until it reached the offending pocket of gas. During my stay this performance was repeated several times and whenever I rang the bell, all that was needed was a nod, and he would, with a wide grin, carry on until the whooshing noise of escaping gas and a sigh of relief told him all was well.

I felt even better when, some few weeks later, we had a surprise visitor from Cairo. It was Sylvia, Erica's twenty-two-year-old daughter. She was gorgeous, laughed easily and had legs that only dreams are made of. And her large blue eyes truly and beautifully reflected an outgoing and affectionate nature. From the very beginning we got on well together and gravitated towards each other on every possible occasion. It was electric, but I couldn't turn on the switch, I was married to her aunt. So we just lit a candle and left it at that. And then, sadly and soon, and after an uncle and niece embrace, she returned to Cairo, to Erica and the business, and to her French boyfriend André.

The Lebanese, in order to improve their training facilities, had ordered three Chipmunk trainers from the UK. They duly arrived in a varied assortment of crates, and we spent several interesting weeks unravelling the jigsaw and assembling them. Two Vampire jet aircraft also arrived but they, thank the Lord, had turned up on the wing and of course became a major source of interest. We were also joined by Squadron Leader Fell, the jet flying instructor, and his wife, making a total of eight families in comfortable exile.

Sylvia (aged 21) by the Red Sea, together with the legs etc that so affected me...

We had naturally been in constant touch with Erica, and everything had been arranged for us to take a three week break in Cairo for the 1954 Christmas.

The time for our departure duly arrived and as we were waiting for the taxi to take us to Beirut, a Lebanese army lorry turned up, carrying live turkeys, one for each family, and each with a card carrying seasonal greetings from General Chehab, the Commander-in-Chief of the Lebanese armed forces.

As Hedy quickly told Jeannette, our 'femme de menage', how to deal with it, I slipped the card into my breast pocket and we left for Beirut, to arrive some three hours before the boat was due to leave for Alexandria, giving us time to get comfortably settled on board.

But the passport control officer had other ideas. Hedy had no trouble but my passport seemed to be puzzling him. I was in civvies and he wanted to know how I had entered the Lebanon, for my passport carried no indication as to how I had arrived there.

Hedy of course, on arrival, had passed through all controls, but as I had been flown direct from Nicosia to Rayak in a military aircraft my passport had no entry stamp. I tried to explain what had happened but without success and, pending enquiries, I was detained in a dark and dismal adjoining room.

Thinking of ways to prove that my presence in the Lebanon was indeed valid, I remembered the card from General Chehab that had accompanied the turkey. I then claimed that I was in the Lebanon as a guest of the General and produced the card to prove it. Within minutes I joined a very worried Hedy in the outer office, and we boarded the boat with just ten minutes to spare. I kept the card in my passport for months, and wondered where I might have finished up had I not fortuitously pocketed it.

The following day and after patiently going through the nit-picking formalities of the Egyptian passport and customs controls, we were met by André, Sylvia's boyfriend. A black haired Mediterranean type, with penetrating brown eyes and an easy smile. Obviously and defensively ambitious. And, as we were to learn years later, even his own father had described him as having a tendency 'de peter plus haut que son cul' which, in acceptable classical English would mean 'to fart higher than his arse'.

The drive to Cairo was fast and luckily uneventful, but in the city itself Monsieur Macho took over, driving with total disdain for other drivers and any traffic laws. He was a Parisian, so how else should he drive?

There was a slight but pleasant churning of the stomach at being once again back in 26 Sharia Antikhana amongst so many old friends. Erica, with the tightest of hugs and a few tears, released two and a half years of emotion and affection and in no time at all 1950 seemed but yesterday. With of

A SHILLINGSWORTH OF PROMISES

course the addition of a new found and loveable niece, who disappointed everyone and eventually herself by marrying her once divorced Latin lover some sixteen months later.

After the Christmas festivities, and early in 1955, I somewhat reluctantly joined the others on a visit to the pyramids. My brain told me that I was close to one of the wonders of the world, and treading the ground of the Ancients, but my mind made little, if any, response.

Apart from the fact that the pyramids are there and have been for four and a half thousand years, nobody knows exactly how or precisely why they were built. Except that they are tombstones, grandiose, gigantic and geometrically perfect, standing stark, silent and sacred in the desert, supposedly providing the necessary comforts for a kingly afterlife. A massive monument to a massive waste of human endeavour, as viewed from the 1990s – but well worth seeing.

And to prove I had, and to aid and abet the commercialisation of the place, I uncomplainingly took part in the obligatory group photograph, choosing a horse instead of a camel. A sad faced little Arab lad dutifully squatting in front, held a numbered card for identification, and looked almost as bored as the overloaded little donkey standing next to him. On our way back to Cairo we stopped at the Mena House hotel for tea, and whilst relaxing

January 1955: Erica, Dina (a friend), Sylvia, Hedy, André, myself.

in the garden a thought that we've all had came to mind. That is that the past is very dead and the future has yet to be born, leaving only a transient and fleeting present. Not much we can do about it, except to get on with it, and so we do. That's why Erica, in dealing with the near future or a prenatal present, had booked a box at the Cairo Opera House, and why two days later, barring accidents, we would all be spending an evening watching the opera 'Porgy and Bess' as performed by a superlative cast of black Americans.

I was no connoisseur and expected to be bored to death. But I was never so wrong, being hypnotised by it all, the atmosphere, the faultless singing, the story, and the infectious enthusiasm of Hedy on one side and Sylvia on the other. It was a total conversion.

We went back to the hotel in high spirits to enjoy a late supper and a few drinks before going to bed around two o'clock. About an hour later we went to sleep, such is the power of a perfect performance.

With the holiday over, on the 11th of January, Hedy and I again said our good-byes and left Egypt for the last time to return to the Lebanon. By coincidence, on entry we were met by the same passport control officer, but this time he was all smiles saying, "Ah the Air Force", as he wielded his stamp with repetitive accuracy, allowing me, after eighteen months, to legally enter the Lebanon.

In February Hedy suffered excessive menstrual bleeding and Doctor Daoud, who was also the hospital surgeon, insisted that a hysterectomy was the only solution. Hedy quickly and willingly accepted, especially on learning that her sex life would not be unduly affected, and it might even be enhanced. Just the same, she said she would like to know and to see exactly what had been taken away.

Within days she was in hospital at Zahle, in the same room that I had had. She also arrived on the operating table in much the same way as I had, but there were two sympathetic nuns to look after her, as well as my young Palestinian wind expert.

The operation was a total success and in the evening I went to the hospital to find Hedy resting quietly in bed but still not totally recovered from the ether. The air was thick and the attendant nurse was having great difficulty in not nodding off, and was visibly relieved to see me. Hedy gave me a hazy greeting and shakily pointed to the bedside locker. I wasn't sure what she wanted exactly, but on opening the door I quickly found out. It was a kidney bowl containing the results of Doctor Daoud's surgical excavations. Not much to look at but enough to reassure Hedy that what she had left would eventually be operational.

Inside ten days she was back at home, recuperating and taking things easy. And I began to learn to cook, all the time remembering my brother's advice, 'Never know where the pots and pans are kept, for the next thing you know you'll be using them – it's fatal'. I needn't have worried for I quickly learnt to like it, claiming that if you can read a recipe then you should be able to cook. But I imagine some of the deified French chefs, fiddling about with their fancy sauces, would argue about that.

It took but six weeks or so for Hedy to return to her cheerful self and, as we were now within three to four months of having to return to the U.K., we invited Erica to spend a holiday with us. The Lebanon, with its beautiful and diverse scenery soon captivated her. And the good progress Hedy had made, made it possible for us to travel about to see and appreciate some of the better known tourist hot spots.

Our first trip followed the well travelled road to Beirut, where we headed north along the coast road to Tripoli, sandwiched between the blue Mediterranean and the foothills to the right, largely and beautifully covered with olive trees, fruit trees and vineyards.

We were heading for the famous 'Cedars of Lebanon', so at Tripoli we turned into the winding road leading up to Beharre. Stopping now and then to drink from the cool fresh water springs shooting out from the rock face. They are reputed to have the purest waters on our planet, and this I could well believe. But the cedars themselves were rather sparse. Hardly surprising since the original forests had been used for boat building since the Phoenicians ruled the trade routes. And each individual tree, although grand, would not match up to the thick trunked, old and beautiful specimen that once stood in the vicarage garden opposite the Saltwood church, where Father is buried.

We happily made our way back to Rayak, feeling touristically content, to have a whisky sour sundowner on the veranda before bedding down to dream our way to tomorrow.

After a day's rest we travelled just twenty five kilometres further up the Bekaa valley to Baalbek to see what is left of the temples of Jupiter and Bacchus. Not a lot. Jupiter, master of the Gods, now has six sixty foot columns; and the God of Wine, forty six, all of about the same height. But the accuracy of the masonry work in the walls was astonishing. Stone blocks tailored perfectly to fit one to the other, the heaviest being some four hundred and fifty cubic metres and weighing about two thousand tons, making the stone blocks of the pyramids look miniscule.

To finish Erica's quick tour we finally took the road to Damascus, encountering major resistance at the Syrian border. I would have turned back but the two sisters smiled our way through and we continued. Only to stay maybe an hour mooching through bazaars not unlike those in Cairo, before we returned to Rayak. At least we could say that we had made some sort of cursory contact with Biblical history.

Erica stayed on for a few days longer, in the meantime becoming acquainted with our hectic social life. A chatty bridge evening with the Hirsts, a mildly lubricated hour in the club, or just a cosy evening at home. Plus of course all the excitement of a few shopping trips.

Naturally there was a sadness when she eventually had to leave, all the more so because our futures were uncertain, and we had no idea when we would all meet again. However, when the time came most of our tears were stoically held back, but the ache of the parting remained with us for days.

We now had another sad good-bye to look forward to, for we had decided that Rolfe's quarantine in the UK would span our own return. So he would be flown back three months before us, leaving only three more months to wait after our own arrival. After making arrangements with Hackbridge kennels near Croydon, the poor lad was reintroduced to his crate, and he made it clear he knew what that meant. But it had to be done, and we took him to Beirut airport, making sure all the paperwork was complete, so that there would be the minimum of delay before he took off. As we watched his aircraft disappear into the distance poor Hedy burst into tears and was barely consolable for days.

But the time for our own departure was fast approaching, and we all progressively prepared for the actual event. Geoffrey Weeks had bravely decided to drive back to the U.K. in his old Hillman Minx. So it was closely inspected and serviced, complete with an engine top overhaul and all seemed well. But the harsh roads of Turkey broke his half-shaft, turning his planned adventure into a series of frustrating but memorable episodes, involving on the spot negotiations, mostly in mime, before he was finally able to ferry his troubles to Italy.

The rest of us were soon saying good-bye to our Lebanese friends, and taking the road over the mountains to Beirut. Hearing for the last time the symphony of screeching tyres as we made the hairpinned descent to the airport. We all sailed through the passport control with no trouble to board an old Dakota for the trip to Nicosia.

Bad weather over Europe kept us pleasantly anchored on the ground for two days before a civilian Hermes took us yawning on our way to Rome. The bad weather was still hanging around over Europe, for, after a delay of about two hours, we took off and quickly found ourselves flying through, and being battered by, a thunder storm. It was a rough ride, and all the passengers kept on the qui-vive, except Hedy who slept, blissfully, as the rest of us twitched our way to Stansted. We arrived late in the afternoon and, after clearing immigration and customs, we all caught the coach to London.

After the carefree, bright and sunny life of the past two years one couldn't help noticing how dowdy and unhappy everyone looked as we travelled through the villages into the suburbs of London. Their clothes, their shopping bags, the prams, everything gave the impression that the austerity of the war years was still with us, and that the intervening ten years had improved little.

It was now too late in the day to travel on to Hythe so we bed and breakfasted at the Charing Cross Hotel, deciding to leave early in the morning. We did, but not for Hythe, for Hedy was aching to see Rolfe, so we went immediately to the kennels at Hackbridge. The dear lady in charge at the time happened to be a Continental, so there was a quick meeting of souls, and she was full of praise for Rolfe, as was his kennel maid. And he knew it, for when he saw us he gave us just one resentful glance and a patronising half wag before giving his whole attention to his new girl friends. We could have been on the moon for all he cared.

Hedy of course was sadly disappointed, and only slightly reassured when I tried to explain that all pets are notoriously fickle, and in any case he had reason, for the poor lad had certainly been shunted around a bit in his short life. And by chance, before we left, we bumped into a newly retired army major, who also had a bull terrier in quarantine and he too had been summarily rejected. And his dog had been with him for nine years, so Hedy felt just a little less offended.

This time, as we travelled through Kent, we were able to study, almost in minute detail, the beauty of the Garden of England, for our train to Hythe was rather more than slow, and stopped at every station. But eventually we slowly slipped into and stopped at Sandling Junction, where we were picked up by Newman's station bus and taken direct to 28 Cobden Road. This bus trip replaced the old branch line to Hythe, a beautiful mile or so of track running through a virtual tunnel of trees and bushes and a pleasantly perfect end to any journey. It had ceased to exist some four years earlier. However, the bus trip was fair compensation, for it too passed through the glorious hinterland of Hythe.

Dear old Mother, placid and loving as ever, welcomed us once again with open heart, and with a home ship shape and shiny and filled with the lovely residual smell of a day's baking.

We naturally and quickly settled in, and this time there were no ablutionary surprises for Hedy, except how to deal with a wet English summer. After a few soakings at bus stops, and a few trips staggering home with saturated shopping, we decided to buy our first car. Something to match the size of our bank balance. So we bought an Austin A30 for around four hundred and eighty pounds. It was just about the right size for two short-arses, Hedy being five foot one and me just five foot six. But we had to wait a week for the chosen colour, and then the car was delivered to the door.

I had almost the same sort of morale lift that I'd experienced when, twenty eight years ago, my brand new bike had arrived. Then I cycled off to Hastings, this time I took a quick familiarisation trip to Seabrook, along the Prince's Parade where, in my cycling schoolboy days there was only a rough track over what was left of the old horse drawn tramway. Three days later came the big initiation, and we all went to Southsea to visit brother Bert. He simply observed, "Neat, isn't it? Petrol or clockwork?"

Having spent some nine hours over the last two days sitting on our bottoms, it was our legs that called for exercise, so we attempted to retrace some of my old rambles. None of which turned out to be quite the same, some being impenetrably overgrown and others built on. Even the seafront stroll, with all the seats and railings torn out and the asphalt unrepaired for years, was almost a voyage of discovery. Poor Hythe. I tentatively tried to introduce Hedy to the rigours of beach fishing and, to my surprise, her casual interest turned to total dedication after she experienced her first catch, a one and a half pound Channel whiting. And then, fully equipped with new and up to date rods and reels, we spent days at Dungeness, quickly becoming expert enough to cast the necessary seventy yards or so.

As Dungeness in those days was relatively remote, some twenty or thirty anglers would have plenty of space to enjoy their sport, and we all became pretty well known to each other. Hedy becoming particularly popular, for they seemed to appreciate her friendly and accented chat, and her peculiar theories as to where the fish were, or weren't, and as she usually out-caught all of us, nobody argued.

My own enthusiasm for fishing centred not so much on the fish, but more on the fresh air and the long blank minded periods of relative inactivity. The psychology of the angler is really quite hard to understand, for if every cast brought a fish then it would be monotonous, on the other hand if nothing is caught it becomes equally monotonous. So the object of the sport revolves around a theory of relativity, but hardly a job for a latter day Einstein.

At the end of our leave Hedy would have to stay on for a while at Hythe, until I found a place to live. So to help pass the time we thought it might be a good idea to teach her how to row. A forlorn hope, for after several hours of patient and detailed instruction, she got no further than rowing from one side to the other, and never under but always into bridges. We quickly agreed that whilst I was away, any travelling along the canal would be by bank and not by boat.

My posting notice arrived early in September, and the following Sunday I drove up to Sutton Bridge on the Wash, to take up duty with No. 56 Maintenance Unit. The function of the unit being to carry out major repairs that were outside the capacity of the holding unit. And I was to have the privilege and responsibility, as a qualified A.I.S. Inspector, to help supervise, check and certify the work done.

My first 'on site' location was at Oakington near Cambridge, and finding somewhere to live in that area was virtually impossible. That's how we eventually found ourselves living in a caravan on a poultry farm, not only close to the airfield but actually bordering it. The caravan at first seemed to be a little restrictive, but adequate enough for two people to be together, as long as they ignored or encouraged a bit of bumping and boring now and then. Our only real complaint was the way the geese cohabited right under the van at night, seeming to take hours before they stopped bonking the floor. But our major worry was Rolfe, for dogs of course were prohibited. So at the first opportunity we went to Hackbridge to discuss with our continental friend the possibility of boarding him after his quarantine period had ended.

But this proved to be impossible, and our problem was no nearer a solution, except we agreed that, as a last resort, we would try to find another owner for him. A while later and when paying a flying visit to Hackbridge we learnt that the retired army major's dog had unexpectedly died. As the major knew Rolfe quite well, we quickly got in touch with him, explaining our problem. He sympathised and immediately agreed to take him, and we overwhelmed him with thanks, meanwhile consoling ourselves just a little by realising that Rolfe, anyway over the last five months, had grown away from us. He subsequently led a very settled life, sharing the major's retirement on a farm somewhere in Sussex.

A somewhat hectic 1955 came to an end, and midway through 1956 my detachment at Oakington ended and I returned to Sutton Bridge to take a permanent job at the base, as Flight Sergeant in charge of local trade training and testing. The job I liked, but the rest made me glad that I was within months of completing my twenty five years of service.

I very quickly found a flat in King's Lynn and Hedy rejoined me. The ten mile journey to and from work each day helped me considerably in my mental preparation for re-instatement to civilian life. And the surrounding countryside, the Norfolk coast and our little car gave us ample opportunity to appreciate the tranquillity, the fresh sea air and the beauty of that corner of England. Enjoyed equally by the occupants of Sandringham House, us, and a few thousand others.

One of the others being Hedy's nephew Yurg from Zurich. He had hitch-hiked all the way he said, and his feet pungently supported the claim. On his return, and to save some thumb work, we took him to Harwich to catch a late night ferry. Coming back in the early hours and just north of Norwich, Hedy had to have a wee, and within seconds of her disappearing into the bushes a police car came from nowhere and pulled up in front.

"Evening. Not in trouble, are we?"

"No, officer."

"Why are we parked here then, not leaving rubbish in the hedge are we?"

"No, not exactly..."

Before I could finish Hedy reappeared from the hedge and, as she pulled down her skirt she gave our surprised friend a big smile and a big 'thank you for the compliment', and we drove off.

Hedy had now been in England long enough to start wondering about some of the war time guests that had enjoyed their hardships at the Pension Suisse. It was a long list and I was unable to help her very much, except for a couple of names that were familiar to me. One being Jasper Maskelyn, connected with Maskelyn and Devants theatre of magic in London, and the other Jeffrey Barling, the Newmarket trainer.

We were unsuccessful in making contact with Jasper Maskelyn, but her phone call to Newmarket brought instant recognition and an invitation for an evening visit. I knew Hedy loved horses, preferring the smell of a good horse to that of a good man. So that, together with our host's obvious delight in retelling and reliving events in war time Cairo, ensured a successful evening. Mrs Barling, with a question here and there, was also pleased and amused to be able to put some meat on the bones of her husband's Cairean war stories.

Our quick escorted trip around the stables brought nothing direct from the horse's mouth, but the atmosphere of it all was exciting, although nothing was actually going on. The only stable I had been near prior to this was Twiddly Twyman's tiny establishment in Prospect Road at Hythe, when I had been sweethearted by Hedy to put my leg over and accompany her on a trek to Saltwood castle and back.

Our journey back to King's Lynn was uncomfortable, for the wet roads kept sludging up our windscreen, for we had wipers but no washers. So on my next day off we drove to the Austin agent in one of King's Lynn's delightfully old and pedestrian filled little back streets to change our A30 for an A35. It was not only plus five but plus a windscreen washer, and that was more to the point.

Hedy also wanted another dog, and this time we chose a small black and white Sheltie and we called him Rolfie. A timid but beautiful little dog who quickly became a force to be reckoned with. For whenever I wanted to read the Sunday papers, he wanted to run around the Sandringham woods. He always won and he always came back smelling of the wonders of the woodland, like hedgehog and fox crap.

Christmas 1956 brought us the news that Erica was now running the Pension Suisse on her own, with the help of a Greek manager, for Sylvia had married Andre in April, had promptly got herself pregnant and was now living, temporarily, in a hotel at Porte D'Orleans on the outskirts of Paris, where Patricia was born on the 19th of January 1957.

The 20th of September 1957 now became my target date, for then I would have completed a quarter of a century with the RAF and a possible half of my life. I had no idea as to what the future would bring, except that we both agreed that it should have a degree of security. So that excluded the idea of taking any high paid job with only short term prospects. So as a safety net, I applied to take the Civil Service entrance examination for Clerical Officers, a better name being clerks. My technical superiors were astounded and critical, in some ways they were right, but in the finality they were wrong.

The months passed slowly, but with great excitement for, after fifteen years as a Flight Sergeant I was 'promoted' to do a Corporal's job as a right guide and marker on the A.O.C.'s annual march past. And on a couple of occasions I had the pleasure of being N.C.O. in charge of the Church Parade, marching twenty or so men a half mile to and from the local church, making sure that any atheists, agnostics or members of alternative faiths knew that they could, if they wished, wait outside with me. None did and neither did I for it rained on both occasions.

I did, however, glean some satisfaction from these last months, for quite a few of the young lads I had been training were successful in their exams and were remustered into higher grades.

Having been notified of the date for the Civil Service exam I naturally made a forgettable mental note. But fortunately, as I was preparing to drive to work on that particular day, Hedy suddenly asked, "Shouldn't you be in Norwich today?" I quickly phoned the camp and we took off together for Norwich, arriving just in time to park the car in the market place and to search out the examination centre, which was in one of the side roads running off from the market place. The examination was over by four o'clock, giving us time for a quick look around Norwich and a light tea before driving back to King's Lynn.

By August the only joy a working day brought was the pleasant ten mile drive to and from Sutton bridge, passing through Clenchwarton and Terence St Clements, which was rumoured to have more banks than pubs. Farmers, it would seem, had many hardships to put up with.

Arriving one morning at the camp during this winding down period, I had a phone call from the orderly room. The adjutant wanted to see me. He was a very young Flying Officer and of post war vintage. His office door was open. I knocked and was invited to enter.

"Flight Sergeant Hitchcock?"

"Yes sir."

"This came with the morning post. I don't know what it's all about, but it's for you."

I picked it up and read the covering letter, which briefly told me that the Lebanese government had awarded me the 'Lebanese Silver Medal of Merit'. The small scroll accompanying it was in Arabic so I had no idea what it said. I looked up at the Adjutant and waited for him to say something. "You'd better sign for it, hadn't you?"

It seemed he thought it to be some sort of inventory item. I controlled my disgust, signed, saluted and left. I prized the award, eventually giving it to the RAF museum at Hendon. It was, and is, the only one they have.

On my final day, the 20th of September, I drove into work as usual. At midday the members of the sergeant's mess presented me with a suitably engraved pewter drinking mug and many good wishes for the future.

I collected my discharge papers from the orderly room and drove home, getting happier by the mile. And thinking that if ever someone were to ask me, "Did you enjoy Service life?" I would have trouble as to what level I should pitch the horse laugh. But if the question were phrased somewhat differently, "Did you enjoy your life in the Service?" Then the answer would be an enthusiastic and unequivocal "Yes!"

7   *Changing jobs, homes & gear*

Hedy, home and Hythe spelt happiness, so I was in no hurry to do anything other than enjoy each moment as it came, free from any restrictive exigencies emanating from the ones above. But we were constrained to a degree by the abrupt drop in income, which now had two elements. An RAF pension of three pounds fourteen shillings a week, and the dole, bringing the total to about five pounds.

The dole office was next to the Co-op at the far eastern end of the High Street where, on my first visit to sign on, I met two of my contemporaries waiting to be dealt with. These same two were well known to be 'dole happy' even before I left to join the RAF I had the urge but not the courage to give life to the thought going through my head, for they both looked as if it might be true.

As the post office was at the extreme western end of the High Street, it meant that, after I had drawn my dole money and walked through the High Street to do the week's shopping, I would be just about skint by the time I reached the post office. But there I would draw my pension to rejoin the ranks of the newly rich.

Living about fifty yards away in Theresa Road were Jack and Joan Hayman. He was an aircraft maintenance engineer working with Silver City Airlines and they operated a car air ferry service to France from Lydd Airport. So Jack and I spent an evening or two together to give me an insight as to how civilian airlines functioned. As a result I wrote to Silver City and the reply promised an interview should a vacancy arise.

Another cross channel air service was being formed at this time, a coach–air–coach link between London and Paris, operating through Lympne airport. I answered a local advertisement for staff and was invited for an interview. It must have been one of the shortest on record, for the interviewer's opening question was, "Are you an engine or airframe engineer?" I told him I was concerned with both and had been since 1935. To which he contemptuously asserted, "That's impossible." I didn't argue, but stood up, gave him a smile and a 'good morning', and returned home to pick up Hedy and to spend the rest of the day fishing.

I had already turned down an offer from Power Jets Limited, a technical school dealing solely with jet engines. They had been given my name by the RAF and they wanted a semi-technical dogsbody to do jobs ranging from making and maintaining sectioned models to operating their cinema equipment. With a footnote saying that I would also be expected to collect and return trainees to and from Reading Station.

I had two more interviews. At Bachelor's newly-opened factory at Ashford, the interviewer asked, "What were your wages in your last job?"

Telling the truth I said, "Seventeen pounds four shillings."

His reply came derisive and quick. "You'll get nothing like that here, mate." As he obviously thought I was some sort of button polishing moron, I didn't give him the chance to prove it.

The second interview was with the Metal Box Company, and at the designated rendezvous a whole gaggle of blokes were hanging about behind a huge lorry, inside which the interviews were being conducted. I quickly decided the Metal Box Company and myself had nothing to offer each other.

I was now beginning to feel, not exactly desperate, but a little perturbed that any future and averagely secure job would again take me away from my roots. So when the Civil Service Commission wrote to me to let me know that I had been successful in the examination and that a post was available in the Valuation Office at Orpington from the first of January 1958, I accepted, albeit with some resignation. And as a half way solution to the roots problem we took a flat in Ashburnham Road, Tonbridge.

Just as we were leaving 28 Cobden road on the 31st of December to go to Tonbridge, a letter offering an interview at Lydd arrived. But the die had been cast and we left. This decision eventually turned out to be the right one, for Silver City, the new coach–air–coach link and Power Jets Limited all ceased to function within a few years. Bachelors and Metal Box survived but that caused me no heart searching.

Within a month of settling in at the Orpington Office I was transferred to Bexleyheath and the fifty two mile journey there and back each day became tedious, even hostile in fog and snow. So I took a half day off to search for another home. But this time it would be our own, ideally about five miles into the country away from any thickly built up areas.

The search took me to Larksfield Road, Hartley, to a brand new semi-detached bungalow with cesspool drainage, no garage and a pot-holed unmade road. It was heaven enough, and an immediate fifty pounds deposit with the agent in Dartford secured the deal. I drove right foot down back to Tonbridge to break the news to a delighted Hedy. Then, after raising a fifteen hundred pounds mortgage, we coughed up the remaining five hundred and fifty pounds and exchanged contracts within three weeks.

Now came the problem, for having bought a new home, it needed to be furnished with every single item from dish cloths to beds, and there was less than two hundred pounds in the bank. So I applied to the Air Ministry to commute part of my pension. This they agreed to, but would only commute enough to settle the bills for household effects, and only then after I had passed a medical examination to make sure that I was not likely to drop dead before they had got their money back.

So we ordered each and every item we could think of and, after taking delivery we sent all the bills, amounting to about five hundred and eighty pounds, direct to the Air Ministry.

They paid the bills and I lost fifteen shillings a week from my pension, which means they had given me a life expectancy of fourteen years. They are already twenty one years to the good, and at 1958 prices that means a loss of eight hundred and fifty pounds to date, or at today's prices, at least eleven thousand. Hardly a brilliant deal but in retrospect it was maybe worth it.

When we eventually moved in and with all bills paid we had seventy two pounds eight and fourpence in the bank, but not for long, for we reduced that to four pounds six and a penny when we bought a television set. So we had everything and we were still solvent.

The RAF pension just paid for the mortgage, so for a few years we lived according to the gospel of Saint Micawber. And practically every minute of our time was spent in changing our virgin plot into something resembling a garden. I erected pre-fabricated fences, an asbestos garage and a garden shed. Hedy planted hedges and turfed the front garden. A bit of crazy paving fronting a low transverse wall, and twenty yards of concrete path killed off this initial burst of back breaking enthusiasm.

Winter came and we transferred our attention to the inside, coving each room, papering the ceilings and finally the walls. All done with the facile ease of two non-critical amateurs, notwithstanding the tendency of long lengths of coving, unless held in position with brooms, to slip away from the corners. Plasterboard nails finally stopped this nonsense. And watching Hedy, the tri-lingual sophisticate, dressed only in slacks, bra and bath cap, bravely fighting a rebellious length of slippery anaglypta, was heart-warmingly funny. Dressed the same way but minus the bra, I joined her and within three weeks of part time effort we eventually finished the job. And in spite of the inexperience and innovation it looked passably professional.

With the home now ready and fit to receive visitors, Mother came to stay for a couple of weeks, together with her two remaining sisters, May and Vi, the oldest and the youngest of the family. They so enjoyed being together that, at the end of their visit, they all went back to Hythe to spend a week or so by the sea.

They hadn't been in Hythe for more than four days when Aunt Vi wanted to go home. So I drove down immediately to take both May and Vi back to Wimbledon. Within six weeks my two dear old aunts had me chasing up to town to take them back to Hythe for another dose of sea air. After just a week they wanted to go home again.

This farce happened just once more, but this time I insisted on knowing why Aunt Vi always found it so necessary to return. It turned out that her life's savings were hidden in little bags, pinned behind her furniture, and she got sad and agitated if she were separated from them for too long. There were no more seaside outings, for I easily convinced her that she would be far happier watching her wardrobes than watching waves.

In August 1960 Erica was in Paris visiting Sylvia, who had spent the three previous years in Rio de Janeiro, and was now living in Paris until her husband took up his new job in Greece. So the girls were able to pay us a quick visit, all three of them, for Patricia was now three and a half years old. A dark-eyed, bright and lively child who quickly captivated us and our neighbours, who sympathetically tolerated the desecration of their flower and vegetable plots as she chased after our new cat, Bella. And Bella would show no appreciation whatsoever to any cooing French flattery, just gazing back at Patricia with that natural supercilious look that all cats have when exercising their divine right to the best that's going.

Sylvia was as attractive and enticing as ever, but was showing signs that the dominating demands of a macho French husband were eating into her own self confidence and sense of worthiness. A point quickly proven when, after she had been with us for less than a week, he sent a curt and authoritative letter demanding that she return immediately.

So after two more days all five of us and the luggage were squeezed into our little A35 for the trip to Heathrow. Then within two and a half hours Andre's family, plus a disgusted and angry mother-in-law, were back under his jealous control. We saw Erica again, and quite frequently, but it was to be some six years before we were to meet up once more with Sylvia.

During their short stay with us, and on a tourists' tour of Kent, we had naturally called in at 28 Cobden Road to visit Mother. She was delighted and happy to meet Hedy's family but puzzled me a little by saying that she was so glad that she had had the time to get to know them.

I had now been with the Valuation Office for twenty months, and I was beginning to doubt the wisdom of my choice. And the thought of being

A SHILLINGSWORTH OF PROMISES

desk bound for years made me seriously consider early retirement. But the introduction of a new range of duties involving outdoor work saved the situation. This new work involved the inspection of properties ranging from houses to factories, to prepare plans, record details of construction, and obtain all other relevant information required by the professional valuers to form their opinions of value. The work was sufficiently diverse and interesting to give me the incentive to carry on. More so because it meant contact with people in all their moods, mostly semi or totally hostile.

Even being told on one occasion when approaching an open door to "Go. Go away, leave me alone". Seconds later a red faced but smiling young housewife invited me in and introduced me to her myna bird, who promptly let her down again by telling me in a slightly deeper tone to "Get 'em off". Trying to help, I suggested, "He's a bit of a sexy lad, isn't he?" By way of explanation she said, "They both are."

As we were now within an hour and a half's drive to the coast, we would often shoot down to Hythe for a weekend to enjoy a few hours fishing, taking picnic meals either on the beach at Dungeness or under the trees on the canal bank, somewhere between Hythe and Lympne Hill.

Mother would usually come with us, but then in October she reluctantly said she didn't feel up to it. When I tried to cajole her into changing her mind she took me upstairs to her room and very quietly and calmly told me that she had been diagnosed as having cancer. She gave me no chance to voice any reaction, simply pleading with me to accept it as she had. She then explained exactly how she had arranged her affairs. So much for this and so much for that, even allowing so much for her funeral and tombstone. All her bills had been paid and she had also packaged the things that her sisters were to have. I was not to tell Hedy until she actually went into hospital, but she would like me to tell my two brothers, Bert in South Africa and Tommy, nearer home in Hayes.

Returning to Hedy downstairs I was amazed to see how naturally Mother carried the conversation. I then realised that her sole concern since she had known the evil truth had been one of total concealment, especially from our wives. But she now knew that the time was fast approaching when they too would have to be told, for the drugged suppression of her pains would soon have to be done in hospital.

And that sadly came all too quickly for Mother was admitted to the Victoria hospital in Folkestone on the 28th of November. On every day that we were able to visit her she would greet us with the softest of smiles, telling us that there was nothing to be sad about as she would leave as she had lived with us, peacefully and happily. She died in the early hours of Monday the 5th of December, and six days later rejoined Father in the churchyard at Saltwood. We planted a small Hydrangea on the grave, their favourite flower, and it's there to this day.

Sorrows never come singly, for when returning home one evening in February 1961 I found Hedy in tears and inconsolable. Poor Rolfie, having found our gate open, had shot off in pursuit of a bitch, and racing across the main road he had run right under the wheels of a passing car, and the unfortunate driver had had no chance. He was himself a dog lover and he brought the lad back in a cardboard box. After the initial shock of breaking the news both he and Hedy shared quite a few tears and a few strong whiskies.

That evening we ate little but talked a lot, deciding that the best thing to do would be to get another dog as quickly as possible. So the following Saturday we drove down to the breeding kennels at Icklesham, between Rye and Hastings, and spent a couple of difficult hours choosing a young brown and white Sheltie puppy. He sat on Hedy's lap all the way back to Hartley and licked his way through her make-up to her heart. We called him Dandy, and within a matter of months he had learnt how to 'stay' at the gate, be it open or shut, even when purposely tempted by a borrowed bitch on heat. I was more than proud of him but hoped his success was due to will power and not simply lack of interest.

The thrice yearly stench when the council tanker came to empty our cesspits was at last to come to an end. For the main drainage system had been completed, and all we as individuals had to do was to pay for our own connection. And by one of those coincidences, the bill for our connection arrived in the same post as a win from Vernon's pools. The bill was for thirty two pounds nine shillings. Not all the money went down the drain directly, for we celebrated with a bottle of plonk and let nature do the rest. Shortly afterwards the road was made up and adopted, ending the daily slalom around the ever deepening pot holes, and bringing us right into the twentieth century.

Often on our walks around Hartley we had been tempted to call in at a bungalow in Stack Lane named 'Berne'. On this particular day, as the lady of the house was pottering in her garden, Hedy couldn't resist a greeting in Swiss. This brought a smile as she replied "It's my husband I think you'd like to speak to". It was, and his immediate delight at being able to chat away in dialect triggered a friendship which lasted the lifetime of both Sam and his wife Millie, who died in 1975, and Sam three years later. Only a month after we had taken him by car to visit his family in Darstetten in the Simmental.

Sam was a son of a poor mountain farmer, and the hard life had sent him in search of a somewhat less bucolic job in Europe. He started from the top room of a Victorian terrace house in London, but after he had eventually realised what all the nightly comings and goings on the lower floors really meant, he moved on. Then, from the lowest rungs of domestic service he progressed upwards to become the butler in various embassies in Sweden, Brazil and Greece. Gathering tolerable fluency in five languages, a wife, and a supreme knowledge of etiquette, which I often fought but never questioned. He was also a 'cordon bleu' cook and he enjoyed the look of appreciation for his cooking as much as he did doing it, so we willingly co-operated and fed his ego as happily as he fed us.

1962 came and with it a visit from brother Bert and his wife Mary, arriving in a motorised caravan on their way to Scotland for their summer holidays, so their stay was short. Long enough though for an appraisal of the bungalow and a good natter, and an attempt to borrow a can of paraffin. I searched our garage but found only a few dregs, and dropping into a not forgotten service vernacular I said,

"Sorry Bert, I've only got a fanny full."

He quickly answered, "That's OK, I've got a five gallon drum."

"I heard that," Mary challenged.

"Sorry love, nothing personal," Bert laughingly replied.

Mary, apparently mollified, climbed into the driver's seat, but as they drove off an apprehensive grin accompanied Bert's wave of good-bye.

Our bank balance now suffered a welcome injection of seventeen hundred pounds from the sale of 28 Cobden Road, so we swapped our A35 for a showy Ford Classic. Then, when pulling up at a house in Danson Road, Bexley, I was greeted at the door by a young housewife saying, "Gorgeous, aren't they?"

I thought she was referring to the car, but it was a Beatles record she was being entranced by.

"H'm Yes," I admitted, adding, "But they won't last long, these new groups never do."

Prophecies should never be based on guess work or disappointment. But I did have more success when forecasting that a close colleague, Don Barker, who had unsuccessfully searched the south east coast for a retirement home, would look no further than a new bungalow in Highfield close, Saltwood. He didn't, and happily lived the rest of his life there, never ceasing to let me know how much he enjoyed the tranquillity and the view across Hythe Bay.

Especially on days when the view was spoilt by the girls from the adjoining school enjoying their hockey.

As Mother's two remaining sisters, Aunts May and Vi, would be alone this Christmas we invited them to join us. May had lost her husband earlier in the year and we had accompanied her to see him in the Chapel of Rest, where she commented that she never realised how tall he really was. The draped lid of his coffin had been drawn back about eighteen inches, misleading poor old aunt May into thinking that uncle Fred was larger in death than in life.

This Christmas was to be a sad one, for on the evening of the 23rd of December and after having enjoyed our evening meal, aunt Vi suddenly collapsed, and remained in a coma. The doctor came and diagnosed a major stroke, and sent her immediately to the Joyce Green hospital in Dartford, where she died on the 27th without ever regaining consciousness. Poor aunt Vi, the timid spinster, she must have missed a lot in life but was never bitter, probably because of the sweet protectiveness of her many sisters. Aunt May, the eldest of the sisters, survived them all. She was the shortest at a mere four foot eleven inches, she was the only one that smoked, the only one that drank, the only one that ever swore, and the only one that never had children. She enjoyed herself to the full until she gave up living and died at the age of eighty four.

The rating revaluation for 1963 had naturally intensified the work at the office, it also involved me in a transfer to a new office at Swanley, which was well within reach of Hartley, so no domestic move was necessary. I had been flattered by being told that they needed a good bloke with a car. But I soon realised it to be quite the reverse, it was a good reliable car they wanted, driven by any sort of bloke, just to help clear their outstanding and outlying cases.

Having sold our old home in Hythe, we now had no base to work from for our fishing trips, so we periodically rented a beach bungalow at Dungeness. It was close to the old lighthouse and called 'Caithness', neatly constructed from old railway coaches camouflaged to a degree with wooden shingles. A comfortable and well used enclosed veranda facing seawards gave greenhouse warmth when the sun shone, and was cosily and completely protective against wind and rain, with a few tentative doubts whenever a strong south westerly blew up.

The area around Hartley being within twenty miles of London, was fast developing into popular commuter country. But it was still peaceful enough

A SHILLINGSWORTH OF PROMISES

to make the routine of life pleasantly acceptable. With the village whist drive the event of the week.

1964 arrived and with it a change of government, and a rather peculiar assumption from the delivery van driver. "You'll soon have to deliver it yourself Tosh, it's the workers turn now mate." I don't know what he had on his mind, but it was certainly some sort of upside down logic. Something like the stock observation, 'The rich get richer and the poor get poorer'. This infers that the rich should get poorer and the poor should get richer. But where does the transition stop? And to assume that some point of balance would be reached and sustained shows a tragic lack of understanding of human nature.

In June Erica finally decided that the difficulties of running the hotel in Nasser's Cairo were too much, so she sold the business and returned to Switzerland and Lausanne. But before attempting to solve the problems of setting up a new life there, she came to us for a period of relaxation.

The two sisters hopefully tried to make contact with some of their wartime friends but had little luck, except to arrange a meeting with a Hackforth-Jones now living in Highbury. They had no luck with Gerald Shaw, the ex-Cairo Odeon organist, or with a Georgie Bastin whom I had met some ten years before when we were in Cairo for the 1954 Christmas. We had entertained him, his wife and daughter when they were visiting Egypt. He and I were in civvies and little did I realise that I was having a noggin with the C-in-C Cyprus.

Erica was introduced to Sam and Millie, and that resulted in several long and revealing journeys back to Sam's birthplace. His stories about the illicit rural rompings in the mountainous and remote villages of his little bit of Switzerland were a mixture of sadness and hilarity, revolving around the ingenuity, success or failure of the temporarily unfaithful in avoiding discovery.

Sam made excuses by saying that anyway, making love is like making money, having done it, it only gives an appetite for more. I accepted his theory, but qualified it a bit by telling him that it was possible that although one might provide happiness and satisfaction, the other might provide neither, and which provided which would not be a matter of choice but a matter of luck.

Sam also regaled us with a story of when he was in Sweden, and became emotionally involved with a young Swedish parlour maid. One evening when she came to his room he felt tired, depressed and unable to react to her overtures. She then became petulantly aggressive, pushed him onto his back, took off her skirt and knickers and silently sat on him. Telling him in accented and basic domesticised English, "If you don't serve me, I 'elp myself."

Sam then quoted the French saying, that 'appetite comes with eating'. We presumed he willingly served a second helping.

Before Erica went back to Lausanne we spent a week at Dungeness, enjoying the silence, the fishing, our composite home, a surfeit of frying pan meals, lengthy aperitifs and daily attempts to clean off a full Mercator's projection of seagull shit from our second new Ford Classic.

With every trip to the coast the urge to return to my roots grew ever stronger. So when an opportunity to transfer to the Dover office was offered I couldn't grab it quick enough. It was a timely and fortuitous coincidence in answer to an oft expressed hope. Had I been at all religious the hope would have been a prayer, albeit a selfish and monotonous one.

We told the good news to Sam and Millie and, although they were disappointed at our leaving, Sam quickly understood. For he himself had fallen in love with Hythe and had been talking it over with Millie in positive terms about moving there. But she being eight years older, thought it was too late, argued against it, and won.

Now came the great joy of choosing a new home in an area I knew so well. There were so many possibilities, so many prices and so little time, for we were in a hurry. I estimated a price of £3,800 for 'Maadi', our Hartley home, but Hedy dealt with the agent and asked for £4,200, and sold it within two days. Proving it's the market and the public that set house prices and not valuers.

Hythe itself proved to be non-productive, sad but true, so we searched a little further afield and found a brand new detached house, number one Tolsford Close, Etchinghill, in the beautiful Elham valley. It was solidly sunk in a sea of mud on a vee-shaped, slightly rising site and looked irretrievably unattractive to me. But Hedy in her mind's eye saw other things, and £3,600 gave her the opportunity to create the picture in reality.

With the help of a young landscape gardener, two teenage assistants, two loads of rocks, two loads of turf and a couple of dozen assorted young trees and bushes, Hedy was able to transform the site within days. It quickly took on the aspect of a mature garden, with a multi-level easily mown 'lawn', a transverse rockery, a peripheral flower border and a line of fir trees topping the bank to Westfield Lane.

It certainly gave the entrance to Tolsford Close a picturesque and lived in look. Making it easier for Mr Ludlow, the developer, to attract attention to his estate. Among those attracted were Mike and Jean Sanders who, later in 1964, bought number 35, and quickly became close friends. And they still are, and they still live in the Close, generously giving us a *pied-à-terre*

A SHILLINGSWORTH OF PROMISES

whenever we come to England, to enjoy Jean's lovely and lively giggles, and Mike's phlegmatic and sincere help with our joys and troubles. He has a fine sense of humour but it doesn't bubble or boil in quite the same way as his wife's. A well matched couple. They must be, for they argue often but Jean always wins. Not surprising and not unusual, for in life's games it's the girls that normally hold or withhold all the blackmailing aces. 1965 came and with it the second sowing of my roots in this lovely area. And these roots were frequently fertilised with heavy doses of nostalgic compost, sometimes expertly applied, for if I returned home in the evening to find the fishing rods leaning on a closed garage door, that meant a quick bite to eat and an evening on the beach at Hythe.

Our favourite spot being just to the west of the big groyne at the end of Twiss Road. The west side being chosen by Hedy, as she figured that the prevailing southwest winds would lodge all the sea food on that side and not the deep side to the east, which was generally favoured by the experts. And one freezing cold November night she quietly and conclusively proved her point by catching a twenty one pound cod. It wasn't a record for her, for some years later, and intuitively choosing a spot just east of Dungeness point and at low tide, she carefully and nonchalantly played in a twenty six pounder. The heaviest fish I ever caught was a shade over sixteen pounds less. In later years and with a fading ego I tried, without success, to propagate the theory and truth that success in fishing is ninety per cent luck, one per cent skill, and nine per cent lying.

Lady Luck it seemed was again looking on me favourably, for in early 1966 the Dover office merged with the Canterbury office in a joint transfer to a new block of offices in Folkestone, on the corner of Sandgate Road and Guildhall Street. It would appear that all I had to do now was to cruise to retirement and settle down to a life of contentment in and around Hythe.

But before my roots could even begin to re-establish themselves they were fertilised with a terminal dose of weedkiller, in the form of promotion and a transfer to the Lowestoft office. However, the staff officer involved promised a return to Kent within the not too distant future.

It didn't materialise, for the Labour government's weird idea of a Lands Commission and my erstwhile staff officer friend's decision to join it, left me stranded on the east coast for the rest of my working days and beyond.

Some few days before we were exiled, our troublesome Ford Classic burst a gasket at Capel-le-Ferne. The A.A. quickly arranged a tow into Folkestone, where it was repaired, and then promptly exchanged for a boxy looking little Vauxhall Viva that proved to be totally reliable and served us well for some six years, starting with our move to Lowestoft. We sadly missed the beauty of the undulating, well wooded landscapes around Etchinghill, which itself was a tiny attractive village, mixing the old with the new in picturesque perfection. And I can think of no better afternoon of discovery than climbing Teddar's Leas road opposite Westfield Lane and driving on through the woods and hamlets to skirt the edge of the Downs overlooking Folkestone and the Channel, before rejoining the coastal traffic at the top of Dover hill, opposite the Valiant Sailor public house.

Also greatly missed were our evening strolls with Dandy after a cloudless summer day to the top of Westfield Lane, across the field past the relay station, to squat on the grass close to the Roman tumuli, and watch the ships, the sea and the French coast. Even on a very clear day being able to see houses nestling on the distant green crests of the cliffs. Bella, our lovely, supercilious white cat, would even condescend to follow us halfway up the lane, and then hide under the same bush each time, to rejoin us on our return and purr her way back to her favourite spot by the back door. Bella was lucky in a way for, as we could only take temporary accommodation in East Anglia, and cats don't take easily to change, she stayed with Jean and Mike at number 35 and was spoilt to death, quickly forgetting her mollycoddled life at number one.

Now, having reluctantly sold our second 'Maadi', we were once again homeless. Lowestoft itself had little to offer so we went one better than a caravan and took a self service studio flat at Satis House in Yoxford on the A12, giving a journey of some eighteen miles to the office.

Some five months later our search for a permanent home ended in Church Road, Blundeston where we bought a detached bungalow next to the graveyard. It had been named Saint something-or-other, so we promptly changed it to Maadi III. We weren't exactly living in the dead centre of the village, but people were dying to be near us. I almost pictured Hedy the spiritualist having a nightly necromantic natter to the more voluble of our neighbours.

We were also in 'David Copperfield' country, the Blundeston Plough Inn being Barkis' starting point for his journey, and the tiny sun dial over the church entrance is presumed to be the one mentioned in Charles Dickens's famous book. And the vicarage opposite Maadi, in Pound Lane, is tentatively mentioned as being where part of the book was written. As our new home had no garage, the first priority was the laying of a sixty foot concrete drive and base. A local lad was recommended and he came to make an estimate for the job, complete with a pencil behind his ear and an opened up fag

A SHILLINGSWORTH OF PROMISES

packet. After an hour's discussion and the taking of copious notes as to length, width and depth of concrete, and what grade of hard-core he should use, and the aesthetic benefits of a slightly curved rather than a straight drive, he promised a figure within a few days. We never heard from him again, but eventually got the job done in three days by two non-smoking amateurs.

Although I had spent eight months in Norfolk during the war, I had not been able to drive around the quiet winding roads and byways of this flat, green and tranquil county. Nor had I been able to appreciate its landscapes, patterned with a thousand fields both large and small, faithfully reflecting all the colours of each changing season. Nor the Broads with their eternal attraction for native and migrating bird life and the not so wildly migrating holiday makers.

My work and weekend wanderings soon familiarised us with the attractions that the countryside and coasts of Suffolk and Norfolk had to offer, northeast of a line from Aldeburgh to King's Lynn. Also greatly appreciated was the slower pace of life, even the urgencies in the office soon lost their impetus, for no one ever seemed to be in a hurry. And the softly accented local brogue plus an adapted and adopted vocabulary added humour to any conversation, even when used in anger.

So our life in exile turned out to be not so traumatic as expected, causing me to search my soul as to where my heart should be. But in spite of continuing seduction I decided it should remain where it belonged. Preferably in a place like the old summer house that used to cap Brockman's Mount. Maybe not and maybe yes, for the story is that it used to be used by its owner as a sound proof swear box, when having an attack of uncontrollable bad temper.

With our now peaceful and undemanding life the days, and indeed the years, flew by, with the highlight of each year being a three or four week touring holiday to and around Switzerland. We did twenty one trips in succeeding years and the scenic beauty of the summer months in this massively spectacular country never ceased to enthral and captivate us.

Hedy of course knew her homeland through all seasons, enjoying the flounderings on the snowy nursery slopes with her father, but never acquiring any degree of expertise. And this accounted for her agreeing with my jealously cynical summing up of winter holiday activities as being exhilaratingly healthy, even the 'apres-ski', but a somewhat punishing form of paradise. I couldn't ski anyway, and messing about in gaudy gear and breaking arms and legs attracted me not at all. If the Almighty had meant us to slide our way through life he would have equipped us with longer feet and shock absorbing arses, built a little closer to the ground. With of course apologies to Jean Claude Killy and others.

Driving on the right on the Continent is really no great hazard, for all the others are doing the same thing, so it takes but a dozen or so miles to feel at ease. The fear comes later, but not much later, when all the Belgian, French, Dutch or German drivers imagine they are alone in the world. Speed restrictions are an insult, inferring that they are not capable of judging a suitably correct speed themselves. And a pedestrian attempting to use a crossing is virtually declaring war, and God help him if he isn't capable of accelerating from nought to sixty in less than a second. Traffic lights are simply a challenge, a red light being approached at a speed which assumes an immediate change to green, and an amber light is considered to be neither one nor the other and therefore meaningless. I must admit they are not helped a lot by their 'priority from the right' rule, which means that an attack from a side road is almost inevitable, and usually unavoidably successful.

But there has certainly been one improvement, for they have at last adopted our 'roundabout' rules of priority, which at least gives some choice as to who hits who. But to appreciate the combative courage of a French driver it is only necessary to join the circulating stampede around the Arc de Triomphe, and to note the look of supreme nonchalance on each driver's face as he or she weaves a way through and across at least six undefined lines of traffic. However, a casual check on any line of parked cars would reveal a high degree of incidental battle damage.

As the parents of Jean from Tolsford Close lived in Littleport, between Ely and King's Lynn, it was easy for her, after visiting them, to make a slight detour on the return trip to visit us at Blundeston.

That was how, on a cold October day in 1967, we found ourselves at Sizewell, taking a refreshing walk along the wide track of grassland between the woods and the sea. And during this walk I suddenly felt the left side of my face go stiff and cold. The following day, with a wide open left eye and a droopy mouth, and suspecting some sort of mild stroke, I visited the doctor. The good news, it wasn't a stroke. The bad news, it was Bell's Palsy, a paralysis of the facial muscles.

I then remembered that Aunt May, who had recently died at the age of eighty four, had had the same thing and had finished up with one side of her face quite badly distorted. I was somewhat more lucky, and will always remember and be grateful to the blind physiotherapist at Lowestoft hospital. His gentle treatment both manual and electrical, left me with only a very

A SHILLINGSWORTH OF PROMISES

slight after effect, an outcome which his super sensitive fingers had been able to detect very early on. And this of course helped me morally, knowing that that evil looking image in the mirror would eventually return to some sort of normality.

On returning to work early in the new year there was one new face in the office, but it wasn't her face I saw first. For she was digging around in the bottom drawer of my filing cabinet, and it being the era of the 'mini' I was willing and able to appreciate all that was on view, from ground to bum level. Not wishing to spoil a magic and lucky moment I took time to greet her. "You're looking remarkably well this morning."

Jeanne straightened up and turned around, and then gave me one of those smiles that turn young men to jelly and cause old men to wobble. I wobbled.

"So you're the Fred I've heard so much about", she said as her smile faded, and that left me wondering. She was dark haired, dark eyed and full lipped, she was nineteen, she was gorgeous.

I soon learnt that all the lads under thirty were in love, and those over thirty were wavering, and I too began to wish that I was twenty five years older. Then she wouldn't be bothering me. But a not totally dream free affinity did develop between us, which was normalised and made harmless by a lunch time invitation to Maadi and an introduction to Hedy. And from that moment a lifetime's friendship began between Jeanne and her family and us. Now, twenty three years later, she is still an easy-laughing, gorgeous forty three year old 'girl', with maybe a few slight signs of having been well nourished over the years.

1969 was the year in which I stopped smoking. For having been told by a colleague that it was the cause of the migrainous flashing lights I sometimes had, affecting my vision, I packed it in completely. Ending forty years of thinking about it. But the flashing lights still persist.

The work at the office could never by any stretch of the imagination be called stimulating, and as there was no possibility that I would ever become totally Civil Service minded, it was necessary to make the most of the outdoor aspects of the work. This meant dealing with the public in their homes and workplaces, and they could be aggressive, caustic, co-operative, derisive, understanding, humorous, or at times downright thick. It was a challenge and what they thought of me no doubt included all the above, plus a few extra B's and F's.

I remember one irate farmer, on learning that his battery hen houses might be subject to assessment, promptly threatened me with the shotgun he was carrying, saying, "I'd like to stick this right up your officious arsehole – both barrels!"

I light heartedly but cautiously replied, "If you do, don't pull the trigger, it might spoil the pleasure."

His smile was slow to come but when it did the tension eased and we parted, if not as friends, then at least less violently antagonistic.

On another occasion, after wasting a half hour or so deep in the country searching for a cottage with no name, up a lane off a road with no name, I was late for an appointment. When I finally found the place I was greeted by its red faced and smelly owner (who probably thought that if you had never wiped your arse with a handful of straw, you hadn't lived) with a half thought out bucolic quip. "You buggers is so daft you couldn't organise a cock-up in a whore shop."

I was taken aback a bit, but then flattered him by telling him, "That means that I'm probably talking to someone that could." He looked puzzled and then slowly gave me a 'no sounding' yes.

Jeanne and her husband Philip, who had been her surprise selection from the office love-lorn, celebrated new year's eve 1969 with us. It had snowed during the evening and then, well oiled and warmly dressed, we spent a laughing twenty minutes treading the virgin snow, greeting the new year, and wishing our neighbours a comfortable and undisturbed 1970. Back in the glowing warmth of the bungalow we cosily sipped our way to the early hours and made arrangements to make our next trip to Switzerland a foursome.

We took off on this trip in the early evening of the 17th of May, enjoying the comfort of a new and larger Vauxhall Viva. Our first 'Swiss' stop was at Berne in Stack Lane, Hartley, for a cuppa with Sam and Millie and to find out the exact location of his childhood home in Steini. Then, after a hurried drive to Etchinghill and a quick hullo and good-bye to Jean and Mike, we arrived at Dover, to spend twenty minutes or so in lane four, before boarding the midnight ferry to Ostend.

We had anticipated having a comfortable snooze across the Channel, but three busloads of young teenage school children hooting and rushing around the ship in a frenzy of excitement, reduced an expected five hours sleep to about two hours of nodding off and nodding on.

It was about half past five when I thankfully drove off the ferry, and with three noisily chatting passengers I bum-bum-bumped my way down the concrete sectioned road to Brussels, just in time to get mixed up in the morning rush hour traffic. I followed a memorised route through the town,

A SHILLINGSWORTH OF PROMISES

along a high level stretch and then down through two tunnels, to pull to the right in order to take the first left turn to Namur. But here 'diversion' signs took me off course, and I found myself eventually needing to cross three lines of bumper to bumper traffic in about fifty metres in order to take my diverted left turn. It was accomplished, but only after a crash course in the art of Continental digital sign language.

Having passed through Brussels Hedy, Jeanne and Philip became silent and a quick look around told me why. They were all fast asleep, leaving me to enjoy a silent and lonely drive through Namur and on to Bastogne, where they all awoke in time for a nine o'clock breakfast of croissants, baguettes, jam and coffee.

Luxemburg, with its tree lined boulevards, was pleasurably negotiated and then Philip took over as a tyro navigator to pass through Metz. A series of unavoidable wrong turns had us corkscrewing our way through the back streets, finally hitting the right exit route by dint of perseverance and accidental good luck.

The road to Nancy was well signposted and the town itself caused no problems. We then approached the Vosges to pass through Epinal and on to Plombiere, where we took a late roadside picnic lunch before climbing up and out of this pretty little town. Now, once more with dozing passengers, I pressed on through Luxeuil and Vesoul to Besancon, to follow an unending series of *toutes directions* signs to finally cross the river Doubs, turn left, pass through an arch and climb steeply out of town.

The picturesque road to Ornans, in places carved right into the side of the mountain, with its marvellous views into and across the valley, and with its balustraded bends, gives an excellent foretaste and appetite for the challenges of the great mountain passes of Switzerland itself.

A straightforward drive to and through the somewhat dreary looking town of Pontarlier, followed by the much more agreeable and winding climb through the Jura woods, took us on to Vallorbe and the Swiss frontier. After another fill up with petrol and coffee and a quick telephone call to Erica, we set off on the last forty five minutes of the journey down a wooded, twisting twenty five mile descent into Lausanne.

Lausanne traffic in those days was reasonably disciplined and pedestrians respectfully waited for the little red man to turn to a bleeping green before venturing onto any crossing. So the journey through the hilly centre of this lakeside town to Chailly was not only easy, but was now becoming familiar, as former trips and already disclosed its twisting hazards.

The approach to Erica's third floor flat in a block overlooking lake Leman was unbelievably steep, giving one the uncanny feeling that at any moment gravity was going to take over completely.

Of course Erica had everything prepared, and the smell of the 'filet mignon' cooking in her tiny kitchen made all the emotional greetings and introductions seem never ending. But then at last, washed and brushed up and with mint clean choppers we all sat down to eat and drink ourselves into a fit state to sleep for ten hours, which we did.

After a full day's rest an early morning start took us up and over the steep undulating slopes behind Lausanne to Gruyeres, to take a purposely delayed breakfast. Gruyeres itself loftily sits astride its own private mountain bump, an old cobble stoned village, touristically profitable and as unique as its famous cheese.

After breakfast we retraced a few miles and then took the narrow, winding and dipping, but continuously rising road to the Jaun Pass. The last steep stretch of which twists its way through the pines which comfortably hide the deep drop awaiting a careless or unlucky driver. The Jaun Pass, although one of the lower passes, still provides the hazards, the joys and the exhilaration of driving high. There was still some two or three feet of residual snow at the summit, adding both beauty and goose pimples. So after a coffee in an overheated restaurant we quickly moved on. The long series of descending hairpin bends giving alternating views up and down the Simmental, quickly wound us down to the river Simmen itself.

We were now in Sam's country and approaching the Alps, with the slightly wooded, wild-flowered meadows, scattered with chalets bordering the road as it faithfully followed the narrow fast flowing, rock filled Simmen. We soon arrived in the village of Darstetten, where a few enquiries directed us to a right hand fork and to a three metre wide track rising sharply to Steini.

A typical Swiss hamlet of half a dozen or so old and ancient timber chalets. One of the most ancient being occupied by the Dreyer family, the head of which was Sam's brother Hans.

June 1970: Philippe, Jeanne, Hedy and Erica high in the Jaun pass.

A SHILLINGSWORTH OF PROMISES

The ground floor occupied by Hans had obviously changed little over the years. White scrubbed timber everywhere, giving a warm feeling of cosy cleanliness. The centrepiece of the living room was the huge wood-fired circular stove, with all round seating accommodation. Outside the running water supply ran cold and clear from an underground spring into a large scooped out tree trunk, forming a trough which overflowed and refilled at the same rate, giving permanently fresh crystal clear water.

The family were naturally talkative about Sam's early life and ceremoniously showed us the bedroom where he was born, and then surprised us by proudly revealing it was even the same bed. We were also surprised to learn that there were two indoor loos, one up and one down. Both of the same uncomplicated design which consisted of a boxed in seat with a lidless hole centred over a pit deep enough to reassure any bare bummed user that there was nothing to fear except an echo. But still not deep enough to discourage the early summer flies angrily and hungrily buzzing their approval.

Steini was pretty but isolated even in this day and age, so one could easily imagine the eerie quietness that must have pervaded the place at the turn of the century, making it easy to appreciate and give life to Sam's story of when, at the age of sixteen and alone way up in the Alms or Alpine pastures with the cattle, he had felt so miserably lonely and so remote from life that he had put both arms around the nearest cow's neck and cried his heart out. It was no wonder he finally decided to leave his native country, the impressive beauty of which he had gotten used to. He just wanted to join the rest of the world and live a little.

Continuing our trip we soon reached Spiez on lake Thun and followed its southern shore to Interlaken, neatly situated between lakes Thun and Brienz. Interlaken although, or because, it is the ideal base from which to start any tour of the Swiss Alps, was over blessed with a plethora of gift shops and has, over the years, slipped from its once Victorian splendour to offering imitative and imperfect fish and chips.

On our return to Lausanne we travelled the whole length of the Simmental to enjoy again all the scenic variations of river, steepled villages, wooded pastures and mountains that had so entranced us in the morning. We then climbed the Col du Pillon, passing through the film stars' paradise of Gstaad, to drop down to lake Leman and reach Lausanne via Montreux and Vevey.

The following day Hedy, Erica and I started our holiday proper, leaving the flat to our two happy newlyweds, who then spent their days making discoveries of their own, one of which shot Philip right out of bed. The rest encompassed lakeside walks at Ouchy and Lutry and boat trips on the lake, to better enjoy the beauty of all the surrounding vineyards and mountains. After four more days they reluctantly returned to England by train, and to the stultifying routine of office work, proving that there is death after life.

Our own destination was Flims in the Graubunden, touring there via Berne with its famous clock and arcaded shops, and on to Bregenz. Then putting our toes into Austria we stayed overnight in the tiny village of Bezau, a winter's paradise but a summertime zero.

We made the most of the good food and the comfortable bed and the noise from the bar. Then waking early we escaped from Austria to pass through Liechtenstein almost without changing gear, to arrive in Chur in the mid afternoon. After an *escalope de veau* with the inevitable half kilo of *pommes frites*, eased along with a nice fresh salad, a glass of wine and a coffee, we followed the tail end of the river Rhine proper before turning off to Flims, to make ourselves at home in our pre-booked chalet.

The next ten days were spent in total relaxation, just sunbathing, sharing short menu cooking and local rambling, interspersed with a few motorised trips to nearby known and unknown beauty spots. We climbed the 365 bend road up to Arosa. The scenery was powerfully picturesque but the town had little to admire except its tiny lake and the high prices in the shops. The impressive Via Mala gorge was of course a must, narrow and deep with the funnelled waters of the Rhine Posterieur rushing to meet big brother further down.

We also made our way up to the highest inhabited village in Europe at Juf, at a height of some 2150 metres, passing through dripping, rough-hewn and unlined tunnels *en route*. The village itself comprised but a few timber houses and of the inhabitants we saw but one man and his dog. Of much more interest were the multitude of marmots, popping up on their hind legs and looking at us accusingly with a curiously unblinking regard, before dropping back again out of sight.

A one day trip over the San Bernardino pass and on to lake Maggiori to Ascona and the return was our last outing before returning to Lausanne. A journey which took us over the 2050 metre high Oberalp pass, with an unmade and gravelly descent into Andermatt. Then we continued over the 2400 metre Furka pass to take the long mountain bordered road to Martigny where the squirting waters from the many 'vachpisse' leave no doubt as to the origin of their name. Two short hours later we were back in Erica's comfortable little flat, reluctantly realising that the next day we would be on our way back to England and Blundeston. And this we did, following a different route via Verdun, Brussels, Ostend and Harwich.

Life's merry-go-round in the office continued, with not a lot to enthuse about, and I began to begrudge the time spent there. But the preparation for the 1973 rating revaluation would add a little sense of purpose to one's endeavours, at the same time providing long hours away from the office, deep in the country.

I remember on one occasion it seemed that practically everyone in one particular village was smoking the same rather obscure brand of cigarette. Curiosity eventually made me enquire as to the reason why from a likely looking young lad who, with a sly knowing grin, passed on the secret. "Them fags in the shop is kept on the top shelf, and she don't wear no knickers."

It being the era of the mini I could appreciate their enthusiasm and maybe the sales technique of the village shop in trying to clear stocks of an otherwise unpopular brand.

One evening on returning home I found Hedy trying to console a tearful Jeanne. It seemed she and Philip were having troubles and she was about to leave him to stay with her sister in Colchester. She had her little Shit-zu dog with her and wanted us to look after him until her problems were resolved. That's how we came to have two dogs, Dandy, our fourteen year old and now Tang, just seven months, for Jeanne solved her troubles temporarily and we kept Tang permanently.

Hedy by now was well known in the village, but I for a long time was known only as the Swiss lady's husband. Her close friends ranged from the local 'Bobby', both shopkeepers, the lads in the garage, the school dentist, the lady who did the church, the elderly council bloke who kept the village tidy, and on to the vicar, not forgetting the two ponies, Whisky and Brandy, kept in the field opposite.

But her closest friend was Elizabeth, the German widow living in Somerleyton. An escapee from Hitler's Reich, who had married a Scot. She lived in Perth until he died, and then came south to be close to her son. A lady of many talents and interests, who enjoyed long challenging chats on almost any subject, and an agnostic to boot. We got on well.

For the Christmas break of 1972 we flew to Switzerland and Erica, leaving Dandy and Tang with Elizabeth. But it turned out to be a sad Christmas, for whilst staying overnight with brother Tom at Hayes, and just before leaving for Heathrow in the morning, we got the news that Dandy had died during the night. He had been unwell for some time and the vet had warned it might happen, so Hedy was not unprepared and took it well.

On our return little Tang reigned alone, and received all Hedy's attention, even more so for I had again been transferred. This time to Norwich, which meant I would be away for some ten hours or so each day. I had also been shifted one up on the hierarchical ladder, but I was still comfortably near the bottom, about four rungs up.

Our journey through life, placid and predictable as it was, continued, almost fitting exactly the pattern I had foreseen all those years ago. Just turning food into faeces and hoping for better tomorrows, and the patience to wait for them.

The 1970's were slowly being whittled away, these years with the sixties bringing an era of conscience easing permissiveness, and a seeming resentment to any sort of authority. The years when homosexuals 'came out' and became 'gay', robbing the vocabulary of a happy adjective, and making the dictionary definition of the word a little ambiguous. Each year the monotony was broken by the now ritual trip to Switzerland. A three to four week holiday at Beatenberg in a beautiful little chalet called 'Sali-Bachli', situated at the western end of this long, 1300 metre high village, aptly named the Sun Terrace of Switzerland. Quite true, unless there happened to be low cloud, then one might as well be in the middle of the Romney Marsh on a rainy day. Except when the clouds lifted and the sun shone at Beatenberg, one would be presented with a wondrous view over trees and a placid blue lake to the near mountains fronting the massive and permanently snow covered, three headed horizon of the Jungfrau, Monc and the Eiger.

A short journey to Kleini Scheidegg would take one close enough to the famous sheer north face of the Eiger to be able to appreciate the strength and courage, if not the seeming madness of those that dare to climb it.

On our 1977 visit to Beatenberg Erica had invited Valy Zaki, now living in Basle, to visit us. This of course linked us all in memory back to our Cairo

days. For Valy was the widow of Hamid Zaki who was the son of Julie who had married Zaki Bey all those years ago in Istanbul.

'Sali-Bachli' with Monc and Eiger in the background.

A SHILLINGSWORTH OF PROMISES

This was also the same year that Sam had accompanied us and we had dropped him off at Steini en route. He had always refused over the years to come with us, but this year he seemed almost willing to give in to our annual bullying. He had been suffering from some internal trouble for a long time, which he wouldn't discuss, and I suppose he sensed that if he wanted to see his family again it was probably now or never.

When we picked him up on our return the poor lad looked really unwell. But that didn't stop him from bringing us up to date with the back-log of the family's history. He appeared to be at ease with himself, and repeatedly thanked us for enabling him to make, what he called his last earthly visit. His only slight and unbitter moan being that over the years he had sent his elder brother Hans a lot of money to modernise the family home. But Hans had simply put it all in the bank, and continued to enjoy life as he knew it, echo and all.

Hans outlived Sam anyway, for two months after our return to England Sam, now living alone, had some sort of crisis and had fallen out of bed, to be found dead by the local vicar some hours later. Sam had a sad beginning and a sad end, but the bit in between, from his stories, had at least made the journey worthwhile. During the funeral service Hedy surprised even me by giving a paused and progressive translation in Swiss, enabling visiting mourners to better understand the vicar's praise and appreciation of Sam's activities within the village, especially and particularly where the elderly were concerned.

By 1970 Sylvia's world wanderings had come to an end, and the family now had a permanent but unhappy home at Arcueil in the southern suburbs of Paris. For by 1978 Andre had acquired a severe drink problem, and the family suffered accordingly, both financially and emotionally.

The family had grown and Sylvia, in search of independence, had taken a congenial and happy job in a small office as a trilingual secretary. Patricia was now twenty one years old and was soon to qualify as a midwife, and was happily engaged to Francois, a trainee doctor. Seventeen year old Christian had as yet to find his feet, and his reaction to conscripted military service.

The stresses of Sylvia's recent troubles had taken their toll, and she had lost weight and was but a pale shadow of her former gorgeous self. So to get away from it all, and to try to rebuild those sunken cheeks and spindly legs, and to put a shine back into her eyes, she spent her 1978 summer holiday with us.

It wasn't long before she began to blossom, with an easier laugh and progressively more to cuddle. Enjoying the days as they came, even laughing off a crashing dent to the roof of her car as a steinschlag in the Gron valley picked on us. Had we been half a second slower the stone would have passed through the windscreen on my side, probably causing irreparable damage to my digestive and reproductive systems.

On a trip a few days later I again had a temporary lack of faith in my future, for we decided to take the tiny, two man, privately operated cable car up to the Arni-see, the last hundred to two hundred metres of which rises practically vertical. The little cab seemed to take an eternity climbing those last few jerking, swaying and bouncing metres, before it eventually ended the suspense and came to a stuttering halt, level with a tiny two man platform. The descent, however, was smooth and quick, with no tingling nerves, proving I suppose that this seeming relic from the era of William Tell will, like his legend, go on forever. But I haven't seen the Arni-see since.

But the real troubles of this particular summer were yet to come, for ten days later on returning to Lausanne, I suffered a massive haemorrhage from the nose, with a blood pressure of 220. After the cauterisation, four days were spent in hospital, during which I nearly became world famous.

Apparently all new cases, minor or major, became the subject matter for all the trainee doctors. Before they visited me my dossier had been placed on the bedside table, to be handy and ready for the instructing medic. He picked it up and read it, and then advised his student audience to take a good and close look at me, for I was about to make history.

"You will all be surprised to learn that this gentleman is in the ninth month of pregnancy and we have to contemplate the possibility of a Caesarean."

I did my best to look concerned. He bawled for the nurse and his class obliged with a sycophantic giggle. I assumed that the details of my cauterised hooter were in the file for the unfortunate lady with the pregnancy trouble.

With my blood pressure normal, and with pills to be taken 'even unto death', we returned to England. With my sixty fourth birthday coming up in October of 1979, I looked forward to my last year with the Civil Service, but with no great enthusiasm. So when the opportunity for an early retirement came in August, I escaped with alacrity, a small pension, a big smile, no regrets and a few friendly handshakes.

A SHILLINGSWORTH OF PROMISES

8   *Retirement, bereavement & reunion*

Having reached what the French politely call the 'troisième' age, and joined the ranks of the world's non-producers, I began to think of mortality, especially my own, and decided to postpone the event for as long as was possible. For I hadn't as yet reached the Shakespearean stage of being 'sans everything'. In fact all my faculties and bits and pieces were in good working order. Except maybe the follicles, which had resisted all attempts at reactivation, leaving one with a long face but with less dandruff.

Like others, I had been looking forward to retirement, to having more time in which to do less, or even nothing. An occupation I felt I could do better than most.

I didn't get the chance to prove it for, as all pensioners know, time is the one thing in short supply, mostly due to having too much to do, work or pleasure, or because the inevitable seems to be creeping up a bit too soon. To solve the 'how long' part of the retirement equation is, I suppose, not just to wait for the inevitable but to let the inevitable wait for you.

1979 as well as bringing retirement, also brought us our twelfth and final new car, and news of Jeanne's second marriage, for she had divorced Philip some eighteen months before. It also brought a fortnight's holiday in Hythe, for we contemplated returning to our favourite corner of England. But poor Hythe had not, even after some thirty four years, totally recovered its pre-war glory. Now devoid of all its old and lovely Elm trees; with the Ladies' Walk looking like a long stretch of disused back garden; the Military Canal tatty and choked with weed; with threats of a new throughway to bring more defacement; my childhood paradise had lost its magnetic appeal. I was disappointed and more than a little sad.

We stayed with Bert and Mary at 26 Cobden Road for the fortnight and, like thousands of others and us, they had spent the previous years eating, sleeping, shopping, do-it-yourself-ing, fishing, visiting and holiday making. Just sling in a bit of culture, opera, ballet and theatre, add a bit of pop and non-pop, a lot of nattering and discussion, mix the lot together, and you have the recipe for living, with death as the dessert. The main course can more or less be chosen 'a la carte' but there is not even a menu for the afters, let alone a choice.

So why the instinct for procreation? The only apparent real function that animal or vegetable is created for, and is happy to perform. The supermarket shelves with their grand displays of dead meat and dying vegetables seem to support the fact that life on Earth is simply a matter of eat and be eaten. This natural chain would appear to be a pretty negative sort of 'Grand Design', and hardly fits in with the human conception of 'live and let live'.

It was the struggle to understand and come to terms with modern existence that proved too much for Andre. For the ultimate effect of his drinking, his depression and the interaction of prescribed drugs, made it impossible for him to continue any semblance of normal family life, and in May 1980 he took his own life. He was fifty four. A shock for Sylvia and her two children, but the beginning of a new and less troubled era for all of them.

Sylvia left Arcueil and bought a flat in Rueil Malmaison, a western suburb of Paris, to get away from sad memories and to be nearer her work. Patricia married a year later and Christian, having completed his military service, married two years after that. They then both, as expected, quickly made Sylvia a very young and happy grandmother by presenting her with three boys. Olivier and Pierre from Patricia and Francois, then Mathieu from Christian and Marie-Jose.

As Hedy and I had by 1981 completely redecorated our Blundeston home, and half finished the backlog of put off repairs and improvements, we were able to vary and extend our annual sorties, to give us the chance to absorb the real beauty of our homeland. I say our homeland, for Hedy had by now become more British than the British, even asserting that the Lake District compared more than favourably with Switzerland. I didn't argue but agreed that maybe when the sun shone, she had a point, but for the other forty eight weeks of the year I would have to be convinced.

But she had more than adequate support from Erica and Sylvia, for they had accompanied us, and they too agreed that the area more than matched the most magnificent and more beautiful parts of their land of birth.

We had hired a bungalow at Glenridding, using it as a base for both the Lake District and Scotland. My memories are of the sheep wandering through the back garden, the Hythe-canal-like rowing boats on Ullswater, the friendly pubs and the good food. The latter presented on the plate as an appetising meal and not as an exercise in geometric design, with little half trimmed carrots radiating out from a tiny moulded lump of something or other, 'à la Française', and costing about four quid a carrot. Their defence being that they cater for the gourmet and not the gourmand!

Although age and laziness prevented me from taking any long uphill or downhill walks, my impression was still that the Lake District was quiet,

A SHILLINGSWORTH OF PROMISES

very beautiful and very wet. Not at all like its inhabitants, who are certainly not all quiet, certainly not all beautiful and certainly not wet.

Especially the lad I overheard giving advice to a pal in one of the pubs. He had been asked by his friend during a boozy confessional how he might know if he was making headway with his girlfriend. The reply was simple but irrefutable. "Once you're on farting terms mate, you've nothing to worry about – you've made it."

Our first forsaking of Beatenberg took us, again with Erica and Sylvia, to St Pierre Quiberon, halfway up the little tongue of land hanging down into the Bay of Biscay from Brittany. It was June 1982 and with the fine weather, it matched the best that the Côte D'Azure could offer, including the renowned sand, sun, sex and sea food. All partaken of but nothing illicit, except in fancy. Who could help it? Surrounded by all that bare flesh, so delightfully and variously sculptured into a thousand deeply cleaved, well oiled rounded breasts and bums, all glistening temptingly in the sun.

Beautifully bronzed and back at Blundeston, and doing the usual Saturday shopping in Lowestoft, Hedy and I passed through the swing doors between Boots and Marks and Spencer and as I held the door for the lady following I heard a half familiar voice say, "It ain't, it can't be, yes it is. How are you, you old so and so?"

The voice belonged to Lofty Mee, and the lady was his wife. A repetitive "Well I'm blowed" followed instantaneous recognition, for neither of us had changed dramatically over the intervening thirty one years since we had last met in Cairo. I had a bit less hair and a bit larger stomach, but lantern jawed Lofty had only acquired a few enhancing wrinkles and an even louder raucous laugh.

Having so luckily bumped into each other after all those years, and as Lofty and Ned lived close by in Kessingland, we kept in regular contact. As in bygone years our meetings usually signalled a move or a journey of some sort, we both hoped that the only foreseeable and possibly final permanent transfer could be avoided, at least for a while. The following year, having rendezvoued in Paris, Erica, Sylvia, Hedy and I again drove to St Pierre for the summer holiday, to enjoy the four S's. But the enjoyment came to a very sudden end when a kidney stone decided to make its presence felt, turning a healthy half bronzed sixty six year old beach boy into a pale sweaty figure paralysed with pain.

Then after a slow gasping walk back to the hotel, and whilst waiting for the doctor, I had an urge to widdle, but nothing happened, and I stood there looking at a non-co-operative Willy and wondering "What next?" The doctor eventually arrived, quickly decided it was an emergency and arranged for me to be immediately hospitalised.

Sylvia drove me to the hospital at Auray, the piercing pain had stopped but my bladder was beginning to complain. It was now almost seven o'clock in the evening and I hadn't piddled for some ten hours.

The young doctor dealing with the emergency was unable to insert a catheter, so my bladder had to be attacked from the outside. A plastic tube was then inserted through the stomach wall some four inches below the belly button. And after a long and diminishing sigh of relief as I gradually got rid of some three pints of piddle, the tube was fitted with a neat little tap, which gave me full manual control of all subsequent urinary evacuations.

An echo graph produced no sign of a kidney stone, so I was now mobile, albeit with a worthless Willy. But with my mechanical cock fitted with a plastic reservoir placed under the seat, I was able to drive back to Paris, stopping only for the convenience of others. I just fiddled with my little plastic widdler as and when required.

After ten days in the Clinique des Martinets, conveniently situated next to Sylvia's office in Rueil Malmaison, and after having had several grams of my prostate whittled away, Hedy and I returned to Blundeston to recuperate from our relaxing holiday.

Hedy had, from our days at Etchinghill, annually suffered in the summer months from some sort of allergy, causing her varying degrees of respiratory trouble, and this summer of 1983 was a particularly bad one for her. And as she had been unable to stop a lifetime's smoking habit, her annual troubles were obviously aggravated. Repeated chest X-rays were all negative, and in spite of religiously following the advice from an allergy specialist from Lowestoft, the only alleviation came with the onset of winter. So in 1984 we decided to spend the summer months with Erica in Lausanne, hoping the Swiss air would be more friendly. We journeyed by car to Paris and then on to Lausanne by rail, to

July 1984: Sylvia, Hedy and myself, just one year before Hedy sadly left us.

A SHILLINGSWORTH OF PROMISES

sample the thrill of travelling on the T.G.V., the much publicised high speed train of the French railways. It proved to be very smooth, very quick and very quiet, with all the added excitement of watching tired business men, grannies and grandads snoozing their way across the beautiful countryside of France and Switzerland.

However, the Swiss air proved to be ineffectual and Hedy continued to cough and wheeze, so we reluctantly had to curtail our stay and return to England, staying with Sylvia *en route*. But at Rueil Hedy began to feel and look very unwell, refusing any immediate medical help, and determinedly insisting that I drive her back to Blundeston. On the way back I spent more time watching her than the road, but each glance brought a wan smile of appreciation, and gave me the courage to press on.

To our disappointment the usual autumn improvement failed to arrive and she reluctantly agreed with me that it was really time to call in the doctor. More X-rays again proved to be unhelpful. Blood tests revealed a lack of potassium and tablets to augment the deficiency did, for a while, bring an improvement.

But as the new year of 1985 wore on it became obvious that Hedy was making no real progress, becoming so weak that she was virtually confined to her bedroom. Further tests in May sadly confirmed our worst fears. She had cancer. Treatment at Norwich hospital failed to halt the rapid progress of the disease, and to be nearer home she transferred to the new hospital at Gorleston.

Hedy of course realised the inevitability of it all and asked only one thing of the doctors. That was a reassurance that she should die without too much physical pain. Her strong religious faith ensured that she would have little other pain.

Poor Erica was unable to come to England to see her dying sister, for she had had a stroke, losing her powers of speech, becoming frustrated and distraught at not even being able to talk and be with Hedy at this critical moment. But Hedy did have many other expected and unexpected visitors, all of whom were astonished at her buoyant and almost carefree attitude to approaching death.

Leisje, the Dutch widow of the vicar at Blundeston, had become a close family friend and accompanied me on virtually every visit to the hospital. And each time Hedy did her best to cheer us up, saying that for the little time she had left she didn't want to be a centre of gloom.

All too soon Hedy lost her wish, for she quietly left us on July 10th, leaving us all to be deeply and uncritically sad. And poor little Tang continued to listen, sniff and search for his mistress, looking at me with big questioning eyes and not understanding the answers.

The only members of Hedy's family left in this world were Erica, two nephews and two nieces, but only Sylvia was able to fly over for the funeral, staying but a few days before having to return. Hedy's ashes now lie under a small memorial stone close to the door of Blundeston church, within sight of Maadi 111, where we had so happily spent the last nineteen years together.

The following days were meaningless and empty and for the first time in my life I felt hopelessly lonely. A half knitted pullover, letters put aside to be answered, and old shopping lists, all once so insignificant, now became eye blurring reminders of all that was. Thought would follow thought, all of which seemed to end with Hedy's last words, which were said with dry eyes and unblinking sincerity. "I do, I do want to die." And then, after a pause, "And I do love you."

I was helped out of these early days of introspection, sadness and near self pity by a surprise visit from the son-in-law of one of Sam's nephews. He was on a holiday tour of England and was on his own, Herman Werfeli by name. He of course was deeply sorry to hear of Hedy's death but was not emotionally involved. This was fortuitous for during the few days that I was able to tour around with him, the sense of self pity, and the haunting image of Hedy's face began to blur. Rationality slowly began to return and I realised that I had to make some sort of solid plan for the future.

One small episode during Herman's short stay, though unusual, did help enormously to reassure me that normality and humour would return. We were passing through the checkout in a mini-market in Beccles and Herman was gargling away in Swiss, when a local lady asserted in a giggling whisper to her pal, "Must be a couple of foreign poofs."

I looked and smiled and said, "Yes, he's gorgeous, isn't he?"

One blushed and looked away but the other one admitted with a grin, "Not bad, not bad at all."

Beautiful and attractive as the area around Blundeston was, I again began to hanker after my roots. And after making repeated trips to Hythe I found that the feeling of belonging was still strong, offering an anchor to my wanderings. The things that had given me such a calm, satisfying and happy childhood had maybe changed somewhat, but memory would paint the picture, and as I stood, watched or listened, I again felt at home. So I immediately set about preparing for a move, meeting some opposition from close friends, particularly Elizabeth from Somerleyton. She was concerned

A SHILLINGSWORTH OF PROMISES

that I might feel out of touch and lonely in Hythe, where surely most, if not all, of my old friends and contacts would have passed or moved on.

And then within a month poor dear Elizabeth, as if to prove a point, had a heart attack and died. It was only a few days before her death that we had been talking of Hedy and how she had been so calm. Elizabeth, an agnostic, then admitted that those that have a strong faith and an unshakeable belief in the hereafter can lean on that faith. Looking on death as just a bit of a nuisance, separating the here from the hereafter. But, as an agnostic or an atheist has only him or herself to lean on, it is only the strength of resignation that helps.

I could only agree, adding that a believer will never know if he or she is wrong, but a non-believer certainly will.

Having, by January 1986, put Maadi 111 up for sale, I left East Anglia, but not for Hythe. For I hadn't been able to find a home there that I could be happy in, one close enough to the sea, for the constant lullaby of wave on shingle to lull me nightly into peaceful slumber, as it had done some sixty five years earlier.

As brother Bert was now living in Tasmania and Tommy was totally occupied with his family and living close to Heathrow, I sweethearted Sylvia into inviting me to Paris for a while. As she was still a working girl it wasn't long before I became fatally familiar with her kitchen, her vacuum cleaner, her washing and washing up machines, and after some months, with Sylvia herself. We then decided to share our troubles and miseries together, and as it turned out to be a very happy solution, we blew out the candle that we had lit thirty two years ago in the Lebanon, and switched on the not now forbidden electricity.

This happy turn of events was made much easier by the early sale of Maadi 111, for Mr and Mrs Hume who had lived just three bungalows away in Church Road, decided to buy it, complete with furniture and furnishings. And as they had been looking after little fourteen year old Tang, they also offered to let him spend his fading years in the home he knew.

Although the journey back to Blundeston in late February to finalise everything was a nightmare of snow and ice, the warm reception I received from old friends soon warmed my heart. It also made the untying of twenty years of attachment and association quite emotional and very difficult.

The kindly Humes had solved the problem of what to do with Tang, and my other big worry was solved when dear Jeanne assured me that she would look after Hedy's grave, making certain that it would always look tended.

Leaving home and friends was certainly not new to me, but as I drove away from Blundeston down the A12, my thoughts kept putting a laughing and light-hearted passenger in the empty seat beside me, and I had to blink away a guilty moistening of the eyes. I felt as if I were deserting her, but it was only an urn of ashes I was leaving at Blundeston, the memories I could take with me.

Life in Rueil quickly assumed a pattern and as time passed I became more and more part of Sylvia's growing family, which now in 1988 included four year old Olivier, one year old Pierre and two year old Mathieu. And I became an ancient, mildly co-operative baby sitter.

I had by now decided to take up permanent residence in France, and that soon started a war of attrition with French bureaucracy. A 'Carte de Sejour', a French driving licence, the intricacies of avoiding double taxation and the regularisation of reciprocal Social Security benefits all provided rich ground for the pedantic idiosyncrasies of even the most minor of French 'Fonctionnaires'.

But the war was eventually won and I finished up with an inch thick file of copies, approved translations (costing the earth), certifications, photographs, signed statements and assorted bumph. After which the renewal of my passport at the British Embassy was child's play.

Sylvia's flat is but twenty five minutes on the RER to the centre of Paris, with all its cultural and architectural attractions, but more importantly it is also only twenty minutes on the same line to Marks and Spencer, British bangers, bacon and baked beans.

Paris, known throughout the world as a centre of romance and dirty weekends, tries hard to sustain the image and certainly caters for most kinds of sexuality, both refined and unrefined. The half naked 'Crazy Horse' and 'Lido' girls with their beautifully choreographed displays of controlled titillation, are obviously refined.

But the Bois de Boulogne, a green haven of calm during the day, becomes at night a vast open air brothel, its trees greeting the dawn gloriously festooned with a variety of discarded *Capote Anglaise.* Quite unrefined, and stretching Anglomania to the limit, I think.

As I hate cities, I'm not really qualified to comment too strongly on one of the world's great capitals. But if I had to, I might admit that the Eiffel Tower is, well – high. And the Grande Arche is, well – big. And the Georges Pompidou Centre, it's –well, it's ugly. And the restaurants, well – McDonald's is the most popular. And the women? Irresistible – well, most of them.

The Louvre, with its multiple galleries displaying the world's largest collection of art created by all the great masters, and with its recently acquired glass pyramid nestling more or less architecturally content in its midst, is of

A SHILLINGSWORTH OF PROMISES

course the Mecca for all the world's art lovers and captured package tourists. All maybe trying to solve the enigma of Mona Lisa's five hundred year old smile, or the mysterious loss of her eyebrows and eyelashes.

Sylvia was still a working girl, so we had been unable to make any grand tours. But as the family had a largish modern house close to the river Loire at Lion-en-Sullias, we could always escape to the country for a break. And for three weeks each summer we would have Erica to stay with us, together with three parentless grandchildren. The parents having slid off on their own to savour again the bonking joys of interference free togetherness.

Caring for three healthy kids on the loose was a bit of a mixed blessing, bringing joy, chaos, headaches, frustration and amusement. They were all well past the wet at both ends stage, chattering away with a fluency which made me jealous. And Pierre also proved that he might just as quickly become fluent in a very basic form of English.

I was working at the desk in the living room when this four year old potential linguist ran through, leaving the door wide open. I called to him to come back, and pleaded, "Pierre, ferme la porte s'il te plait." Nothing happened and I closed it myself.

A while later he ran through again, leaving the door open. I raised my voice a little and called, "Pierre, ferme la porte."

Nothing happened. After a third repeat performance, and now getting angry, I shouted, "Pierre, shut the bloody door!" This time he stopped in his tracks, gave me a grin and immediately closed it.

Some time later Pierre again ran in, followed by five year old Mathieu. Pierre suddenly stopped and whispered to his colliding cousin, "Fred – il veut que tu 'shut the bloody door'." Mathieu looked blank and Pierre shrugged, and then closed it himself.

A few days later Pierre was sitting in the loo with the door open, peering intently between his legs.

I asked him, "Pourquoi tu regard ton zi-zi comme ca?"

I got a sideways glance and a quick response. "Je ne regard pas mon zi-zi, et ferme la porte s'il te plait."

I was pleased to hear him revert to his mother tongue, it eased my conscience considerably.

On another visit to the country, and again acting as temporary childminders, we were amused to hear Olivier and Mathieu nattering together in a matter-of-fact way about where babies come from. Mathieu asserted emphatically, "C'est les dames qui fabriquent les bebes."

Olivier, not impressed, asked, "Comment tu sais ca?"

"Parce que quand Pascal etait ne son papa etait en Afrique." It was unassailable childlike logic, to assume that if Papa wasn't there when the baby arrived then it had nothing to do with him.

Sylvia's flat in Rueil is but three hundred metres from the banks of the river Seine where it winds its way out of Paris *en route* to Rouen and the English Channel. So we often spent and hour or two strolling along its beautiful tree lined banks, just for pleasure, or to walk off the soporific effects of too much plonk and irresistible nosh. In any case the banks were more than adequately benched, so more often than not the walk deteriorated into a spasmodic meander.

Sylvia and I had now been together for some five years, and on one particular morning my mind floated back ten years to our holiday in the Lake District and the alcoholic advice given by one wordly wise inebriate to his equally inebriated and enquiring mate. For judged by his criteria our relationship was certainly on very firm ground.

For I had listened over the years to beautiful Sylvia's complete repertoire, ranging from her subdued and discreet supermarket bleep to the robust and unrestricted blast of the first of the day. Daring me to do better. I couldn't, but I showed my appreciation by flatteringly complaining that I couldn't understand how such a beautiful instrument could produce such rotten music.

In 1992 Sylvia finally took her retirement, so we were now able to begin our contemplated exploration of those parts of France that we hadn't so far reached. Using our house at Lion-en-Sullias as a base, for it had recently been redecorated and replumbed by Messieurs Salgado and Bernard from the village. All to a standard far superior to that which one would get from any polite and smiling Paris based smooth talker.

As two years previously I had spent four days in hospital having my prostate rebored for the second time, long journeys were now no longer a bother. Although, after eleven years of measuring each stage of a trip by the distance between loos, I had accumulated a rare knowledge of the location and state of literally hundreds of them.

And if I have any advice at all to pass on, I would simply suggest that you imagine that the person who designed those little figures on the doors was a transvestite. It might help.

Strangely it was a choice of loo that took me accidentally to Joan of Arc's birthplace at Domremy. And the same sort of urge that took me some twenty two years later, and again by chance, to the site in Rouen where she had been burnt at the stake. Hardly a potted history of her life, but a peculiar coincidence just the same.

Apart from this incidental link with the distant past, our travels inevitably took us to the sites of some of the more infamous events of the not so distant last war. The horrors of which were shockingly brought to life at Oradour sur Glane, where the Germans after having vengefully and cold-bloodedly killed all it's inhabitants, set fire to the whole village, razing it to the ground.

The village remains to this day as :they left it, and is a potent reminder of the unbelievable depravity of war, leaving one with feelings of sadness and utter revulsion repeatedly asking the simple question *"How could they? - How could they?"*.

As previously mentioned, the landing beaches of Normandy were also visited, where the somewhat different horrors of war triggered the same question *How could they? - how could each and every one of them have found that sort of selfless courage...*

Now as 1994 approached it wasn't courage I needed but some sort of progressive resignation, for my so far intermittent attacks of arthritic pain decided to become more intrusive, stiffening a few joints from neck to knee. Age had decided to make itself felt, but it could have been a little more selective in what it decided to stiffen, or soften for that matter. Old Father Time it would seem had decreed that it was now time I thought of joining the ranks of those despondent old gents who slowly steer their way around the supermarket aisles, surreptitiously using their trolleys as mobile Zimmers, at the same time sadly contemplating the relevance of some of the advice stuck to it's contents - 'Keep in a warm dry place' - 'Keep away from children' - 'Shake before use' - 'Use by' - and a thought provoking - 'Recyclable'.

Later this same year we had bad news from Erica. Her long years of diabetes were taking their toll, and at the age of 85 she felt unable to carry on. A new nursing home had recently been completed within a throw of her home, and proved to be the answer to our immediate problems. But sadly not for long, for soon after, she began to deteriorate, eventually giving up and joining her Maker (for she was a strong believer) in January 95. Leaving Sylvia and I to grieve and to realise we were now the last remaining remnants of the family's Cairean connection.

It wasn't morbidity but logic that now told me it would probably be my turn next, and that if my days were not exactly numbered, their regression to zero was a not too distant certainty. This conclusion enabled me with some satisfaction to deflate an over zealous salesman, who, when trying to flog me a high priced settee, proudly asserted it would last for 50 years, or more. I pointedly explained to him that at least forty of them would be of no interest to me. A request for something less durable and proportionately cheaper, brought a resigned shrug, a forced smile and a new settee of undefined longevity and 40 years cheaper.

1996 has not brought an end to my 'and then what' – but I do feel inclined to ask Sylvia to accelerate a little when passing an undertaker's parlour or a cemetery. At the same time fighting the temptation to give a two finger salute as they disappear from view in the rear mirror, for I'll not be able to keep the mercenary so and sos at bay for ever.

These thoughts not so strangely took me back some 35 years, when in the process of inspecting a newly extended undertaker's premises, I bumped into a live ex RAF Carpenter Rigger, now happily employed making coffins. A livelihood which would seem to have a very secure future. To a double-edged enquiry as to the state of business, he replied.

"It varies - sometimes good, sometimes bad - snag is, we never get a lot of notice and nobody dies to order - makes reaching the deadlines a bit difficult."

His face was dead pan so I presumed the pun to be unintended. He then went on to describe a local air crash that had recently occurred when the plane had rolled right over on landing, trapping the 3-man crew underneath. Thinking our past mutual interests had occasioned this bit of unhappy news, I politely enquired.

"Anybody hurt?"

1995: Sylvia and I with her daughter Patricia and son Christian and the three grandsons, Pierre, Matthieu and Olivier.

A SHILLINGSWORTH OF PROMISES

"Yes, one lad bought it - he had a lovely funeral though, with a beautiful oak box - cost a fortune. I should know – I made it!"

Not knowing whether to be congratulatory or sympathetic, I offered, "A bit sad though wasn't it?"

He carried on with his chiselling, and without looking up, straightfacedly answered. "Yes it was, the other two got away with it!"

A trifle accusingly, I said, "You sound a bit disappointed".

He didn't answer. But after a little more chat, and as I said my cheerios at the door, he half smiled as he half waved goodbye, saying "Be seeing you..."

'Not at your prices you won't' I thought.

Xmas 96 was fast approaching and in spite of my creeping decrepitude, I'm thankfully not yet ga-ga and it still can't be said that "Outside the loo I'm often seen wondering if I have or haven't been". No doubt it will come in due course, but until then I'm sure life will carry on in blissful certainty.

And now after an average sort of life, conforming to most so called Christian ideals, I still could not possibly be called a lapsed agnostic. Probably something more like a non-practising atheist.

I think young Pierre in a moment of youthful candour and clear sightedness, summed up my present position to perfection. For after looking at me intently for a while, he said, *"Fred, tu es blanc et tu es vieux..."* and then a few moments later he casually warned me *"Et tu seras bientot mort".*

I laughingly thanked him for his prophecy of an early death, hoping at the same time that my bits and pieces would hang together at least long enough for me to see my uninhibited miniature Jeremiah reach a happy but less perceptive boyhood.

Meanwhile I shall carry on at a leisurely and light hearted pace until the inevitable intervenes to end my particular unplanned and unwished for journey from creation to cremation. And as I won't have earned a ticket to either heaven or hell en route, a nice little nudge back into nothingness will be all that I'll need, and reward enough.

NB. Since this book was written, all sexual activity within the Bois de Boulogne has been officially restricted to the flora and fauna.

THE END

August 1996: Pierre and I waiting for lunch at Spiez on lake Thun.

A SHILLINGSWORTH OF PROMISES